ALSO BY WILLIAM KNOEDELSEDER

Stiffed: A True Story of MCA, the Music Business, and the Mafia

In Eddie's Name (with Bryn Freedman)

*I'm Dying Up Here: Heartbreak and High Times
in Standup Comedy's Golden Era*

THE RISE AND FALL OF
ANHEUSER-BUSCH
AND AMERICA'S KINGS OF BEER

Bitter Brew

WILLIAM KNOEDELSEDER

HARPER
BUSINESS

An Imprint of HarperCollins*Publishers*
www.harpercollins.com

Dedicated to my sisters—
Mary, Ann, Kate, and Martha—
who have helped make me the man I am.

A hardcover edition of this book was published in 2012 by HarperBusiness, an imprint of HarperCollins Publishers.

FIRST HARPERBUSINESS PAPERBACK EDITION PUBLISHED 2014

Designed by William Ruoto

Library of Congress Cataloging-in-Publication Data has been applied for.

ISBN 978-0-06-200927-2

14 15 16 17 18   OV/RRD   10 9 8 7 6 5 4 3 2 1

ACKNOWLEDGMENTS

For their aid and encouragement, I would like to acknowledge the following:

- My agent for life, Alice Martell, who has been my dear friend and champion for nearly thirty years.
- My most excellent editor at HarperCollins, Hollis Heimbouch, who should start a brewery with a name like that;
- Adolphus IV, Billy, and Trudy Busch, and Lotsie Busch Webster, and Lotsie Hermann Holton—members of a great American family who shared their story on the record;
- Gary Sgouros, who shared his memories of Gussie's last days at Grant's Farm;
- Former Anheuser-Busch executives Denny Long, Andy Steinhubl, and my brother-in-law Mike Brooks, who helped make a great American company what it was;
- Former Pima County deputy sheriff Ron Benson and former St. Louis Police detective Nick Fredericksen, who did their jobs;
- All the dozens of other people who contributed to this narrative but prefer to remain anonymous;
- Glenn Jamboretz, PR consultant par excellence, who helped every time I called (and sometimes when I didn't);
- Pat Crane, Nancy Cason, John Crotty, and Suzanne Otto—old St. Louis friends who did likewise;
- Michael London, John Sayles, Barbara Wall, Kevin Beggs, and all the

good people at Lionsgate Television, who believed in this book even before it was finished.

- John Mettler, Deborah Rybak, Jeff Kwatinetz, Bill and Nancy Cason, and Dennis McDougal—members of my finance committee, who made it possible for me to eat regularly and sleep under a roof during the writing process.
- Father John Rechtien, Don Crinklaw, and, especially, Irv Letofsky—who set me on the road to a writing career years ago and inspire me to this day;
- Dennis McDougal, a fellow traveler on that road who deigns to talk to me every morning;
- Matthew, Colin, and Halle Knoedelseder, my three astonishing, creative children, who keep me young at heart and hopeful about the future.

CONTENTS

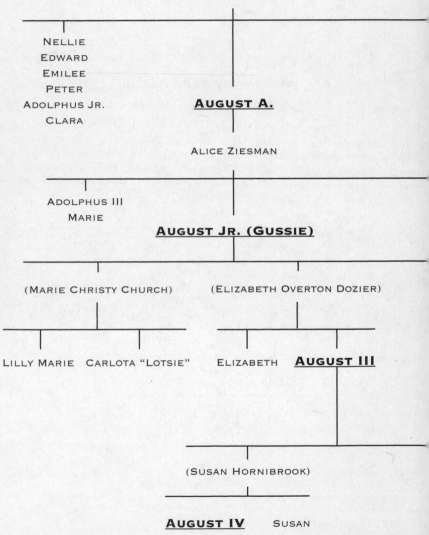

ADOLPHUS BUSCH

LILLY ANHEUSER

NELLIE
EDWARD
EMILEE
PETER
ADOLPHUS JR.
CLARA

AUGUST A.

ALICE ZIESMAN

ADOLPHUS III
MARIE

AUGUST JR. (GUSSIE)

(MARIE CHRISTY CHURCH)   (ELIZABETH OVERTON DOZIER)

LILLY MARIE   CARLOTA "LOTSIE"   ELIZABETH   **AUGUST III**

(SUSAN HORNIBROOK)

AUGUST IV   SUSAN

BUSCH FAMILY TREE

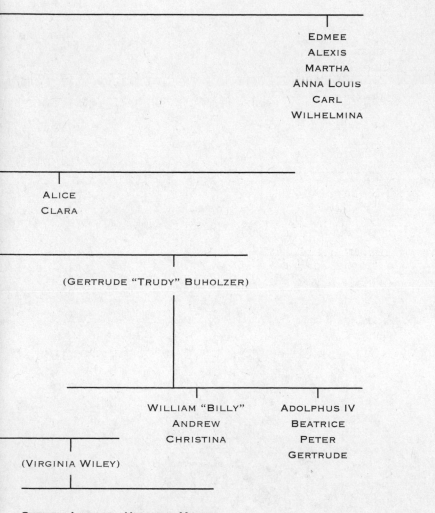

EDMEE
ALEXIS
MARTHA
ANNA LOUIS
CARL
WILHELMINA

ALICE
CLARA

(GERTRUDE "TRUDY" BUHOLZER)

WILLIAM "BILLY"   ADOLPHUS IV
ANDREW   BEATRICE
CHRISTINA   PETER
                         GERTRUDE

(VIRGINIA WILEY)

STEVEN AUGUST   VIRGINIA MARIE

"AUGUST IS NOT FEELING WELL"

In the grand ballroom of the Hyatt at Capitol Hill in Washington, D.C., on the afternoon of May 13, 2008, several hundred Anheuser-Busch distributors sat in rows of uncomfortable chairs, restlessly awaiting the arrival of August Busch IV, the forty-three-year-old president and CEO of Anheuser-Busch, Inc., America's premier brewery.

"The Fourth," as he was commonly called in the industry, was twenty minutes late, and no one from the company had appeared with an explanation for the delay.

The distributors were among 1,200 beer professionals from around the world attending the eighteenth annual National Beer Wholesalers Association/Brewers Legislative Conference. This year's three-day event coincided with the seventy-fifth anniversary of the repeal of Prohibition, and Anheuser-Busch had taken the opportunity to schedule a separate meeting with its distributors, the independent operators who—by a law passed in Prohibition's wake—serve as the middlemen between the brewery and retailers.

There was much to talk about. Beer sales were on the decline globally, and the industry was weathering a period of rapid consolidation that threatened A-B's century-long dominance. In the past few years, Milwaukee's Miller Brewing had merged with London-based South African Breweries to form SABMiller; Canada's Molson had merged with Colorado-based Adolph Coors to form Molson Coors, which then merged its U.S. operations with SABMiller to form Miller Coors; and Belgium's Interbrew SA had merged with Brazil's AmBev to create InBev, which had knocked A-B out of its perennial position as the world's largest brewer. A-B was still the most profitable brewer, with its brands accounting for about 50 percent of beer sales in the United States, the world's most lucrative market. But the company's drop to No. 2 in volume, coupled with the fact that its stock price had remained flat for nearly five years, or roughly the period that August IV had been in charge of the brewing division, was fueling speculation that the aggressively acquisitive InBev was eyeing A-B as a possible takeover target. Busch had dismissed the talk of a takeover during a meeting with distributors in Chicago the week before, drawing a standing ovation when he declared, "Not on my watch."

The Fourth was actually the sixth Busch to head the St. Louis–based brewery, a responsibility handed down from father to first-born son since his great-great-grandfather Adolphus founded the company in the wake of the Civil War. With the exception of the Fourth's great-uncle, Adolphus III, each of his predecessors had left an indelible imprint, not just on the company but on American commerce as well. Over the course of five generations they'd taken a tiny, bankrupt brewery that made bad-tasting beer on the banks of the Mississippi River and transformed it into a colossus that pumped out more than 100 million barrels a year. They had steered the company through two world wars, Prohibition, and the Great Depression, building their signature lager, Budweiser, into the best selling beer on the planet, making Anheuser-Busch, in the words of the Fourth's father, August A. Busch III, "the world's beer company."

Thanks to their beer, the Busch family had tasted all that America ever promised the immigrant class from which they sprang—wealth almost beyond comprehension, political power that provided access to presidents, and a lifestyle rivaling that of history's most extravagant royals. Along with that, of course, came a king-size portion of heartbreak, scandal, tragedy, and untimely death. But they had endured. Nearly all the other German immigrant brewers who'd built their businesses by hand, branded their factories with their family names—Schlitz, Miller, Pabst, Blatz, Schaefer, Coors, Lemp, Stroh, Hamm, Griesedieck—and turned America into a beer-loving nation were gone, their paternalistic empires swallowed up by foreign-based conglomerations of amalgamations with soulless names like InBev. Of the brewing giants that boomed after Prohibition and fought fierce and sometimes desperate battles for market share in the last half of the twentieth century, only Anheuser-Busch remained as a freestanding, independent company, still operated by the family that founded it.

So a lot was riding on the shoulders of August Anheuser Busch IV as the audience at the Hyatt waited for him to make his appearance. His "watch" had come at a portentous time for the company, bridging a glorious past and a perilous future. His vision going forward could determine the fate of the distributors' families, and the families of thousands of A-B employees and suppliers.

Thirty minutes into the wait, one of the Fourth's trusted lieutenants, vice president of marketing David Peacock, materialized at the podium and apologized for the "tardiness." He explained vaguely that the company plane had had trouble landing at the airport and promised, "August will be here shortly." He then added that Busch was "taking medication for a sinus infection." The audience registered a collective "Huh?" at the seeming non sequitur, and it quickly became apparent that Peacock was vamping for time.

Another ten minutes passed before Busch finally entered the room from stage left, surrounded by his ever-present phalanx of inner-circle executives, "the entourage," as they were called inside the company. Tanned and perfectly coiffed, wearing his trademark open-neck dress shirt, slacks, and cowboy boots, he stepped up to the microphone and, barely acknowledging the audience, launched into his prepared remarks. Casual about rehearsing for his public speaking engagements, Busch was known for sometimes going off script, losing focus and relying on his good looks and charm to get him through. Most often he had not even looked at the speech before reading it in the teleprompter. Once, in an appearance before the Beer Institute in Boca Raton, Florida, he was supposed to say, "When our forefathers arrived on these shores, one of the first things they did was to erect a beer house." What came out of his mouth instead was, "When our forefathers arrived on these shores with erections . . ." He laughed off the arguably Freudian flub ("Did I really say that?"), and many in the audience laughed along with him, but his twenty-seven-year-old wife, Kate, sitting next to him on the dais, dropped her forehead to the table in embarrassment.

There was no laughter on this day. From the outset, it was clear that something was wrong. As Busch attempted to address the effect of the slowing economy on the beer business, he slurred words and stumbled over phrases. At first, some in the audience thought he was having trouble with the teleprompter, but it soon seemed that the Fourth was seriously impaired, and not from overindulging in an A-B product or taking some mystery sinus medicine. No, this appeared to be a deep state of stoned. Unmindful of the rising murmur and the concerned looks on the faces in the crowd, he plowed on for several excruciating minutes, speaking in a kind of slow-mo monotone. Finally, mercifully, David Peacock intervened. He leaned in to the microphone and said, "Obviously, August is not feeling well." He then took Busch by the arm and led him off the stage. Busch went docilely, stumbling once before he disappeared from view.

The meeting was over, but the audience remained seated, stunned, absorbing the impact of a quintessential "holy shit" moment. It wasn't so much that Busch was bombed. His reputation as a party animal stretched back to his college days, when a Chappaquiddick-type incident left a twenty-two-year-old cocktail waitress lying dead in a roadside ditch next to Busch's overturned Corvette and Busch, who had walked away from the scene, telling police investigators hours later that he couldn't remember what happened or who was driving his car. His father had extricated him from that jam and a number of others over the years, and A-B security men had cleaned up countless lesser messes that "the Third" was never told about. In a way, bad-boy behavior was expected of the Fourth. He was a Busch, after all, a member of a family in which hard drinking, fast driving, womanizing, and gunplay were part of the male curriculum. Both his father and his grandfather, the legendary beer baron August A. ("Gussie") Busch Jr., had hard-earned reputations as hell-raisers in their youth.

But the incident at the Hyatt was different; it crossed a line that hadn't been crossed before. All of the Fourth's previous escapades could be dismissed as after-hours personal indiscretions. But this occurred on the job, in the course of his daily duties as chief executive of the publicly traded, $19 billion-a-year Fortune 500 company, and in full view of the entire industry. That's what really shocked the audience at the Hyatt. There had always been questions inside the company about the Fourth's fitness for the top job, and when August III prevailed upon the board to name his son CEO in 2006, the widespread assumption was that the elder Busch had made sure there were loyal retainers in place among management and the board of directors who would protect August IV and the company from just this sort of thing. But all the king's horses and all the king's men hadn't been able to prevent the debacle. Clearly, the wheels had come off the beer wagon.

Word of the Fourth's performance poured out of the Hyatt ballroom and into the bar, and flowed down the escalator to the main reception room. Within minutes it was the talk of the NBWA conference. Cell phones flashed the information back to A-B home base at 1 Busch Place in St. Louis, where it was treated as a potential PR disaster.

It proved to be worse than that. The Fourth's personal problems, which for years had been denied, ignored, or covered up by those around him, were about to have worldwide repercussions. Three and a half weeks later, on June 11, InBev, a four-year-old company based in Belgium but controlled by a trio of Brazilian billionaires, made an unsolicited and utterly unwelcome bid to acquire Anheuser-Busch for $46.5 billion. When the dust settled on what became the largest cash acquisition in history, America had lost one of its most beloved companies, and more than a thousand A-B employees in St. Louis had lost their jobs.

The Fourth and his father were among the executives who made fortunes in the deal—they walked away with nearly half a billion dollars between them—but their long-rocky relationship was by then irrevocably broken. They no longer spoke to each other.

Untethered from both family expectations and company responsibilities for the first time in his life, August IV quickly descended into an abyss. According to friends, family members, and court documents, when the police came for him in February 2010,

America's last king of beer was holed up in his mansion, grievously addicted to drugs, gripped by paranoia, beset by hallucinations, and armed with hundreds of high-powered weapons, including several .50-caliber machine guns.

"It's like the final scene in *Scarface*," sighed one Busch family member, slipping almost unconsciously into an imitation of Al Pacino as doomed drug kingpin Tony Montana: "'Say hello to my little friend.'"

"BEER IS BACK!"

A crowd began gathering at the brewery gates in the early evening of April 7, 1933, milling around near the intersection of Broadway and Pestalozzi Streets on the south side of the city near the river. As the hands of the lighted clock on the Gothic Brew House tower approached midnight, the number of people swelled to an estimated 35,000, standing shoulder to shoulder for blocks around, growing increasingly boisterous in anticipation: America's thirteen-year prohibition against the sale of beer was about to end.

"Happy days are here again, the skies above are clear again," they roared out in a raucous chorus, "Let us sing a song of cheer again."

Similar scenes played out in smaller scale all around town. Over at Kyum Brothers Café at Ninth and Pine, patrons sang Irving Berlin's teetotaler's lament "The Near Future"—*How dry I am . . ."*—while hundreds of customers at the German House restaurant joined in an old Deutschland drinking song, "Was Wilst du Haben?" (What will you have?).

Inside the iron gates of the giant brewery complex, 300 trucks pressed up to the loading dock, while 1,200 more lined up bumper-to-bumper on the street outside, ready to take their place. From within the plant the rumble of machinery signaled that the long-hibernating giant was now fully awake, as seemingly endless columns of brown Budweiser bottles, with their famous red-and-white labels, clattered along snaking conveyor belts to be packed in wooden crates proudly stamped, "Property of Anheuser-Busch, St. Louis Mo."

On the bottling plant floor, brewery president August A. Busch Sr. and his two sons, Adolphus III and August Jr., posed for photographers as they packed a twenty-four-count crate destined for President Franklin D. Roosevelt, who'd swept into office in November on the promise of a "new deal" for America that included the repeal of the Eighteenth Amendment, which banned the manufacture and sale of alcoholic beverages in the United States.

Full repeal would not come for eight more months because it required another constitutional amendment and thus needed ratification by the legislatures in thirty-six (three-fourths) of the forty-eight states. But FDR had already made good on his campaign promise to the nation's brewers. On March 13, nine days after his inauguration, he asked Congress to immediately modify the so-called Volstead Act, which had set the maximum legal alcoholic content of beverages at .05 percent, to allow the sale of beer with a 3.2 percent alcohol. "I deem action at this time to be of highest importance," he said. Both the House and the Senate quickly complied, setting April 8 as the date when the sale of beer could resume.

The Busches had been preparing for this moment ever since the election, spending more than $7 million to refit and modernize their plant, purchase supplies, and gather the ingredients for the brewing process, notably the expensive Bohemian hops they considered crucial to the character of Budweiser, which had been the No. 1 selling beer in the world when America's state lawmakers shut off the tap.

Eager to reestablish their brand as the "King of Beers," the company's board of directors had authorized August Jr., the superintendent of the brewery, to buy several teams of Clydesdale draft horses "for advertising purposes." Gussie, as he was called, purchased sixteen of the massive 2,000-pound animals for $21,000 at the Kansas City stockyards. He also found two wooden wagons from back in the days when the company employed eight hundred teams of horses to deliver its beer, and set about having them restored to the exacting standards of his late grandfather, brewery founder Adolphus Busch, who liked to conduct weekly inspections from a viewing stand, with his son August at his side as all the drivers passed in parade, hoping to win the $25 prize for the best-kept team and wagon.

Gussie's wagon restoration was conducted in secrecy behind locked doors in the brewery's famed Circular Stable because he wanted to surprise his father with this majestic symbol of the company's history and the old man's youth. Gussie even tracked down Billy Wales, who had been the company's best eight-horse driver for years prior to Prohibition, when he left to work in the Chicago stockyards because he couldn't bear to be away from horses.

When all was ready, Gussie and his brother Adolphus III called their father out of his office, telling him they wanted to show him a new automobile. Instead, as they walked across the street toward the stable, the big doors swung open and the first team of perfectly matched Clydesdales—each with white stockings and feathers, a white blaze on its face, and white ribbons braided into its mane and tail—high-stepped into view, pulling a bright red brass-trimmed wagon with Billy Wales sitting up in the driver's seat. Speechless, the old man wept at the sight.

And now, finally, the big moment had arrived. A brass band was playing outside the brewery as the crowd counted down the Brew House clock. At the stroke of midnight, the plant whistles shrieked, setting off widespread jubilation, with cars honking and bells ringing all across the city. At 12:01, beer trucks began rolling through the gates and onto the streets. Sirens wailed as police cars escorted the first truck to the St. Louis airport, where one case of Budweiser was loaded onto a Ford Trimotor plane bound for Washington, D.C. and President Roosevelt, and another was put aboard a flight to Newark, New Jersey, for former New York governor Al Smith, a hero to August Sr. because of his anti-Prohibition presidential campaign against Herbert Hoover in 1928. A six-horse hitch of Clydesdales had been sent ahead to Newark, New Jersey, where it now waited on the tarmac to carry the precious cargo on the last leg of the journey.

In the train yard of the Anheuser-Busch complex, newly hired workers loaded cases of bottled Budweiser onto 130 freight cars while the brewery's fleet of bright red trucks fanned out through the city, making priority deliveries to the Jefferson, Mayfair, Lennox, and Chase Park Plaza hotels, where crowds of well-heeled patrons waited. In the lobby of the bottling plant, Gussie Busch stepped to a microphone that had been set up by the fledgling CBS Radio Network for a nationally broadcast report on the celebrations going on in three "beer cities"—St. Louis, Chicago, and Milwaukee. As his ailing father listened to the radio broadcast at his home, Gussie addressed the nation for the first time:

"April seventh is here, and it is a real occasion for thankfulness, marking a newfound freedom for the American people, made possible by the wisdom, foresight and courage of a great president and the cooperation of an understanding Congress. There is a song in our hearts: it's 'Happy Days Are Here Again.' And they *are* here again," he said, "for out of a maze of confusion and anxiety has come a beacon light to guide the way to better times. Happy, grateful men are back to work after what seemed an endless idleness."

Reading from a script he surely had not written but every word of which he certainly believed, Gussie went on for more than two minutes, linking the country's economic future to that of the brewing industry. "Once again freight cars are rolling in, loaded with grain from American farms, bottles and cases and various equipment, as well as coal and supplies from industries long suffering from the Depression, while others soon will be rolling out and onward, contributing their share toward the rehabilitation of industry, agriculture, and transportation." With brewers and politicians now working together, he said, "a new and greater era looms on the horizon for our people, one that will result in a happier and more secure existence for all of us."

He closed with a sign-off that would be made famous some years later by newsman Edward R. Murrow, "Good night and good luck," then walked over to a VIP table and announced, "Beer is now being served."

Indeed it was. Over the next eight hours, America's beer cities went on a bender unlike anything ever seen before, not even after the Armistice in 1918. Back at Kyum Brothers Café, a local politician named Larry McDaniel squeezed his ample belly behind the bar, raised a ten-cent glass of golden liquid, and hollered to the cheering crowd, "This is *Democratic* beer." At 2:30 a.m., four apparently democratically inclined beer lovers attempted to hijack an Anheuser-Busch truck but were interrupted by the police. By breakfast time, Anheuser-Busch had moved the equivalent of 3,588 barrels out of its plant, and the citizens of St. Louis had literally drunk the town dry; there wasn't a drop of beer left anywhere outside the brewery.

The situation was the same in all the big brewing towns, as demand outstripped all capacity for supply, prompting Gussie Busch to make a public plea for moderation. "We are asking people to hold back their orders," he said. "I believe they are for not less than five million cases. Our Pacific Coast division has ordered 74,000 cases, and a man in Seattle has asked us to send him a seventy-five-car trainload as soon as we can." In what would become a recurring theme in the decades to come, he explained, "The reason the supply is so limited is that beer must be thoroughly aged. This process takes more than three months, and cannot be hurried even under present exceptional conditions."

In New York on the morning of April 8, thousands gathered to watch as the Clydesdales clopped through the Holland Tunnel into Manhattan and down Fifth Avenue to the Empire State Building, where Al Smith was waiting with a live radio microphone. In Washington, the White House was inundated with shipments from breweries all over the country, but Anheuser-Busch's huge bay horses with their white-feathered hooves caused a sensation when they pranced proudly along Pennsylvania Avenue with their package for the president.

The Clydesdales were featured prominently in the company's full-page newspaper ads the following day, along with heroically rendered images of American male archetypes—the Farmer, the Laborer, the Hunter, the Athlete. "Beer is Back!" the ads proclaimed, expounding on the same patriotic, Depression-busting theme as Gussie's radio address the night before:

Beer is back. But is that all? No. To cheer, to quicken American life with hospitality of old, the friendly glass of good fellowship is back. Sociability and good living return to their own, once more to mingle with memories and sentiments of yesterday. America looks forward, and feels better.

No one felt better than the Busches, of course, because no one had more to gain—or regain—from the repeal. Before Prohibition, they had been to beer what Rockefeller was to oil and Carnegie to steel, and the story of their rise in America rivaled that of the most famous robber barons of the Gilded Age.

A dolphus Busch, the second youngest of twenty-two children born to a well-to-do wine merchant in Kastel, Germany, arrived in the United States in 1857 at the age of eighteen, in the midst of a massive influx of German immigrants. More than a million of them had arrived in the previous decade, a "Teutonic tide," in the words of one historian. Unlike the Irish, who were pouring into the country desperately impoverished, the German émigrés tended to be middle-class liberals seeking social and economic freedom following the failure of a political revolution in 1848. They came to America with money to spend and migrated inland, with huge numbers of them settling in an area of the Mississippi River valley that became known as the German triangle, the points of which were Cincinnati, Milwaukee, and St. Louis.

Adolphus landed in New Orleans and traveled up the Mississippi River to St. Louis, where the German-born population had swelled from a mere sixteen families in 1833 to fully one quarter of the city's 161,000 residents the day he stepped off a steamboat. A June 1857 editorial in the newspaper the *Republican* described how the city had been transformed by his countrymen: "A sudden and almost unexpected wave of emigration swept over us, and we found the town inundated with breweries, beer houses, sausage shops, Apollo Gardens, Sunday concerts, Swiss cheese and Holland herrings. We found it almost necessary to learn the German language before we could ride in an omnibus, or buy a pair of breeches, and absolutely necessary to drink beer at a Sunday concert."

St. Louis even had a German-language newspaper. The *Mississippi Hansel-Zeitung* reported in detail on the operations of the city's thirty to forty breweries, which were producing more than 60,000 barrels a year, or about 18 million five-cent glasses of beer, all of which were consumed locally.

Adolphus worked for two years as a clerk on a riverboat. When his father died in 1859, he used his inheritance to buy into a brewery supply business, forming Wattenberg, Busch & Company. One of his early customers was Eberhard Anheuser, a prosperous soap manufacturer who had come into ownership of the failed Bavarian Brewery through a defaulted $90,000 loan, and was trying to make it profitable.

On March 7, 1861, three days after the inauguration of Abraham Lincoln, Adolphus married Anheuser's daughter Lilly in St. Louis's Holy Ghost German Evangelical Lutheran Church. It's unlikely that Anheuser's beer was served at the wedding reception; it was so foul tasting that tavern owners were accustomed to patrons spitting it back across the bar at them. Anheuser, struggling to sell 4,000 barrels a year, soon ran up a sizable debt to his son-in-law's supply house. In 1865, after a four-month stint in the Union Army, Adolphus went to work for his father-in-law, and by 1873 the E. Anheuser & Co. brewery was profitably producing 27,000 barrels a year. Eberhard rewarded Adolphus in 1879 by making him a partner in the rechristened Anheuser-Busch Brewing Association and allowed him to purchase a minority stake in the company, amounting to 238 of the 480 shares of stock. When Eberhard died in 1880, he divided his stock among his five adult children. With Lilly's 116 shares added to his own 238, Adolphus controlled a majority, and his own destiny.

One of the first things he did as president of his own brewery was to acquire, through a close friend and local restaurant owner named Carl Conrad, the recipe for a beer that for years had been produced by monks in a small Bohemian village named Budweis. The crisp, pale lager was known in the region as Budweiser. Adolphus adopted the name along with Conrad's refined recipe and, now armed with a competitive product, set about revolutionizing the brewing industry.

Adolphus was the first brewer in the United States to pasteurize his product, which enabled him to bottle Budweiser and store it longer without fear of spoilage. He built a system of rail-side ice-houses and became the first brewer to distribute his beer far beyond the local market. The icehouses morphed into a national distribution network when he pioneered the use of artificial (non-ice) refrigeration, first in his plant and then in a fleet of 250 railroad cars that transported his beer throughout the country. A proponent of vertical integration before there was even a name for it, he bought a controlling interest in the company that built the rail cars he used, as well as the company that made the glass bottles his brewery consumed in huge quantities. He bought two coal mines on the Illinois side of the river and built his own railroad connecting them to the brewery.

And he extended his control of the process all the way to the other end of the supply line by acquiring an interest in countless taverns, often paying for a new proprietor's liquor license, permits, and sometimes even rent, and providing promotional light fixtures and glassware, all in exchange for a signed agreement that the establishment would sell only Anheuser-Busch products.

As other brewers scrambled to compete by buying into their own saloons, abuses abounded, with proprietor-partners dabbling in prostitution and gambling on the side, bribing local police and politicians to look the other way. Those corrupt practices would come back to bite the brewing industry, but not before Adolphus Busch had built Budweiser into the first national brand of beer.

Of course, Adolphus got an assist from the U.S. population, which more than doubled between 1820 and 1870 with the arrival of 7.5 million immigrants, two-thirds of whom came from the beer-drinking countries of Germany and Ireland. He saw the dramatic population growth in St. Louis's German neighborhoods of Carondelet and Soulard and in the Irish section of the city known as the Kerry Patch, and he concluded that beer was on its way to becoming America's national drink. So he plowed profits back into the company, building more and more production capacity. Sure enough, between 1870 and 1900 per capita consumption of beer in the United States quadrupled, rising from four gallons a year to sixteen, and Anheuser-Busch became the largest brewer in the country, pumping out more than a million barrels of beer annually by the turn of the century.

Adolphus turned that river of beer into a mountain of money that he lavished on himself and his large family (Lilly gave birth to thirteen children, nine of whom survived to adulthood). With a personal income of an estimated $2 million a year at a time when there was no income tax, he maintained baronial mansions in St. Louis; Cooperstown, New York; Pasadena, California; and Bad Schwalbach, Germany, on the banks of the Rhine River. He called the Pasadena estate Ivy Wall, but it became known to the public as Busch's Garden due to the thirty-five acres of surrounding flora, which cost $500,000 to plant and required fifty gardeners to maintain. The estate was the envy of his fellow tycoons Andrew Carnegie and J. P. Morgan, who hurried to build their own mansions nearby, creating Pasadena's famed "millionaire's row."

Adolphus traveled between his American estates in a private rail car, immodestly named the *Adolphus* and outfitted sumptuously enough to earn its description as "a palace on wheels." He built his own rail spur so the *Adolphus* could roll right up to the back door of the family's principal home at 1 Busch Place, located in the middle of a large park dotted with ponds and fountains on the grounds of the brewery. Everything he did was in the grandest style; some would say over-the-top or gauche. Indeed, the French-descended, blue-blooded banking class in St. Louis so disdained his showiness that they coined an adjective to describe it—"Buschy." But Adolphus didn't much care what they thought. He didn't need their money; he did all his own financing. And he didn't need their social acceptance; he numbered among his friends Presidents Theodore Roosevelt and William Howard Taft. The latter called him "Prince Adolphus."

Among the general population in St. Louis, Adolphus was viewed as a benevolent monarch whose carriage whooshing past would cause common folk to catch their breath and cry out, "Oh, look!" And he played the part with flair. Always resplendent in the latest European tailoring, his flowing gray hair, twirled mustache, and elaborately long goatee trimmed daily by his personal servant barber, he greeted passersby in a booming, heavily accented voice and had a habit of handing out silver coins to the children who, understandably, came running whenever he appeared on the street. It wasn't so much affection he inspired among the populace as it was awe. He exuded power and privilege; he personified the American possibility. When he and Lilly celebrated their fiftieth wedding anniversary, more than 13,000 people showed up at the St. Louis Coliseum for a party in their honor. The fact that the couple was 1,400 miles away at their Pasadena estate was more than made up for by the fact that the beer was free and unlimited. The crowd managed to consume 40,000 bottles in a few hours.

For all his Old World–liness, Adolphus had a genuine feel for his adopted country, and he exhibited a keen understanding of America's symbols and myths. In 1896, for example, he conceived a brilliant advertising campaign based on an epic painting of the Battle of Little Bighorn that he saw hanging on the wall behind the bar in a St. Louis saloon. Titled *Custer's Last Fight*, the eye-grabbing nine-by-sixteen-foot oil on canvas was the work of a local artist named Cassilly Adams, a descendant of Founding Father John Adams. The painting depicted General Custer with his long hair flying, saber in hand, fighting desperately in the last few minutes before he and his men were overwhelmed by thousands of Sioux and Cheyenne warriors. The saloon was about to go into bankruptcy, and Adolphus was among the major creditors, so he acquired the painting along with its reproduction rights for a reported $35,000. He commissioned another artist to paint a smaller, modified version of Adams's work, instructing him to add more blood and scalpings. Then he distributed 150,000 lithographic prints of the painting to taverns, restaurants, hotels, and anywhere else that Budweiser was sold. There was no product mentioned or beer bottle pictured, just the legend "Anheuser-Busch Brewing Association" emblazoned at the bottom.

In a masterstroke of associative advertising, Adolphus had branded a piece of American history and made both the painting and the brewery part of the nation's popular culture. The campaign proved so successful that fifty years and an estimated million prints later, customers still crowded around a framed copy of *Custer's Last Fight* that hung on the wall in one small-town Missouri tavern. According to an article published in 1945 by the Kansas Historical Society, "It is probably safe to say that [*Custer's Last Fight*] has been viewed by a greater number of the lower-browed members of society—and by fewer art critics—than any other picture in American history." More to the point, untold millions of those lowbrow barflies became loyal Budweiser drinkers, and Adolphus's promotional genius became part of his company's DNA.

Adolphus's one professional failure was his inability to turn back the rising tide of Prohibition, a fight that consumed his final years. He spent a fortune trying to promote beer in general—and Budweiser in particular—as a "beverage of moderation," an antidote to the devil whiskey that so incensed the temperance movement. One of the company's pre-Prohibition ad campaigns even featured the tagline "Budweiser Spells Temperance." In his effort to create a wholesome, healthy image for his product, and to differentiate it from that of the nation's distillers, Adolphus went so far as to host a party at his Pasadena estate for seven thousand members of the American Medical Association. He railed against the anti-alcohol movement as an attack on individual rights. One particularly florid newspaper ad for Budweiser invoked the name of his hero, German chancellor Otto von Bismarck:

"Bismarck, like all Germans, prized Personal Liberty as the breath of life—a NATURAL RIGHT to be guarded and defended at any cost. Among our millions of law-abiding German-American citizens there is not a man who does not consider it insolent tyranny of the most odious kind for any legislation to issue this command: 'Thou shalt NOT eat this; Thou shall NOT drink that.' Germans know that there is no evil in the light wines and beers of their fathers. EVIL IS ONLY IN THE MAN WHO MISUSES THEM."

Adolphus became the Prohibitionists' favorite poster boy when they figured out that he and the other major brewers owned or controlled a majority of the country's saloons, which sold most of the whiskey they believed was destroying American life. Author Ernest Barron Gordon, then the foremost chronicler of the anti-alcohol movement, denounced him as a "promoter of villainous dives."

Adolphus took his case against prohibition directly to President William McKinley. Upon being introduced to the president at a political function, he launched into an impassioned thirty-minute lecture warning of the danger in outlawing the "light, happy" beverage that he claimed was "demanded" by 85 to 90 percent of the adult population.

"Mr. President, the demand I speak of is prompted by human nature itself," he said, his voice rising. "And believe me, if the fanatics should ever succeed in preventing its being satisfied legitimately, the people will resort to narcotics or stimulants so injurious as to eventually undermine the health of the nation."

On June 10, 1910, as Adolphus and Lilly were about to set sail from New York on their annual summer trip to Germany, he told reporters that, "if given full sway," Prohibition would "ruin the whole world."

Adolphus lived to see his vision of beer in America borne out. In 1911 the United States surpassed Germany as the No. 1 beer-producing country in the world, with an output of nearly 63 million barrels, 1.6 million of which were the product of Anheuser-Busch, Inc. of St. Louis, Mo. In 1912 the U.S. Census Bureau ranked brewing as the country's seventeenth-largest industry.

Adolphus did not live to see his worst nightmare come true. On October 10, 1913, after a day of hunting with his friend Carl Conrad in the woods near Villa Lilly, he fell ill, and several days later he died. His body was brought back to New York aboard his favorite steamer, the *Kronprinz Wilhelm*, and then carried home to St. Louis by a special five-car train that included the *Adolphus*. Back at his mansion, 30,000 people—more than 5,000 of them brewery workers—viewed his body before the funeral, and an estimated 100,000 lined the route to the cemetery. At the time, the cause of death was reported as heart failure. Years later, it was disclosed that the heart failure may have been caused by cirrhosis of the liver.

Adolphus left an estate worth a staggering $60 million. His stock was divided equally among his seven surviving children, with each receiving thirty-eight shares, except for the eldest son, August Anheuser Busch Sr., who received an additional three shares for serving as a trustee along with his mother, Lilly. In addition to the 116 shares she had inherited from her father, Eberhard Anheuser, Adolphus's Lilly held in trust the shares bequeathed to four of the children: Nellie, who Adolphus considered a spendthrift, Clara and Wilhelmina, who were married to German citizens, and Carl, who was disabled from a prenatal injury suffered when Lilly fell down the stairs the night her father died.

With an original par value of $500 per share, A-B stock paid huge annual dividends, usually between $3,000 and $5,000 per share, $8,000 in 1913. It was said that Adolphus once bought back a share from a member of the Anheuser family for $60,000, and that any bank in St. Louis would lend $25,000 against a share.

August Sr., referred to in the family as "August A.," inherited his father's position as president of the company, which was valued at $40 million in property and equipment. He also inherited a series of interlocking problems that threatened to destroy everything his father had built.

In the last decade of the nineteenth century, the Anti Saloon League emerged as the leading organization in the fight to ban alcohol, lobbying for Prohibition on a state-by-state basis. But the ASL changed its tack in December 1913, when it staged a demonstration in Washington that featured five thousand anti-alcohol activists singing "Onward, Christian Soldiers" as they paraded down Pennsylvania Avenue to the Capitol steps, where they presented two "dry" congressmen with a petition for a constitutional amendment imposing *national* prohibition. Around the same time, the ASL's superintendent, a Methodist minister named Purley Baker, launched a well-financed "public information" campaign that demonized the producers of alcoholic beverages, particularly the nation's mostly German-American brewers, who, according to Baker, "eat like gluttons and drink like swine." League posters referred to them as "Huns" and portrayed them as apelike Neanderthals who threatened the American way of life.

Making matters worse, in June 1914, eight months after Adolphus's death, the assassination of Archduke Francis Ferdinand of Austria set off World War I. The Busch family was summering at Villa Lilly when hostilities broke out. August A. and his wife and children quickly fled the continent, but his mother, Lilly, remained in Germany with her two married daughters. Even before America entered the war in 1917, anti-German sentiment swept the country when the Germans became the first to use mustard gas in combat and a German submarine sank the British ocean liner *Lusitania*, killing nearly 1,200 of the 1,959 passengers, including 128 Americans.

The Busch family's ties to the fatherland and their longstanding support for Kaiser Wilhelm were well known. Fearing a backlash against his family and the brewery, August A. did everything he could to show his patriotism. He wrote a $100,000 check to the Red Cross. He announced that he was buying $1.5 million worth of Liberty Bonds. He offered to produce submarine engines for the war effort through a company his father had established, the Busch-Sulzer Brothers Diesel Engine Company. He changed the label on all Budweiser products, eliminating the double eagle design that some people believed represented the Austrian coat of arms. He began wearing an American flag button on his lapel. He abolished German as the official language at the brewery and ordered busts and paintings of Chancellor Bismarck removed from the premises.

Despite these efforts, Budweiser sales dropped from nearly $18 million in 1913 to $12 million in 1917. Lilly Busch's continued presence in Germany became a public embarrassment to her son and the brewery when it was revealed that both of her daughters' husbands were involved in the German war effort. Lilly finally returned to the United States in 1918, but only after President Woodrow Wilson established the office of Alien Property Custodian, which was empowered to seize all American assets owned by people living in an enemy country. Upon her arrival in Key West, Florida, the ailing seventy-five-year-old widow of Adolphus Busch was detained for forty hours and subjected to a strip search that included "a very thorough examination of her vagina and womb," according to her lawyer, who decried the treatment as "unexcelled in brutality, an examination not perpetrated on the poorest prostitute or female pick-pocket."

Lilly's property was seized pending the results of an investigation by the U.S. Senate Judiciary Committee into the activities of Anheuser-Busch and other German-surnamed breweries in the United States, based on the flimsy suspicion that they might be secretly funding the German war machine. The Busches and the brewery were eventually given a clean bill of health and an apology from the U.S. attorney general, and Lilly's property was returned to her by order of President Wilson shortly after the Armistice was signed. But August A.'s problems were just beginning.

On December 8, 1917, Congress passed the Eighteenth Amendment, banning the sale of alcoholic beverages nationally. The amendment was to take effect one year after the ratification by the states. However, on September 16, 1918, with more than half a million U.S. troops fighting in France, President Wilson issued a ban on the production of beer in order to conserve grain for the war effort. The ban was short-lived, ending with the signing of the Armistice on November 11, 1918. But two months later, on January 16, 1919, the Nebraska legislature became the thirty-sixth to ratify the Eighteenth Amendment. Manufacturers of alcoholic beverages howled that the American people would have rejected Prohibition overwhelmingly if it had been put up to a popular vote, a claim that appears to have been borne out by the bootlegging success of Al Capone and his gangster cohorts during the bloody, booze-soaked Roaring Twenties that followed. August A. angrily dismissed the amendment's passage as "an attempt to substitute the authority of law for the virtue of man," and he predicted that the experiment ultimately would fail. He vowed to keep his company operating, one way or another, until it did.

In the meantime, Anheuser-Busch sought to rally the public against the amendment with promotional pamphlets and ads that testified to the societal benefits of its product. "The temperate use of a temperate alcoholic beverage like beer makes for the advancement of individual progress; the evils incident to outlawing it make for demoralization," proclaimed one. "Pure beer, such as Budweiser, is the nation's greatest aid to temperance, a home beverage which promotes both physical and moral well being."

Another brochure quoted Dr. Benjamin Rush of Philadelphia, one of the signers of the Declaration of Independence, as saying that fermented beverages were "generally innocent, and often have a friendly influence upon health and life." It cited records from the *Mayflower* indicating that beer was on the Pilgrims' minds when they put in at Plymouth Rock rather than push on to their intended destination in Virginia, "for we could not now take time for further search or consideration; our victuals being much spent, especially our beer." If that wasn't enough, a translation by George Smith of the British Museum of text on clay tablets found in Nineveh in 1872 purportedly proved that beer was part of the cargo on Noah's Ark: "with beer and brandy, oil and wine, I filled large jars."

As the official start of Prohibition approached—midnight, January 18, 1920—August A. called his two sons into his office. They were grown men—Adolphus III was twenty-nine, Gussie, twenty-one—and their inheritance guaranteed that they would never need to work again if they didn't want to. "You can afford to ride this out and retire," their father said, "but in my book Prohibition is a challenge and we owe it to our employees to keep going."

Given that they had 6,500 employees and an annual payroll of more than $2 million, it was a challenge that even Adolphus would have found daunting. And there was some question as to whether August A. was up to the task. As a young man, he'd shown little interest in the family business, announcing at age nineteen that what he really wanted to do was be a cowboy. He even bought himself an outfit and a six-shooter and, much to his father's chagrin, embarked on a six-month sabbatical at a ranch in Montana. But the prodigal eventually returned to St. Louis and dutifully submitted to Adolphus's strict program for learning the business from the bottom up, starting as a brewer's apprentice and rising methodically through the ranks under the unwavering eye of his father, who ceaselessly bombarded him with letters of instruction, exhortation, criticism, and praise, some running as long as twenty pages. A typical passage reminded him, "Our whole welfare and happiness . . . depends solely and only on the success of our brewery; its earnings are sufficient to make us happy for all time to come."

August A. was a gentler personality than Adolphus, shy and soft-spoken, adverse to publicity, and more attuned to the life of a country squire than that of a hard-driving industrialist. Unlike his father, he didn't enjoy travel. On a 281-acre parcel of land 8.5 miles from the brewery, he built a $300,000 French Renaissance Revival chateau that was easily the grandest residence in the state of Missouri. The estate featured a $250,000 stable for his prized horses, a private zoo that included what he boasted was "the world's tiniest elephant," named Tessie, and a 175-acre "deer park" with a large pond and a clear, burbling stream that serviced his world-class collection of bison, antelope, elk, and deer from Japan, Siberia, India, Europe, Canada, and Virginia. Deer parks—enclosed hunting areas for royalty or the aristocracy—dated back to medieval times in Europe and were popular among the upper classes in Germany during the eighteenth and nineteenth centuries. August A. was especially proud of his herd of European roe deer, similar to the ones his father had hunted from the time he was a boy in Germany right up until a few days before his death.

The property upon which August A. built his mansion was steeped in American history. A previous owner, Colonel Frederick Dent, acquired it in 1821 and used it as a country home, which he called White Haven. One of Dent's sons roomed with Ulysses S.

Grant at West Point, and when Grant was stationed at the nearby Jefferson Barracks, he became a frequent visitor and a suitor to Dent's daughter Julia. The couple married in 1848 and lived at White Haven on and off for the next three decades. At one point right before the Civil War, Grant built a two-story log cabin on the property with the help of several of Dent's slaves. He called the handcrafted residence Hardscrabble. During his years in the White House, he managed the farm from afar and planned to one day retire there. But after a financial swindle left him bankrupt, he mortgaged the property to William Vanderbilt, along with many of his Civil War trophies. When Grant was dying of throat cancer, Vanderbilt offered to forgive the debt, but Grant refused.

August A. Busch bought the property in 1903, by which time it had become known simply as Grant's Farm. Four years later he bought Hardscrabble Cabin, which had been sold, disassembled, and moved elsewhere, and had it reconstructed on the southern edge of the property, bordered by a fence made from 2,563 rifle barrels he purchased from a local armory that was shutting down.

Grant's Farm became the wild frontier refuge that August A. had sought as a young man out West. It was here, away from the unceasing sound and odor of the factory, that he engaged in his favorite pastimes—hunting, breeding livestock, and spoiling his five children.

Over the years, however, as three of his brothers died (Edward, Peter, and Adolphus Jr.) and the fourth was born profoundly handicapped, August A. shouldered more and more of the burden of leading the company. When his father passed away and he assumed the presidency at age forty-eight, he was as schooled and experienced in the art and business of brewing as any man could hope to be. Unfortunately, four years into his stewardship, the American brewing industry was in effect legislated out of existence.

As they sat in their father's office in January 1919 discussing their uncertain future, both Adolphus III and Gussie agreed to join him in the fight to keep the company operating, even if they had no idea how he was going to manage it. In the end, he did it by diversifying. Over the next thirteen years, Anheuser-Busch survived by making products that were spin-offs of its brewing business: rail cars, truck bodies, refrigeration cabinets, ice cream, a nonalcoholic form of Budweiser, a malt-based soft drink called Bevo, barley malt syrup, and baker's yeast. The latter two products—branded with the Budweiser name—proved the most successful, not coincidentally because they were the key ingredients in the nation's booming illegal home-brew trade. As Gussie would admit years later, "We ended up as the biggest bootlegging supply house in the United States."

Anheuser-Busch lost $2.5 million in 1919, $1.6 million in 1920, and $1.3 million in 1921. Before the company returned to profitability, August A. had been forced to borrow $6.5 million from family members and banks and to sell off most of the animals at Grant's Farm, including his beloved Tessie, who was purchased by the Ringling Brothers Barnum & Bailey circus. He saw Tessie one last time some years later when the circus came to St. Louis. According to a story told by his grandson Dolph Orthwein, as Tessie led a parade of elephants into the ring, August A. rose from his seat and called out her name. At the sound of his voice, she raised her head, broke ranks, and trotted around the ring to where he stood in the third row, reduced to tears. After the performance, he tried to buy her back, but the circus refused to sell.

Prohibition took a terrible toll on St. Louis, wiping out an estimated 40,000 brewing-related jobs as dozens of breweries shut down. But even when the unemployment level reached 30 percent in the city during the Depression—80 percent among blacks—August A. managed to keep the Anheuser-Busch brewery operating, with 2,000 workers still on the payroll. For that, his employees and the city loved him.

August A. never stopped fighting against Prohibition. For the entire thirteen years, he argued indefatigably that beer should never have been banned because, unlike distilled liquor (which he did not drink), beer wasn't intoxicating. Rather, it was a "wholesome" and "mildly invigorating stimulant." He once told reporters, in all seriousness, "I have always believed that in making a pure, light beer, I was contributing to the temperance progress of the nation." In May 1921, when a congressional committee was considering a proposal to authorize the limited sale of beer "for medicinal purposes," he sent members a letter opposing the idea as elitist. Saying he was speaking "on behalf of the great mass of men, those with the dinner pail but not the prescription price," he urged the committee to push instead for full legalization: "Beer for all, or beer for none."

He peppered two presidents—Warren G. Harding and Calvin Coolidge—with letters complaining about inequity and hypocrisy in the enforcement of Prohibition. In June 1922 he informed Harding that he had learned through associates that the chairman of the shipping board had obtained presidential approval to allow the sale of all alcoholic beverages—including beer, wine, and hard liquor—on U.S. cruise ships. On one ship alone, he said, the United States was operating five saloons. His charges caused a sensation when he sent copies of the letter to all members of Congress and the Washington press corps. The U.S. attorney general quickly declared that all U.S. ships were prohibited from serving alcohol and that foreign ships could not enter American waters with alcohol on board.

To President Coolidge, August A. sent a nearly book-size missive alleging, among many things, that "quite recently there appeared in the newspapers of the country a series of syndicated articles under the name of Roy A. Haynes, Prohibition Commissioner of the United States. The articles bore evidence that they were written from official information gathered at great expense to the taxpayers. It is within our knowledge that they were offered to certain newspapers at $1,500 for the publication rights. It is a matter of current knowledge that the Prohibition Commissioner received a large sum of money for the articles."

His most effective broadside came in the summer of 1930, when he issued a pamphlet titled *An Open Letter to the American People*, which argued that the relegalization of beer was the perfect antidote to the nation's economic woes because it would return 1.2 million Americans to work in the brewing industry, put money in the pockets of farmers, coal miners, and railroad workers, save the government the $50 million it was spending each year on enforcement, and recoup nearly $500 million in lost taxes. He sent the pamphlet to every senator and congressman, and reprinted it in full-page ads in national magazines. Franklin Roosevelt, then governor of New York, was among the politicians who took his argument to heart. Running on a platform that included the total repeal of Prohibition and supported by former Republican August A., Roosevelt swept to victory over Herbert Hoover in 1932. Nine days after his inauguration, he recommended that Congress sanction the renewed sale of beer immediately, saying, "I deem action at this time to be of highest importance." Congress quickly approved a law authorizing the sale of beer with 3.2 percent alcohol content.

On February 20, 1933, Congress proposed the Twenty-First Amendment to the Constitution, repealing the Eighteenth Amendment. Eight months later, on December 5, Utah became the thirty-sixth state to vote for ratification. Prohibition was dead, and Anheuser-Busch was very much alive.

In one way, Prohibition had benefited the company, wiping out most of its competition, including St. Louis's Union Brewery, whose owner, Otto Stifel, shot himself to death in 1920, and the William J. Lemp Brewing Company, the maker of the popular Falstaff brand, which shut down in 1922 and was sold to the

International Shoe Company for $588,000, less than 10 percent of its pre-Prohibition value. Several months later, the brewery's president, William J. Lemp Jr., committed suicide by shooting himself twice in the heart. Nationally, of the more than 1,300 U.S. breweries operating in 1914, only 164 survived to celebrate the repeal, and a mere handful of those were in any kind of position to challenge A-B for market share.

But the end of Prohibition did not end hard times for the company. After an initial surge, Budweiser sales slumped badly; American consumers had grown accustomed to mixing their bootleg alcohol with ginger ale and other sweeteners. As a result, many former Budweiser drinkers now complained that it tasted bitter. Some among the sales staff argued in favor of changing the formula to make the beer sweeter. August A. wouldn't hear of it. "No one will tinker with the Budweiser taste or the Budweiser process as long as I am president of Anheuser-Busch," he declared, predicting that consumers eventually would come around and the brand would rebound. He also predicted that before that happened, "somebody is going to suggest that we can sell more Budweiser and make more money if we produce it faster. This we will *never* do," he said, recalling his father's insistence that Budweiser had to be aged for at least two and a half months, or it was not Budweiser.

He was proven right about the customers eventually coming back, but it brought him little joy. By then, it was too late; the triple whammy of the war, Prohibition, and the Depression had worn him out. At age sixty-eight, he was in rapidly failing health, suffering from heart disease, gout, claustrophobia, and edema, which caused his legs to swell painfully with fluid. On the morning of February 13, 1934, following a night spent doubled up in pain and crying out, "I can't stand this any longer; please do something," he went to his bedroom, wrote a note that said, "Goodbye precious mama and adorable children," and shot himself in the chest with a pearl-handled .32-caliber pistol he kept in a drawer by his bed. The bullet just missed its intended target, his heart, so he lay on the bed in agony for about fifteen minutes as his wife and other members of the household watched him die.

In his will, August A. requested that his funeral services be conducted "with the utmost simplicity," and so they were, at least by Busch standards. More than ten thousand people paid their respects during an open-casket viewing in the living room of the mansion at Grant's Farm, and members of the St. Louis Symphony Orchestra played for the funeral service while 2,000 spectators gathered outside listened. He was buried on a grassy hilltop in a nearby cemetery, in a pine-shaded plot he had picked because it afforded a view of his mansion. "I can see my home from here," he had said. "This is where I want to be buried." His gravestone served to further differentiate him from his father, whose final resting place is a quintessentially "Buschy" pink granite and marble Gothic mausoleum, built at a cost of $250,000, festooned with gargoyles and vaingloriously inscribed with the quote from Julius Caesar—"Veni, Vidi, Vici" (I came, I saw, I conquered). In stark contrast, August A.'s grave is marked by a small slab of red Missouri granite inscribed, in utmost simplicity, "Busch."

August A.'s estate was valued at $3.4 million, a huge fortune by most standards of the day, but a small fraction of what Adolphus had left behind. The bulk of it consisted of 23,889 shares of Anheuser-Busch stock, which made him a minority shareholder. At the time of his death, there were 180,000 shares outstanding, all but 4,000 owned by descendants of the two original partners, Adolphus and his father-in-law Eberhard Anheuser. August A. had maintained voting control over 167,000 shares, and before his death he established a trust that transferred the voting power of the stock to his two sons, Adolphus III and Gussie. He also left "the boys" joint ownership of his beloved Belleau Farm, a 1,500-

acre duck-hunting retreat that the family always referred to as "the Shooting Grounds." As the firstborn son, Adolphus III inherited his father's position as president of the company, while Gussie had to settle for the title of first vice president and general manager.

Still, no one who really knew Gussie doubted that he would one day take control of everything. And when that happened, the company, the family, and the brewing industry would never be the same.

THE ALPHA BUSCH

August A. "Gussie" Busch Jr. first entered the public consciousness on April 27, 1918, the day he married Marie Christy Church. The event had all the earmarks of an arranged marriage, a union of old class and (relatively) new money. Gussie was nineteen years old; Marie was twenty-two. Beautiful, refined, and polished, the product of a young women's finishing school in Bryn Mawr, Pennsylvania, she could trace her ancestry to General William Clark, one of the leaders of the Lewis and Clark expedition, and to Rene Auguste Chouteau, along with French fur trader Pierre Laclede, one of the founders of St. Louis in 1764, nearly a century before Adolphus Busch stepped off the boat. St. Louis blood didn't get much bluer than hers. The couple first met at a Junior League charity event. He spotted her in the dance lineup, liked what he saw, and introduced himself.

No one ever called Gussie Busch refined or educated. He'd grown up in almost feral bliss in the mansion at Grant's Farm, where his father's indulgences included letting him skip school whenever he wanted, which after the fourth grade was most of the time. "I never graduated from anything," he boasted later in life. Instead, he spent much of his boyhood as a stable rat, homeschooling himself in horsemanship, becoming a championship rider and carriage driver by the time he was a teenager. He was coarse, blunt, and brash, a young man of unbridled appetites and a reputation as an incorrigible carouser, habitual barroom brawler, and insatiable lothario known for romancing women of varying age, social station, and marital status. He bragged that while he was still in grade school he snuck out of the house late at night to visit a brothel. One of his cousins once walked in on him in a bedroom at Grant's Farm, locked in a passionate embrace with the wife of another cousin.

The Busch-Church wedding took place in the home of Marie's widowed mother, but newspaper accounts played up the upper-crust aspects of the event—the diamond-encrusted platinum bracelet the groom gave the bride, the $10,000 check his grandmother Lilly presented to the couple, the plans for a European honeymoon while a small army of craftsmen redecorated the gray stone mansion his father had given him on Lindell Boulevard, the city's most fashionable thoroughfare.

The Busch family had not been embraced by St. Louis high society, which disapproved of their earthy exuberance and the fact that their fortune, massive though it was, flowed from such a plebeian enterprise as making beer. Denied membership in the WASPish St. Louis Country Club, Gussie's father, August A., built his own weekend social club in south St. Louis County, a few miles from Grant's Farm, starting with an elegant hotel, the Sunset Inn, then adding a golf course and swimming pool in 1918 to complete the Sunset Country Club. In a typically Buschy touch, the pool at Sunset was the first in the St. Louis area that allowed men to swim topless.

August A. also founded his own foxhunting club, the Bridlespur

Hunt, which rode in full regalia twice a week through the woods and pastures of Huntleigh Village, an estate-studded suburb that was becoming something of a Busch family enclave. Gussie's sister Clara and her husband Percy Orthwein maintained a mansion there, as did his brother Adolphus III and his cousin Adalbert von Gontard, the son of Gussie's great-aunt Clara and her German husband, Baron Paul Kurt von Gontard. Most of the Busch–Orthwein–von Gontard clan participated in the hunt, but Gussie stood out. In his mid-twenties, compact and muscled, clad in the hunt's traditional pink jacket, white breeches, and black velvet hat and knee high English boots, always riding headlong in the lead as the club's Master of Fox Hounds, he was without question the alpha Busch.

The marriage to Marie produced two daughters—Lilly in 1923 and Carlota in 1927—but it didn't alter Gussie's womanizing ways. He had begun a dalliance with a married woman in their social circle, Elizabeth Overton Dozier, when Marie contracted pneumonia and died in January 1930. By all accounts, Gussie was devastated by the death of his beautiful young wife (she was thirty-three), but it didn't cause him to break off his relationship with Elizabeth. When he married Dozier three years later, the society pages practically clucked with disapproval. One article noted that the bride was "recently divorced" and the ceremony was "performed in a New York hotel with few present," while recalling that Busch's previous wedding had been "an outstanding social event."

The second marriage didn't yield much in the way of domestic bliss: Elizabeth moved into the mansion with the three children from her previous marriage, but Gussie's youngest daughter, Carlota ("Lotsie"), didn't get along with her, and the six-year-old promptly ran away from home to impress the point on her father. Elizabeth was asthmatic, a condition exacerbated by horse dander, which kept her from participating in one of the great passions of Gussie's life. Their relationship was stormy from the start, and got worse over the years as Elizabeth developed a dependence on alcohol and prescription drugs. Decades later, Lotsie would recall that her stepmother "was in bed much of the time." Fortunately for Gussie, he had a company that required his attention, and he threw himself into the task with the same hard-charging energy he applied to chasing foxes and women.

During Prohibition, Gussie had been given the unenviable job of overseeing daily operations of the all but moribund brewery, while Adolphus III had focused on the company's default profit center, the Yeast, Malt and Corn Products Division. The minute the taps were turned back on, however, the relative importance of their respective roles was reversed. Gussie, ostensibly the No. 2 man, now held the power. Publicly, he deferred to his older brother as the president of the company, but privately, he was determined to run the brewery as he saw fit, and to hell with anyone who didn't like it.

The task ahead of him was enormous. As part of the price of repeal, Congress and the president had imposed new regulations on the industry, outlawing some of the sales practices that had helped make his grandfather Adolphus so successful. Roosevelt created the Federal Alcohol Control Administration to establish codes for fair competition, and one of FACA's new rules prohibited breweries from owning any financial interest in retail establishments. Now they had to sell their product in arm's-length transactions with independently owned distributors who in turn sold to the taverns and restaurants. The so-called three-tier system meant that Gussie had to put together a network of hundreds of wholesalers around the country, teach them how to sell his beer, and cut them in for a commission.

Further adding to his cost of operation, Congress had raised the federal excise tax on beer from $2 a barrel to $5. Gussie didn't think he could offset the new costs by raising prices in an economy just starting to recover, and he refused to skimp on ingredients or cut corners with the forty-five-day Budweiser brewing process. The good news that orders were exceeding production meant he had to invest heavily to increase plant capacity or risk losing market share to his two national competitors, Pabst and Schlitz. As a result, even as Budweiser regained its No. 1 position, with more than a million barrels shipped in 1934 and 1935, the brewery division continued to run in the red, subsidized by his brother's yeast operations and the proceeds from the government-ordered divesture of the company's ownership interests in taverns and restaurants.

In February 1936 Gussie was elected president of the newly established Brewing Industry Inc., a self-described "organization of leading American brewers." One of his first acts was to issue a state-of-the-industry report pointing out that since April 1933, America's brewers had paid $800 million in federal, state, and municipal taxes, another $200 million in wages to labor, and $150 million to farmers for grain and other agricultural products used in brewing.

"The records show that more than 50,000 union wage earners are employed directly in the brewing plants," Gussie was quoted as saying. "The products of the industry are distributed by 15,000 wholesalers, each of whom employs from two to four men. The products are sold to consumers by 175,000 retailers, each of whom employs at least two men. The agriculture products needed require at least 65,000 100-acre farms to produce them, so the industry, directly in the manufacture and distribution of its products, has given employment, and better than average wages, to 650,000 persons."

The report was practically a point-by-point affirmation of his father's 1930 *Open Letter to the American People* pamphlet proposing the relegalization of beer as a cure for the Depression. As it turns out, economists now mark March 1933, the month Congress voted for the return of beer, as the official end of the Great Depression. Over the next three years the economy experienced a robust recovery, with unemployment falling from 25 to 14 percent as beer sales soared. In 1937, however, the economy went into a tailspin, and unemployment shot back up to 19 percent. Economists ascribe the "Great Recession of 1937" to a confluence of factors that sounds familiar today—an attempt by the Roosevelt administration to reduce the deficit by slashing government spending, coupled with a tax increase on the wealthy and a tightening of the money supply by the Federal Reserve. There was widespread fear that the country was going to slip back into a depression.

Viewed from an era of egregious corporate greed, Anheuser-Busch's reaction seems extraordinary. The company announced that it was going to devote its entire 1938 advertising effort to a series of newspaper and magazine ads aimed at calming the nation's economic fears and restoring confidence in the ability of the country's institutions to deal with the problems. The idea was "to sell America to Americans," according to a statement A-B sent to its employees and the industry at large. "Our challenge is more important than selling beer, more important than making profits."

The ads contained no pictures of the product, no statements about its merits. Instead they offered patriotic pep talks that might have made Ronald Reagan blush. "Each sunrise in America ushers in new opportunities to those who keep their chins up . . . who never lose that lusty courage and willingness that made ours the most envied nation on earth," said one. "Confidence sailed our pioneer forefathers across the turbulent Atlantic," said another. "Confidence helped our grandfathers extend the stubborn frontier, and made ours the strongest and most abundant land on earth today. Confidence is ready now to take America further still."

The only mention of Budweiser came in the ads' tagline: "Live life, every golden minute of it . . . Drink Budweiser, every golden drop of it."

Without question, there was self-interest behind the ads—Gussie and Adolphus III figured that confident wage-earning men were likely to drink more beer than fearful unemployed men. But the campaign was hardly a cynical ploy. Gussie believed in his gut that serving the public good also served the company, and that goodwill was always the best salesman. It all went back to the beginning, when his grandfather Adolphus first explained to his new partner and father-in-law, Eberhard Anheuser, that their business was not just making beer. "Making *friends* is our business," he said. Gussie had made that his motto; rarely did he go a day without uttering it. Over the years, he came to the conclusion that the company could never go wrong by doubling down on patriotism and the public good. "If we do something in the public interest which at the same time is profitable to the company, then this is, indeed, *very* good business," he said.

As it turned out, Anheuser-Busch did very good business in 1938, selling more than two million barrels, surpassing its pre-Prohibition high by 400,000. At a time when the industry as a whole grew by 26 percent, A-B sales increased 173 percent. For the first time in nearly twenty years, the brewery division turned a profit.

All of which helped boost Gussie's public image in St. Louis. No longer was he seen as merely a beer baron's playboy son. Now he was considered a bona fide captain of industry, cut from the same cloth as his grandfather Adolphus. Cocksure and playfully extravagant, he was great copy for the local newspapers, which gleefully reported on his extracurricular activities, whether it was his arrest for driving 70 miles per hour on a city street in his Pierce-Arrow sedan or his purchase of an eleven-ton, thirty-three-foot private bus equipped with a kitchen, bathroom, and sleeping berths for eight. He got the idea for the bus, which he called "my land yacht," from his pal silent film cowboy Tom Mix, who had customized his traveling horse trailer to include sleeping quarters for humans. On a trip to New York City, Gussie entertained himself by taking a shower as the bus cruised down Fifth Avenue, lathering up and laughing uproariously at the thought that he was probably the first person ever to do that. A reporter for the *St. Louis Globe-Democrat* was on hand when Gussie returned home from an Arizona vacation accompanied by "12 cow ponies, two cowboys and a cowgirl" that he planned to employ in a calf-roping exhibition at the St. Louis Spring Horse Show. To practice for the event, in which he intended to perform, Gussie built an elaborate corral, "patterned after those on Western ranches," at Belleau Farm. As he watched his hired cowpokes put on a roping demonstration for the newspaper, he boasted that the pony named Indian Summer had cost him $1,000 and was "one of the best roping horses in the nation today." He was, said the newspaper, "like a kid with a new toy."

In the years immediately following Prohibition, it was good to be Gussie. He had a valet, a personal barber, and a driver to attend to his daily needs. Tailors came to his office to fit him for his business, formal, and sporting attire. His household staff included a butler, two cooks, several maids and nannies, a laundress, and a yardman. If he was not yet a king, he was definitely a crowned prince. The only thing lacking in his life, as far as he was concerned, was a male heir. Over the course of nineteen years and two marriages, he had fathered three daughters—the youngest, Elizabeth, was born in 1935—and each birth had been more disappointing for him than the last. He loved his girls, and doted on them, particularly Lotsie, whom was spunky and free-spirited and reminded him of himself at her age. But he needed a son to carry on the family name and run the family company; it was an ancestral imperative. His grandfather and father were never far from his mind. He adored August A., whom he invariably referred to as "my good Daddy," and was awestruck by Adolphus. "Grandaddy would take us hunting, let us smoke and have a drink of whiskey," he recalled. "I was a big man when I was with him. And everything he touched turned to gold."

Gussie wanted to be a big man to his own boy—teach him to ride and hunt and run a brewery, encourage him to drink deeply of the golden American dream that his forebears had realized.

He finally got what he wanted on June 16, 1937, when Elizabeth gave birth to August Anheuser Busch III. As if to make it clear to the world that the future leader of the company had been born, Gussie arranged for the baby to be fed a few drops of Budweiser even before he tasted breast milk.

The arrival of August the Third would prove a classic case of "Be careful what you wish for." Gussie's firstborn son would lead the company to heights his father never dreamed of, but in the process he would commit an act of betrayal that Gussie would never fully forgive.

"BEING SECOND ISN'T WORTH SHIT"

At the outbreak of World War II, fearful that a wave of anti-German, anti-alcohol hysteria would once again devastate their industry, America's brewers fell all over themselves trying to prove their patriotism. They retooled sections of their plants to manufacture parts and equipment for the military. They conducted highly publicized programs encouraging their employees to buy war bonds. And they launched ad campaigns that seem almost laughable today, tying their product to the war effort by suggesting that drinking beer would help defeat the enemy.

Hoping to head off any government-imposed rationing of grain similar to that which occurred during World War I, the industry dispatched its lobbyist to Washington to convince lawmakers that beer was not only vital to the American economy, it was also a necessary ingredient to maintaining morale among the troops *and* the civilian population. The U.S. Brewers Foundation borrowed a page from Adolphus Busch's pre-Prohibition playbook with an advertising campaign that promoted beer as "America's Beverage of Moderation." Working with the government, the trade association created what became known as the "Beer Belongs" series of magazine ads, which contained the tagline, "Morale is a lot of little things." A typical ad featured a Norman Rockwell–style rendering of a young man, perhaps a college student, lying on his bunk reading a letter from the folks back home. "A cool refreshing glass of beer . . . a moment of relaxation. In trying times like these, they, too, help to keep morale up." Anheuser-Busch ran an ad that said, "Every sip helps somebody."

The brewers' main contribution to the war effort was, of course, beer—millions of bottles and cans of it, shipped to military bases around the world under contracts with the government. "Every fourth bottle of Schlitz goes overseas," blared one of that brewery's most memorable wartime ads, which pictured a ship bristling with big guns and slicing through the waves as if chasing down a German U-boat. The Big Three national breweries—Anheuser-Busch, Pabst, and Schlitz—sold the lion's share of the beer to the military because the smaller regional firms didn't have the production or distribution capacity to service the contracts.

In addition to providing hundreds of thousands of olive-drab cans of Budweiser to all the service branches, A-B manufactured ammunition hoists for the navy, and arranged with the Army Air Force to earmark the company's employee war bonds program for the purchase of B-17 bombers. A-B employees bought enough bonds—nearly $900,000 worth—to pay for two of the so-called Flying Fortresses, which, in a smart bit of branding, the company got the army to name *Miss Budweiser* and *Busch-whacker*.

When the government suggested that the big national shippers temporarily cease distribution on the West Coast in order to free up railroad freight cars for the military, only Anheuser-Busch agreed to do so. In a move that was both classy and clever, the company withdrew from the region with a published statement to its customers commending "the many fine beers now being brewed on the Pacific Coast," as opposed to those brewed in Milwaukee.

When it came to personal displays of patriotism, Gussie Busch outdid all of his competitors. Six months after the Japanese attack on Pearl Harbor, at the age of forty-three, with four children, he joined the army. To be sure, he didn't sign up for combat duty; he accepted a commission as a major in the U.S. Army Ordnance Department, stationed in Washington, D.C., a posting arranged by his good friend, Missouri senator Harry S. Truman. The assignment was without doubt a cushy one, but it did require Gussie to take a leave of absence from the brewery, forsake the services of his valet and butler, and submit to the authority of the military chain of command, which couldn't have been easy for him. He reported for duty at the Pentagon in a beautifully hand-tailored uniform and by all accounts served with distinction, earning a promotion to lieutenant colonel within six months and another to full colonel in November 1944. He eventually was awarded a Legion of Merit medal for distinguished service, which was pinned on him personally by the secretary of war and worn on his lapel for the rest of his life. He couldn't have been more proud if it were a Purple Heart or a Silver Cross for battlefield heroism.

Contrary to the brewers' initial fears, anti-German sentiment never became a factor with American beer drinkers, and the war actually proved a boon to the business. Per capita consumption in the United States increased by 50 percent during the course of the conflict. Anheuser-Busch shipped nearly 3.7 million barrels in 1944, 2 million more than was ever shipped in Adolphus's time.

But all was not well back at the St. Louis brewery. That summer, Gussie got a phone call from a trusted employee at the plant telling him that a batch of beer had overfermented and tasted bad, but his brother, Adolphus III, was going to bottle and ship it anyway.

Gussie was appalled. He immediately countermanded Adolphus and ordered that the tainted beer, a million dollars' worth, be poured down the sewer. Adolphus was furious and threatened to resign as president, but the board of directors talked him out of it. Still, he never forgot what his younger brother had done.

Gussie returned to St. Louis in June 1945, but not to the mansion on Lindell Boulevard. His time in Washington, and his rumored romantic liaisons there, had left him and Elizabeth utterly estranged. Along with his eighteen-year-old daughter Lotsie, he moved into a six-bedroom apartment in the so-called Bauernhof at Grant's Farm, an elaborate U-shaped medieval German–style structure his father had built to house his prized horses, cows, cars, carriages, and farm staff. The main house at Grant's Farm had been vacant since shortly after his father's suicide in 1934, but was still maintained and used for family get-togethers at Christmas and Easter and occasional company parties. Gussie's mother, Alice, lived a few hundred yards down the lane in a two-story colonial home the family referred to as "the cottage," which was built for her after her husband's death and qualified as a cottage only in comparison to the three-story, thirty-four-room, fourteen-bath mansion.

Gussie's homecoming was attended by speculation in the newspapers that he would run for mayor, but he dismissed questions about his candidacy as abruptly as he did the tendency on the part of some people to address him as "Colonel Busch." He was flattered by the talk, but not tempted. His eyes were focused on the brewery, and he didn't like what he saw.

In many ways, business had never looked better. Americans were drinking more beer than ever before; overall production had doubled during the war. Anheuser-Busch, Pabst, and Schlitz were gaining significant market share at the expense of regional brewers thanks to returning GIs who had tasted their beer for the first time while on active duty. Profits were up; the St. Louis plant could not brew enough to fill its orders.

The problem, as Gussie saw it, was that for the first time since the turn of the century, Anheuser-Busch was No. 2. On his brother's watch, Pabst had taken the lead. Pabst was A-B's longtime archenemy. Gussie's grandfather Adolphus had competed maniacally with "Captain" Frederick Pabst for decades, no doubt in part because Pabst, too, had gotten his start in the business by marrying the brewery owner's daughter. In 1894, after a panel of judges in Chicago awarded Pabst lager the first-place blue ribbon in a competition for "America's best beer," Adolphus personally pursued one of the event's judges across Europe in an unsuccessful attempt to get the decision overturned in favor of second-place Budweiser. The rebranded "Pabst Blue Ribbon" beer outsold Budweiser for the next six years.

Like his grandfather, Gussie couldn't bear to be beaten, whether in equestrian competition, gin rummy, or business. A-B's fall from first place reportedly caused him to grouse that "being second isn't worth anything," but the quote seems uncharacteristically tepid for a man given to coarse expression. People who knew him always suspected that a reporter had cleaned up what he really said, which could not have been printed in any publication at that time— "Being second isn't worth shit."

As for his own No. 2 position, fate intervened in August 1946 when, after eight days in the hospital, Adolphus III died of cardiac failure brought on by stomach cancer. He was fifty-five and had been ill for some time. Six days later, Gussie was named president of the company at a special meeting of the board of directors, where there were mixed feelings about the passing of the torch. Adolphus had not been a particularly dynamic or visionary leader, and his drinking had troubled some members of the family and the board, who thought it sometimes impaired his judgment, as in the tainted beer incident. For the most part, however, they regarded him as a calm, competent, reasonable steward of the company, and a gentleman. Gussie, on the other hand, was volatile, bumptious, hot-tempered, tyrannical, rude, obstinate, impatient, and vindictive. Yet he was also charismatic, fun-loving, infectiously exuberant, and possibly the most brilliant beer salesman who ever lived. Not even his grandfather worked a saloon with such determination or delight—striding across the room, his hand outstretched, his distinctive voice overpowering the din: "My name is Gussie Busch, and I'd like to buy you a Budweiser."

Gussie bounded onto the Anheuser-Busch throne determined to return the company of his father and grandfather to its rightful place at the top. His first order of business was increasing capacity to meet demand. His plan called for a $50 million upgrade of the Pestalozzi Street plant and the construction of a new $34 million plant in Newark, New Jersey. Some board members worried about the cost of the new plant and argued for the cheaper option of acquiring an existing plant and refitting it, as Schlitz and Pabst were already doing in New York. Even though it was duly incorporated, with stockholders and a board of directors, A-B bore little resemblance to a modern corporation. It was in every sense a family business. Of the fifteen members of the all-male board, seven were either direct descendants of Adolphus Busch or married to direct descendants, two were grandsons of Eberhard Anheuser, and the rest were cronies of Gussie. One local writer likened the board to "the cast of a rousing Rudolph Firml operetta, with Adolphs, Augusts, Eberhards and Adalberts crowding each other off the corporate stage. . . . There's a Wagnerian air to the whole enterprise."

Family members held more than 70 percent of the company stock, with Gussie controlling the largest block. In addition to his own shares, he had the power to vote the shares that his father left to his mother in trust, so it was not particularly difficult for him to get his way. If all else failed, his temper usually did the trick. When told he couldn't do something, his response was typically, "I can't? Just watch me."

Gussie won board approval for the expansion plan, including the new plant, but climbing back into first place took a lot longer than he thought it would. Despite a big increase in Budweiser sales, Schlitz came out on top in 1947, while Anheuser-Busch dropped to fourth place. For the next six years, Gussie worked tirelessly to knock Schlitz from the No. 1 position, personalizing the battle in the same way that Adolphus had done with Pabst half a century before. His near obsession with beating Schlitz was partly due to a personality trait—throughout his life, he'd always needed an enemy to compete against; it's what energized him and inspired him to do his best. But it also derived from his realization that the war had changed the brewing landscape, and the future would be determined by which of the three superpowers came to dominate. As it was with geopolitics, so it was with beer.

In the summer of 1949, Gussie took a break from the brewery and traveled to Europe with his buddy Tony Buford, A-B's chief counsel. After a stay in Paris and a visit with Gussie's aunt Wilhelmina (Adolphus's youngest daughter) in Munich, they took a train to Lucerne, Switzerland, where they stopped for lunch one day at a restaurant called the Swiss House. Gussie was immediately taken with the hostess, a tall blue-eyed blonde named Gertrude Buholzer. Partway through his meal he approached the proprietor and asked, "Who in the hell is that beautiful girl?"

"That's my daughter," said Willy Buholzer. "Why do you want to know?"

Gussie replied awkwardly that they were in town looking to purchase schnauzers to breed at his farm in the United States and wondered if she knew where they could acquire some of the dogs. The two Americans paid their bill and left, but they returned the next day. This time, Gussie asked Willy Buholzer if he could meet his daughter. "Trudy" was accustomed to male customers making a fuss over her. At twenty-two, she was stunning, vivacious, and educated. She spoke four languages—French, German, Italian, and English. Her father told her she didn't have to meet the Americans if she didn't want to, but she said she'd be happy to take them to some people she knew who had the dogs. At the end of the day with her, Gussie proposed, never mind that he was twenty-seven years her senior and still married.

Trudy was more amused and intrigued than smitten. She was already engaged to a man named Hans, who was thirty-eight and owned a house on Lake Lucerne. "My parents were crazy about Hans," she recalled later. Still, she agreed, and her parents acquiesced, when a besotted Gussie invited her to visit him in America.

Gussie paid for her ocean passage and met her boat in New York, where they stayed for a week at the Plaza Hotel. They went shopping for "New York shoes," took a carriage ride through Central Park, and hit the hottest show on Broadway, *South Pacific* with Mary Martin. Then he pulled out the stops with a journey to St. Louis via private train car with its own chef and waiters. Stepping off the train in St. Louis's Union Station, Trudy was struck by how ugly the city looked, choked with smoke and covered in soot, so far removed from the lakes and trees of her homeland. She was unnerved, too, by the number of black people on the street; they were a rarity in Switzerland. Belleau Farm, where Gussie put her up during her stay, was much more like home, with its rustic lakeside lodge and fields full of wildlife.

It was her first visit to the brewery, however, that sealed the deal. "That's when I fell in love with him completely, because of the way he handled himself, his assurance and knowledge in telling everyone what to do. It was very sexy to me." More than sixty years later, seated in the dining room at Belleau Farm, eighty-three-year-old Trudy smiled at the memory and confided, "I was in love and lust. He was the first man I made love with. I had never had sex before."

Trudy returned home and broke the news to her family—she was in love with the rich American brewer who wanted her to come to the United States to be with him. While she was in Switzerland, Gussie besieged her with love letters, which, she found out some years later, were actually written by his longtime secretary, Dora Schoefield. "She had a beautiful way of writing, and she knew him so well; they were wonderful letters."

Gussie brought Trudy to St. Louis again in the spring of 1950. This time she stayed at Grant's Farm, where he put on a show for the ages, hosting a reception for President Harry Truman, who was in town to attend a reunion of his World War I army unit. Gussie and the president had been friends since Truman was an up-and-coming state politician in Kansas City. As Truman rose to prominence—as FDR's vice president in 1944 and then as his successor following FDR's death in office in 1945—Gussie liked to tell the story of how he once took Truman to Union Station to catch a train back to Kansas City and had to lend him a quarter to make the fare. He contributed a great deal more than that to Truman's come-from-behind campaign for reelection in 1948.

At Grant's Farm, Gussie greeted his old friend at the front gates while Trudy served as one of the hostesses at a dinner party for a thousand guests who were seated at canopied tables in the courtyard of the Bauernhof, surrounded by the Busch collection of antique carriages, coaches, landaus, tally-hoes, phaetons, buggies, Russian sleighs, and German hunting wagons.

After dinner, like two young boys bent on mischief, Gussie and Harry climbed aboard one of Gussie's favorite carriages, the Vigilant, and clattered off into the deer park behind four shiny black horses, leaving the president's Secret Service detachment in their wake. They were gone for more than half an hour, and it's not difficult to imagine that they used the time to enjoy a nip or two from one of Gussie's silver flasks.

Over the next year and a half, Trudy became more and more visible as Gussie's companion, appearing with him at A-B events around the country and traveling with him on vacations to Florida and Europe. All the while, he was trying to extricate himself from his marriage. In 1948 he published a notice in the local newspapers disavowing Elizabeth's debts. "You are hereby notified that, having furnished my wife, Mrs. August A. Busch Jr., with adequate funds to maintain her household, I will no longer be liable to you, or any other person whosoever, for any accounts contracted by Mrs. Busch for any purpose whatsoever, or for any accounts contracted by her on behalf of our two children."

He finally filed for divorce on August 7, 1951, six years after separating from Elizabeth. Citing "general indignities," he claimed that she had exhibited "the most violent wrath and hatred" toward him and had told him on several occasions that she didn't love him. For the next six months, *Busch vs. Busch* played out in the court and in the newspapers, with each side visiting indignity upon the other, making it appear to the public that the main issues between them were her drinking and his philandering. His lawyers questioned "how much she paid the yard man in 1940" and "how much was spent for whiskey, wine and gin." Her lawyers demanded to inspect his books and records, because "how else could we find out how much Mr. Busch has been spending on other women." The judge, however, denied her request to examine her husband's financial records, saying they were "immaterial," and the Missouri Supreme Court upheld his ruling. A few weeks later, Elizabeth accepted what the newspapers trumpeted as the state's first-ever million-dollar divorce settlement. It consisted of a lump sum of $450,000 for alimony, a property settlement of $480,000, to be paid over a number of years, and the house on Lindell, which was valued at $100,000. She also was awarded custody of the couple's two children, Elizabeth and August III.

August was only five when his father went off to Washington. Raised mostly by his troubled, often impaired mother, he had developed into a moody, withdrawn adolescent with a spotty school attendance record and only a few friends. As the ugly dissolution of his parents' marriage dragged on in public, he began acting out. One particularly antisocial episode occurred on Halloween night in 1949, when two neighbor girls accused him of shooting them with a pellet gun when they came to his house trick-or-treating. The girls told the police that when they rang the doorbell at the Busch residence on Lindell, they were greeted with a barrage of eggs, tomatoes, and water from a second-story window, so they ran home and got some eggs to respond in kind. But when they returned, August stood at the second-floor window with a rifle and shot them. The girls were treated for minor contusions, and two police officers went to the Busch house. The story they got from August was that a "swarm of girls" had engaged in an unprovoked attack on the house that started when the butler answered the front door and an egg "came flying through and splattered in the living room." August admitted that he had stood at the window with a gun and warned the girls to go away, but he claimed the gun was partly dismantled and could not have been fired even if he had attempted to do so.

August's version of events did not pass the smell test, but his mother and the butler backed him up about the gun and took the police upstairs to see it lying on the bed, partly dismantled, just as August claimed. Even though no charges were filed, the preteen contretemps earned a headline in the next day's paper: "August A. Busch III Questioned by Police in Halloween Fracas." It's unlikely that it would have been reported if his name had been anything other than Busch.

Gussie's physical and emotional absence from August's life during this period would eventually have serious consequences for the family and the company. Years later, in describing to a colleague what it was like to grow up as Gussie Busch's firstborn son, August ruefully related an incident that occurred at Grant's Farm when he was a boy: He'd put on an old pair of his late uncle Adolphus's old chaps and had taken one of the farm's tractors on a joyride around the lake when he lost control of the machine and wound up in the water, standing on the seat as the tractor slowly sank. Suddenly he heard his father calling and saw him standing on the bank. He thought he was about to be rescued. Instead, Gussie shouted at him, "August, what the hell are you doing wearing your uncle Adolphus's chaps?"

4

"THE MAN WHO SAVED
THE CARDINALS"

On March 22, 1952, the day after Gussie's divorce from Elizabeth became final, he and Trudy were married. The ceremony took place in Gussie's cottage on the grounds of the Majestic Hotel in Hot Springs, Arkansas, and was performed by a justice of the Arkansas Supreme Court. It was a brewery family affair: Eberhard Anheuser gave away the bride; Gussie's cousin Adalbert ("Addy") von Gontard, an A-B vice president, served as best man; and Gussie's two daughters by his first marriage, Lilly and Lotsie, were Trudy's bridesmaids.

Press coverage of the event was carefully managed. Gussie's public relations man, Al Fleishman, had alerted the local newspapers to the impending nuptials just the day before, telling reporters that August III "was expected to attend." He did not, however, and neither did his sister Elizabeth. Following a breakfast buffet reception that featured unexpected entertainment by comedian Joe E. Lewis, who "just happened to be in town," the newlyweds boarded Gussie's motorbus and left for a two-week Florida vacation.

As Busch weddings went, it was a low-key, seemingly inauspicious event, an impression the newspapers furthered by devoting nearly as many words to Gussie's two previous unions as they did to the one at hand. Trudy's name wasn't even mentioned in the society-page headlines, one of which said, "August A. Busch Jr. Will Marry Swiss Girl Today" (she was twenty-five).

A lot of people underestimated Trudy Buholzer in the beginning, but marrying her turned out to be one of the best moves Gussie Busch ever made, ranking up there with his decision less than a year later to purchase the St. Louis Cardinals baseball team. Together these two "acquisitions" defined the rest of his life.

The Cardinals weren't even his idea. He was approached in February 1953 by a contingent of local businessmen that included several A-B board members and Fleishman, who was fast becoming one of his most trusted confidants. The men told Gussie that the owner of the Cardinals, Fred Saigh, was in talks to move the team to Milwaukee, where an investor group had offered him more than $4 million for the franchise. Saigh had financial problems and was about to begin serving a fifteen-month prison sentence for tax evasion. He needed to sell the team, they said, but he preferred that the Cardinals remain in St. Louis; he just hadn't been able to find a local buyer. If Gussie was interested, then Saigh might sell the team to A-B for less than the Milwaukee people had put on the table.

Gussie didn't give a good goddamn about baseball or the Cardinals. He was a "sportsman"; he enjoyed hunting, fishing, horseback riding, and coaching—all gentlemanly pursuits. He had never followed professional team sports; that was for the masses. He knew that St. Louisans loved their "Red Birds," of course, and that first baseman Stan Musial was considered one of the greatest players in the game. The men who worked at the brewery idolized "Stan the Man" or "Stash" (pronounced *stosh*), as some of them liked to call him, a childhood nickname bestowed by his Polish-born father.

The Cardinals were in fact one of the most successful teams in the major leagues, having won nine National League pennants and six World Series titles in the previous twenty-seven years. That paled in comparison to the New York Yankees' record of nineteen pennants and fifteen World Series wins, but the Cardinals boasted a broader fan base than the Yankees. As the farthest west and farthest south major league franchise, they were the home team of more Americans than any other ball club. If you lived in Kentucky, Kansas, Arkansas, Oklahoma, Nebraska, Texas, Tennessee, or a dozen other southern and western states in 1952, you likely rooted for the Red Birds. They were, arguably, "America's team." Which made the radio and TV broadcasting rights to their games all the more valuable. Those rights were then held by Griesedieck Brothers Brewery, owned by members of the German family brewing dynasty, whose Falstaff brand was the No. 1 seller in the city, a fact that galled Gussie no end. He knew the electronic media's potential for selling beer. In 1950, Anheuser-Busch became the first brewery to sponsor a network TV program, *The Ken Murray Budweiser Show*. The one-hour Saturday-night variety program ran on fifty-one CBS stations and often showed the host and his guests sipping the sponsor's product live on the air. Budweiser registered sales increases in those fifty-one markets that were double those in other cities.

Gussie liked everything he heard. With one move, he could deny the city of Milwaukee, home of Pabst and Schlitz, a professional baseball team, wrest the Cardinals' broadcasting rights away from Griesedieck Brothers, and turn Sportsman's Park, where the Cardinals played, into a giant outdoor tavern—thirty thousand Budweiser drinkers held captive for two or three hours at a time in the sweltering St. Louis heat. Better yet, as Al Fleishman explained, the acquisition could be sold to the public as an act of good citizenship on the part of Anheuser-Busch, and Gussie would be celebrated as "the man who saved the Cardinals for St. Louis."

Done deal. Gussie agreed to pay Saigh $2.5 million and assume $1.25 million of Saigh's debt. He bludgeoned the A-B board into going along with the plan, which included naming himself president of the team. The board also acquiesced when, after an inspection tour of Sportsman's Park, Gussie decided to buy the stadium for $800,000 and spend another $400,000 on badly needed repairs and refurbishing.

The local newspapers played the story just the way Al Fleishman said they would. "Busch Saves the Cards for St. Louis" blared the banner headline on the front page of the *St. Louis Globe-Democrat*.

On March 10, 1953, a stockholders meeting at A-B headquarters drew a record one hundred people (only twenty-one had attended the previous meeting) who voted 99 percent of the outstanding shares in favor of the acquisition. In a room with blowups of recent press coverage displayed on the walls, Gussie spoke about the tremendous public relations potential of the team. "Development of the Cardinals will have untold value for the development of our company," he said. "This is one of the finest moves in the history of Anheuser-Busch." At a subsequent press conference, however, he played up the benefits to the city and delivered a line that Fleishman obviously scripted to preempt any impertinent questions from reporters about the new owner's love of the game.

"I've been a baseball fan all my life," Gussie said. "But I've been too busy to get out to the park in recent years, unfortunately."

In all the excitement surrounding the announcement, Gussie stumbled when he told reporters off-the-cuff that he intended to rename the ballpark Budweiser Stadium. Howls of protest went up immediately, decrying the crass commercialization of the great American pastime. Baseball commissioner Ford Frick called Gussie directly to tell him the organization could not condone naming a ballpark after an alcoholic beverage. Al Fleishman drew the unpleasant task of trying to talk Gussie out of something he wanted to do. Suggesting that there might be a more appropriate name for the ballpark, Fleishman deftly pointed out that when chewing gum magnate William Wrigley Jr. bought the Chicago Cubs in the 1920s, he named the ballpark Wrigley Field, not Juicy Fruit Field. Gussie got the point, admitted he made a mistake, and Sportsman's Park became Busch Stadium, supposedly in honor of his grandfather, father, and brother.

Gussie wasted no time establishing himself as a hands-on owner. Three days after the stockholders meeting, he pulled into the Cardinals spring training camp in St. Petersburg, Florida, behind the wheel of his motorbus, trailed by a caravan of Cadillacs containing a retinue of cronies and company executives that, according to *Post-Dispatch* writer Jack Rice, "looked like it had been recruited from a P. G. Wodehouse March on the Rhine." He strode into Cardinals headquarters at Al Lang Field with his hand out and voice booming: "My name is Gussie Busch and I'm the new owner." He donned a Cardinals cap and a white flannel team jersey, which he tucked goofily into his baggy gray suit pants, and he posed for pictures in the batting cage with Stan Musial and manager Eddie Stanky. Awkwardly holding a bat as if it were for the first time, he stood at the plate with an uncomfortable smile frozen on his face. A sportswriter described the ignominy: "After fanning on half a dozen softball pitches from the mound, he dubbed a couple of dribblers and called it a day."

Meeting the players, he was surprised to see only white faces. "Where are our black players?" he asked Stanky and the coaches. He was told there weren't any. "How can it be the great American game if blacks can't play?" he replied, angrily. "Hell, we sell beer to *everyone*." In fact, Anheuser-Busch sold more beer to black people than any other brewery. Gussie feared that A-B's ownership of an all-white team at a time when Jackie Robinson and Willie Mays were in ascendance could spark a black boycott of Budweiser. He also thought it was morally wrong. He ordered Stanky and the Cardinals management to find some black players, fast. They quickly acquired a black first baseman named Tom Alston, but when Gussie learned that Alston was two years older than he'd been told, he demanded $20,000 of the purchase price be returned because he figured he'd been gypped out of two years of Alston's career. Manager Stanky seemed to understand the new situation perfectly. "Gussie likes me," he told reporters. "We play gin rummy. I take his money. And when he decides I'm bad for beer, I go."

If the Cardinals thought Gussie's interest in their daily affairs would wane as the novelty of ownership wore off, they were disabused of that notion when it was announced that he would be "following the Red Birds on the road" in a new $300,000 private railroad car that could be hitched to the train that carried the team. The custom-built, eighty-six-foot car had four bedrooms, three conference rooms, a dining room, a kitchen, two bathrooms, an observation lounge, quarters for two attendants, and a communications system that included two-way radios, telephones, and a television set. Stainless steel on the outside and oak-paneled within, it sported an Anheuser-Busch "A & Eagle" trademark insignia on one end and a Cardinals team logo on the other. It was as Buschy as all get-out, and a harbinger of Gussie extravagances to come. A company spokesman hastened to clarify that "the car will be used in the nationwide operation of the brewery, which *could* coincide with the Cardinals road schedule."

A-B's purchase of the Cardinals drew the ire of Colorado senator Edwin C. Johnson, who embarked on a one-man crusade to undo the deal, claiming that Gussie had "degraded" baseball by reducing it to "a cold-blooded, beer-peddling business." Johnson introduced legislation to "bring under anti-trust laws any professional baseball club owned by a beer or liquor company" (the U.S. Supreme Court had recently held that baseball teams were not subject to the Clayton-Sherman antitrust laws as they were written).

With encouragement from Al Fleishman, St. Louis civic leaders jumped to Gussie's defense. Mayor Raymond Tucker sent a telegram to Senator Johnson praising Gussie as "an outstanding leader in St. Louis affairs" and stating that "the people of St. Louis do not believe the Cardinals are being run for business purposes." The president of the Chamber of Commerce sent a similar telegram "to inform you that this 100-year-old company and its president have brought great credit to this community through their business practices, civic spirit and community services."

Undeterred, Johnson prevailed upon North Dakota Republican senator William Langer, chairman of the Senate judiciary committee, to hold a subcommittee hearing on his proposed bill. Testifying as the leadoff witness, Johnson described Gussie's purchase of the Cardinals as "a lavish and vulgar display of beer wealth and beer opulence," and warned that it threatened the very existence of baseball because it would force other brewery owners to buy major league teams in order to remain competitive. "When that happens, sport goes out the window," he said. "It just becomes a contest between big businesses. Not only will there be a monopoly in beer, but there will also be a monopoly in baseball."

National League president Warren Giles countered that the Cardinals sale had, in fact, "stabilized the national league and helped stabilize baseball."

Johnson's motives were called into question in that day's newspapers, which reported that he was also the president of the Class A Western Baseball League and, as such, was worried that Anheuser-Busch's plan to broadcast Cardinal games in cities with minor league teams would cut into attendance. The press also revealed that Johnson's son-in-law was the majority owner of the Denver Bears Class A Team, on whose board sat none other than Adolph Coors III, the chairman of the Colorado brewing empire.

Johnson admitted that his bill was aimed solely at the "St. Louis combination," which he described as "an unholy alliance" that was having "an unhealthy influence on the youngsters of America." To press criticism that he was "picking on" Anheuser-Busch while conveniently forgetting that the New York Yankees had been owned for years by brewer Jacob Ruppert with no apparent harm to the team or the sport, he retorted, "The business of brewing and baseball always were kept separate by Colonel Ruppert. Not one cent of Ruppert's beer money went into baseball."

Not surprisingly, Gussie was the only brewer called to testify at the Senate hearings. For the most part he held his temper in check and hewed to the line that the Cardinals purchase was purely an act of community service, not of commerce. "Anheuser-Busch was a leader in its field before any baseball broadcast, and even before organized baseball itself made an appearance on the American scene," he said. "If anyone wants to buy the Cardinals, they're open. All I ask is that they be kept in St. Louis." When Johnson asked what his price would be, Gussie responded sharply, "Exactly what we paid for them and put into them." Addressing the other subcommittee members, he said, "Gentleman, this was and is the only means known to me that would have kept the Cardinals in St. Louis." After a pause, he added, "St. Louis without the Cardinals wouldn't be the same."

From a public relations standpoint, he hit it out of the park. Illinois senator Everett Dirksen and Missouri senator Stuart Symington, both subcommittee members, came out strongly against Johnson's proposed legislation and praised Gussie and his "illustrious family."

At day's end, Senator Johnson called it quits, telling reporters, "I'm through; I closed up shop." Then, in the face of all evidence to the contrary, he claimed victory: "The hearing accomplished its purpose of awakening baseball to the dangers it faces from corporate ownership of individual clubs."

Al Fleishman could not have hoped for a better outcome: the city had retained a beloved and badly needed sports franchise; the brewery had acquired a potent marketing tool; and St. Louis's most famous family had been cast in a favorable new light. As *St. Louis Post-Dispatch* writer Jack Rice put it, "For 100 years, the Busches had been baronial and remote, now they were right down here with the people, playing baseball."

For Gussie, the episode resulted in an extreme makeover: his image as a bad-tempered, foxhunting, skirt-chasing millionaire was wiped from the public consciousness and replaced with that of benevolent city father and man of the people. And the city was busting its buttons with civic pride. America may have had Mom and apple pie, but St. Louis had Budweiser and baseball, Gussie Busch and the Redbirds. Happy days were here yet again.

Not everyone was applauding, however. P. K. Wrigley, the owner of the chewing gum giant and the Chicago Cubs, cited his own company's experience when he harrumphed, "August Busch and his beer company right now believe the Cardinals are going to be a great advertising agent for them. But they are in for a rude awakening if things start going wrong for the ball club."

Wrigley couldn't have been more wrong. The Cardinals had a so-so season in 1953, coming in third in the National League, while Anheuser-Busch blasted back into first place by turning out 6.7 million barrels, 1.5 million more than second-place Schlitz. The Cardinals dropped to a dismal sixth-place finish in 1954, but A-B still bested Schlitz by 400,000 barrels that year. And so it went for the next forty years as the Anheuser-Busch–Cardinals combo proved to be one of the best marketing team-ups in the annals of American business.

One unforeseen effect of the Cardinals purchase was that it turned Gussie Busch into a national celebrity almost overnight. "Not many people wrote to me when I was just a brewery president," he said. "But as owner of the Cardinals I began to receive thousands of letters."

Sportswriters flocked to him and fed greedily on his salty observations about baseball and horses and women. It didn't matter if half the things he said couldn't be printed; he rarely disappointed and frequently astonished. As the *Post-Dispatch*'s Jack Rice observed, "He so obviously says what he means, wants what he says he wants and expects to get it, that the simplicity of his drive and candor can be upsetting to people more accustomed to the subtleties of business. Or society." A perfect example occurred the day he was talking to a reporter about a longtime brewery employee who was retiring. After praising the man profusely, he blurted, "Of course, this has nothing to do with his wife, who is the biggest bitch that ever happened."

In the summer of 1955, he hit a national magazine trifecta. *Ladies' Home Journal* profiled him as one of "The 10 Richest Men in America." *Life* magazine published a nine-page pictorial by famed photographer Margaret Bourke-White, "The Baronial Busches," depicting him as the patriarch of a large and colorful clan whose "way of life adds a memorably exuberant and expansive segment to the American scene." And finally, *Time* magazine put him on its cover, dubbing him "The Baron of Beer" and lionizing him as an American business icon—"Trim (5 ft. 10 in., 164 lbs.), graying, hard as an oaken keg at 56, Gussie Busch operates on a simple formula: 'Work hard—love your work.'"

Both *Life* and *Time* mentioned Trudy in a single sentence, describing her in the exact same words—"his handsome third wife." No doubt it was the chauvinism of the age that led them to dismiss her so blithely, but she was much more than met the eye. When world leaders and Hollywood celebrities began coming to Gussie's castle door in the 1950s, it was Trudy who welcomed them in and saw to it that they were made comfortable, catered to, entertained, and cared for. It was a role she seemed born to play: Guinevere to Gussie's King Arthur. Without her in the years that followed, there would have been no Camelot.

THE MAGICAL BEER KINGDOM

During the first two years of their marriage, Gussie and Trudy lived in the Bauernhof at Grant's Farm, a quarter of a mile from the main mansion. The Bauernhof (which means "farmstead") was modeled on the traditional "fortress" farms of medieval Germany, which combined living space for the family with shelter for animals and storage for farm equipment, all behind a protective wall.

This, of course, was an American millionaire's farmstead, with five apartments for servants and farm staff and a private two-story, six-bedroom "clubhouse" residence for the family. Gussie's father, August A., had his architects design a system for the stables and dairy barn that watered the animals automatically on the half hour, with the water temperature controlled by the stable master. Styled to resemble the buildings in Bavaria's medieval walled city of Rothenberg, the dramatic U-shaped structure was built around a huge wood-block courtyard enclosed by a white stone and timber wall, with an arched entry on the southeast side and sculptures of nesting storks along the roofline, an ancient symbol of good luck.

As luck would have it, Trudy gave birth to two children while they lived in the Bauernhof—Adolphus IV in July 1953 and, less than a year later, Beatrice in July 1954. Shortly after Beatrice was born, at the urging of Gussie's mother, Alice, they moved into the mansion, which the Busch family always referred to as "the big house." Alice, nearing ninety, remained in the sixteen-room "cottage" nearby. The move was not an easy decision for Gussie, who worried about the expense of operating such an immense household. He was reportedly the highest paid executive in St. Louis, with an annual income of more than $200,000. But he'd borrowed $600,000 from his mother to pay his ex-wife's divorce settlement, and he constantly complained that he was cash poor; all his wealth was tied up in company stock. He even sought the advice of his daughter Lotsie, who shared the Bauernhof quarters with him and managed the household accounts until she got married in 1948. "How much do you think I should give Trudy to run the big house?" he asked. "Would $1,000 a month cover it?" Her response was, "You must be kidding."

The big house had gone to seed somewhat since Gussie's mother and father had lived there. The ground floor was in need of new curtains, carpets, and furniture. When the huge Aubusson rugs in the living room and dining room were replaced twenty years before, it had cost several hundred thousand dollars. The children's bedrooms upstairs were now empty. The kitchen was obsolete.

"Okay, you can start to order things," Gussie told Trudy, "but make it as cheap as possible, because I can't afford it."

She ignored him completely and went at the task like the future Jackie Kennedy redecorating the White House. "I just bought and bought and bought," she recalled later. "The man from Lammert's Furniture came out to the house and we got the very best carpets from New York. It was amazing what [Gussie] had to spend."

Having grown up in the big house, Gussie knew its every secret hiding place and historic secret. The most stunning feature was the main staircase leading to the second floor, where a curved seven-panel window of Tiffany glass depicted a majestic stag standing in the forest. The ornate molded ceiling above the stairway was perforated so that the sound of an orchestra playing in the third-floor ballroom could permeate the house. Gussie's favorite places were the gun room—a parlor off the living room with a score of his father's animal-head trophies mounted on the wall and a marble fireplace big enough to burn five-foot logs—and his father's bed-room, with its large window providing the perfect vista onto the deer park right where a small creek cut across a rolling meadow and the herds gathered to graze and drink. Once, in an attempt to cheer up his bedridden father, Gussie led a newly acquired horse up the main staircase and into his father's bedroom.

Gussie was not a religious man, but the deer park passed for his house of worship. Whenever weather and work permitted, he and Trudy loved to ride or "coach" through the park together, es-pecially in the evening after dinner. On one such excursion, they had driven into the park in Gussie's convertible and were taking a walk around the lake when suddenly a huge stag confronted them. Trudy recognized the animal as Ike, an English red deer she had bottle-fed and cared for two years earlier after it was abandoned by its mother. Ike had followed her around for months, until he was old enough to be released back into the park. Now he was fully grown, it was the middle of rutting season, and by all indications he wanted to mate with her. He charged them with his antlers down, snorting, challenging Gussie. They ran back and jumped into the car, but Ike stood in front of it, locked his antlers onto the front bumper, and began lifting the car on its suspension. Gussie told her to put the top up while he got out, ran around to the trunk, and took out a rifle. When Ike came at him again, he fired.

Ike buckled, but then recovered and staggered off into the darkness. The next morning, Gussie went out and found him dying. He finished him off and had his magnificent head mounted on the wall in the gunroom.

With Gussie and Trudy in residence, the big house once again became the focal point of activity for the extended Busch clan and the company. No one loved a party more than Gussie, so he ordered them and Trudy organized and executed them with the help of her twelve-person household staff. Thanksgiving, St. Nicholas Day, Christmas, New Year's, Easter, family birthdays, team parties, employee dinners—they seemed to never end. One of them almost didn't. In the summer of 1954, after a drop in Budweiser sales in St. Louis, Gussie decided to invite every distributor, retailer, and bar owner in the area—anyone who had a hand in selling his beer—to a dinner party in the courtyard of the Bauernhof. In order to accommodate the 11,000 invitees, he and Trudy played host to 1,000 people a night for eleven straight nights. "When midnight came, my hand would be so swollen I couldn't move my fingers," he told *Time* magazine, which reported that Budweiser sales in St. Louis went up 400 percent after the marathon.

At a party for the Cardinals and their families, one of the players' wives gushed to Gussie that his wooded kingdom was so "magical," he should consider opening it to the public, "because children would love it." He jumped on the idea. He'd already begun replenishing his father's herds; now he started expanding his menagerie of more exotic animals to include tropical birds, monkeys, chimps, llamas, camels, longhorn steers, mountain goats, even black and grizzly bears. The cherry on top of the ice cream was his acquisition of a baby elephant, just thirty-nine inches tall and named Tessie II. Next he purchased a fifty-four-passenger, seventy-two-foot "trackless train" that could carry kids safely on guided tours past President Grant's log cabin and through the deer park, the animal enclosures, and the fifty-one-acre Clydesdale breeding farm. Naturally, he named the kiddie tram "the Budweiser Special." Finally, he set up a concession stand in the Bauernhof courtyard that offered refreshments at the end of the tour—hot dogs and sodas for the children and beer and pretzels for their parents—all of it, like the price of admission, free. He funded the operation, including the sixty-head Clydesdale farm, by having the company lease most of the property from him at a price that covered his costs.

Grant's Farm quickly became one of the most popular tourist attractions in St. Louis, with many children preferring it to the world-renowned St. Louis Zoo because most of the animals roamed free and could walk right up to the train and sniff you—or bite you, depending on their mood. Either way, it was an indelible experience. Visiting days were Monday through Thursday from May through August, and reservations were a must because the entire season was booked in a matter of days, forcing schools to reserve for their annual class trips a year or two in advance. More trains had to be ordered.

The tours were routed away from the big house to preserve the family's privacy, but Gussie frequently walked over to the Bauernhof and waded into the crowds, shaking hands and kissing babies, running Tessie II, his chimps, and his blue-eyed cockatoo, Cocky, through their routine of tricks. He loved being the center of attention, the ringmaster of the circus. And he never lost focus on the fact that each person he touched was someone who could eventually buy his beer. He did not—perhaps could not—separate himself from the company. In his mind, they were all one—the Clydesdales, the Cardinals, Grant's Farm, and the family—joined together in the furtherance of a greater cause, the promotion of Anheuser-Busch and Budweiser. "My happiness is my business," he once told the *St. Louis Post-Dispatch*, maybe a bit too candidly. "I eat it, sleep it, and dream about it. My family, of course, comes a close second to my love of my business."

Trudy, or "Troodles," as he called her, understood that better than anyone. She knew from the outset what he needed her to do and what the benefits would be. In addition to managing the household staff and the grueling entertainment schedule at both Grant's Farm and Belleau Farm, she accompanied him on business trips when he deemed it necessary, either because he didn't want to go alone or felt her feminine charm would be an added value. On his annual hops-buying trips to Europe, for example, her fluency in German and French proved enormously helpful in his dealings with the growers. Trudy not only shared Gussie's passion for horses, she became one of the top competitive female equestrians in the United States. The "Swiss girl" who had seated customers at her father's Lucerne restaurant quickly blossomed into the world-class hostess of one of America's most glittering residences. She beguiled Frank Sinatra on the ballroom dance floor, ministered to Ed McMahon after he fell down drunk in the living room and pulled the curtains along with him, covered for Andy Williams when he drank too much to sing for the guests as promised, and saw to it that Yul Brynner had a late dinner and good conversation waiting for him every night when he stayed at the cottage during his two-week run of *The King and I* at the St. Louis Municipal Opera. Gussie was powerfully proud of her; she made him look good.

He was proud of himself, too, when she gave birth to five more children after Adolphus IV and Beatrice—Peter, Gertrude, Billy, Andrew, and Christina—all seven of them in the span of eleven years. He beamed when his older daughters Lilly Marie and Lotsie teased him about his remarkable motility, calling him "miracle man."

For the first time in his life, now in his mid-fifties, Gussie seemed settled. When he wasn't traveling on brewery business, he was home in time for dinner with Trudy and kids at 7:00 p.m. sharp. He and Trudy always sat side by side at the head of the enormous dining room table, speaking to one another in German when they didn't want the children to know what they were saying. In the fall and winter, when it was dark outside, the children were expected to show up at the table bathed, in their robes and pajamas, and ready for bed. The three-course menu was planned by Trudy but prepared and served by a kitchen staff that could be summoned to the table by a bell. Gussie brought his work home with him, of course, but in an inclusive way, enveloping them all in the latest tale of triumph or challenge at the brewery. He took pains to refer to it always as "our" company rather than "the" company, and he corrected them whenever they made the mistake, just as he did when they carelessly called their product beer. "Not beer," he would chide gently, "Budweiser." As a result, by the time the children reached the age of reason, they understood they were part of something bigger than themselves and even bigger than the family.

"Our father led us to believe that the business and the family were one and the same," Billy Busch recalled fifty years later. "We knew we were in the limelight, not because we were better than anyone else but because we were also a company that sold a wonderful product that people loved."

Gussie didn't involve himself in the minutiae of child-raising—what they were going to eat, wear, do, or which schools they would attend. He left all that to Trudy, along with the discipline. While he did not believe in hitting, she believed in it wholeheartedly. "She would beat you with whatever she could get her hands on," said her oldest, Adolphus IV, chuckling. Her favorite weapons were the "switches" fashioned from saplings that she seemed able to pull out of thin air. At the same time, she made the rounds to their bedrooms at night to read and say prayers with them before tucking them in. A devout Catholic, she herded them all to mass every Sunday, either at Our Lady of Providence Church nearby or in the small chapel she had built on the grounds, named St. Hubert's after the patron saint of hunters and designed to resemble her family's chalet in Switzerland. The Irish priests at Our Lady of Providence, Fathers Duggan and O'Reilly, were all too happy to celebrate mass at the private chapel of the impossibly rich parishioner that Providence had put in their path. They became, in effect, the house priests at Grant's Farm. A lifelong agnostic, Gussie did not attend services on Sunday morning, but he was there on Sunday night when the family gathered together in front of the TV to watch *Bonanza*.

Gussie insisted that the kids always kiss him hello and goodbye, but he rarely engaged in intimate conversations with them. Mostly, he dealt with them as a group, offering his counsel and dispensing advice at the dinner table. "Hold on to your gun until they convince you that their way is better," he'd say. Or, "You can always correct someone when they are wrong and back them in the corner, but always remember to leave a door open for them to get out." However, he made a point of telling them individually exactly where he stood as their father: "Right or wrong, I'm always behind you," he'd say. "But I expect you to do the right thing."

He also expected them to work. Growing up at Grant's Farm may have been comfortable and privileged, but it was not easy. With nearly three hundred acres to maintain, more than a hundred animals to care for, and thousands of tourists traipsing through, the estate provided endless potential for chores. The Busch brood was required to labor alongside the paid staff after school and on the weekends—pulling weeds, repairing fences, feeding animals, working the concession stand. April was always the cruelest month, as they prepared for the annual start of the tram tours. "It was almost like getting ready for a festival," recalled Billy, who was No. 5 among the children born at Grant's Farm. "Everything had to be made beautiful for the arriving tourists."

Gussie was a particularly difficult taskmaster because he'd inherited one of his grandfather's quirks, a fastidiousness that bordered on obsessive-compulsive disorder. Legend had it that Adolphus once decided not to buy a competing brewery because he thought the alley behind the plant was too messy. Gussie's children joked that he could "spot a broken branch from two miles away." As a result, a casual walk or a coach ride with him could turn suddenly into heavy lifting.

"You never saw Dad sitting around reading a book," Billy said. "When he was home he would be out on the grounds, and with his eye for detail there was always something he thought needed to be done—the grass here was too long, this needed painting or that wasn't clean. Sometimes it kind of got you down: 'Gee, Dad, this was supposed to be fun!'"

Gussie's quest for visual perfection extended to the pigeons that roosted in the eaves of the big house. He loved the all-white ones that he had cultivated, but could not abide the gray, black, and mottled ones that constantly flew in from the city. So there was a standing order to exterminate the interlopers, which prompted Gussie's loyal black valet, Frank Jackson, to tease him: "I notice you only shoot the colored ones."

By the mid-1950s, the Newark and Los Angeles breweries were producing at capacity. Gussie's plan to help pay for the latter plant with a 15-cent-per-case increase in the wholesale price of Budweiser had been a disaster, causing a steep drop in sales that let Schlitz regain the No.1 position in 1954. But he'd redeemed himself by acknowledging his error at the annual stockholders' meeting—"We made probably the worst mistake in our company's history and, as your president, I take sole responsibility"—and by spending most of the next year traveling the country in his rail car, repairing relations with distributors and enlisting them in the battle against Schlitz.

"That was the turning point for the company's sales," he said later. Lest anyone think his job was easy, he boasted that in one tour of local taverns on that trip he was required to consume forty-eight beers in eight hours. "I had to take a few shots of whiskey to warm up my stomach," he said. "That beer sure gets cold."

By 1957, Anheuser-Busch and Budweiser were back in first place on the heels of what turned out to be an historic ad campaign. Using photography instead of illustrations for the first time, and depicting real people in everyday situations rather than formal ones, the ads marked the debut of Budweiser's nickname: "Where there's life, there's Bud."

After Newark and Los Angeles, Gussie set his sights on Florida for further expansion of A-B's production capacity. Construction began on a new plant in Tampa in 1957, but this time he envisioned something more than a brewery. The company had been offering guided tours of the St. Louis brewery since the repeal of Prohibition. Other breweries had tours, but A-B's were considered the gold standard. The historic Brew House—with its two-story turn-of-the-century chandeliers, dark stained wood, and baroque Germanic art—combined with the ornate Clydesdale stables to make the Pestalozzi Street plant a field-day destination for every junior and senior high school in the area, and one of the top tourist attractions in the state. The entire place was so brightly painted and sparkling clean that it resembled a Disney-designed diorama more than a fully operational manufacturing facility, giving the impression that you could lick the factory floor without fear, and it would probably taste like sugar. For those over the age of twenty-one, the tour offered a bonus of free beer at the end.

What Gussie had in mind for Tampa was a combination of the St. Louis brewery tour and Grant's Farm, with birds. He had an abiding passion for beautiful birds. In addition to Cocky the cockatoo, he had a full-blown aviary in a screened room off his office at Grant's Farm and several cages of finches and songbirds around the big house. Without seeking the approval of his board of directors, he ordered that a fifteen-acre park be built adjacent to the new plant. Called Busch Gardens after his grandfather Adolphus's Pasadena estate, it would offer visitors a chance to sit and enjoy free beer in a lush tropical setting filled with parrots, macaws, toucans, cockatoos, flamingos, and various birds of paradise. Gussie was so intensely involved in the development of the park that he and Trudy went to Miami on a buying spree and brought cages full of brightly colored birds back to Tampa on the train.

Opened in March 1959, Busch Gardens was, more than any other aspect of the company, a pure expression of Gussie Busch's passion. He would eventually expand it to seventy acres, adding a free-roaming wildlife enclosure that simulated Africa's Serengeti Plain and an incongruously themed restaurant called the Old Swiss House, a replica of the Buholzer family's restaurant in Lucerne, where he first met Trudy. He spent $13 million on the restaurant and presented it to her as a Valentine's Day present. Gussie's pet project became the cornerstone of the second largest theme-park operation in the United States (after Disney)—ten parks with 25,000 employees and 25 million visitors a year. "The parks were part of the old man's magic, like the Clydesdales," said Denny Long, who ran the division in the early years. "Gussie's magic was very expensive. His idea was to build goodwill. There was no concern for cost controls, but it sure helped sell the beer."

In May 1958 Gussie's mother Alice passed away peacefully while taking an afternoon nap. She was ninety-two and had been suffering from Parkinson's disease for some time. Still, Gussie took it hard. Even though her house was just a few hundred yards away from the big house, he held off telling the children that "Gannie" had died. "I can't talk to them about it," he said to Trudy. "It would be too upsetting for them." In truth, it was too upsetting for him. The flip side of his vaunted joie de vivre was that he "always had a problem dealing with sadness and death," Trudy recalled later. He relented after a few weeks when five-year-old Adolphus kept asking why they didn't have dinner with Gannie anymore.

In her will, Alice left Grant's Farm to Gussie and forgave the $600,000 loan she'd given him for his divorce settlement with Elizabeth. The bequest didn't sit well with his sister Alice, who had expected to inherit an interest in the historic family home. His brother Adolphus's heirs were already upset that he had somehow managed to acquire their father's half interest in Belleau from August A.'s estate. And his cousin, longtime pal and most recent best man Adalbert von Gontard, was none too happy that Gussie had fired him as head of advertising. "Adie" had been with A-B for more than thirty years; he was an officer of the company, a member of the board of directors, and a large shareholder. The Busch and von Gontard families were close; the children were friends. Nonetheless, Gussie banished Adie from the kingdom. The perception was that he blamed his cousin for the company's drop to second place behind Schlitz. His only stated reason to the family was that Adie had purloined spent grain from the brewery to feed to his pet peacocks, which they thought was laughable; the grain was worthless and would have been thrown out otherwise. They knew Gussie would have given the grain to Adie if he'd asked for it. That was the point, Gussie said. Adie had not asked his permission, but had done it "behind my back."

If Gussie felt bad about all the family discord he'd sown, he didn't show it. As the 1960s dawned, he was a man in full. With four breweries running flat out and a fifth planned for Houston, the company was setting record after record for barrels produced, revenue earned, profits returned, and dividends paid. A close friend of both former President Truman and future president Lyndon Johnson, Gussie was now a kingmaker in national politics, having played an important fundraising role in the election of John

F. Kennedy. As Kennedy's campaign coordinator, Massachusetts congressman Tip O'Neill, recalled later, "All you had to do was tell Gussie that money was getting tight and more was needed. In a few days, a package would drop from heaven. Gussie raised it faster and easier than anybody in that era."

Gussie and Trudy traveled to JFK's inaugural in the Adolphus, along with their guests Harry and Bess Truman and Gussie's longtime pal Tony Buford and his wife. But when they got there, Gussie wasn't satisfied with their seats at one of the inaugural events. He yelled at Buford, "You're supposed to have a lot of pull in Washington, Buford, so get us a better box." Pointing to where the president and First Lady were sitting, he said, "I want to be up there." When Buford told him that was impossible, Gussie responded, "Either you get me up there with the Kennedys, Buford, or I'm sending you back to Jefferson City where I found you." Buford reportedly quit on the spot, and he later went to work for Falstaff, for which Gussie never forgave him.

Every spring, Gussie and Trudy took the kids to Florida on the train and spent time at the three-house compound Gussie had purchased on the beach in Pass-a-Grille, outside St. Petersburg. That's where the Anheuser-Busch "fleet" was moored for his use—an 84-foot yacht named *Miss Budweiser*, a 41-foot Rybovich deep-sea fishing boat named *Miss Bavarian*, and a 120-foot million-dollar yacht called the *A & Eagle*. Trudy and the children typically returned to St. Louis after a few weeks, and when they were gone, a group of Gussie's buddies—usually including St. Louis Cardinals announcer Harry Caray—would descend on St. Petersburg and take up residence in the compound for another few weeks of fishing, drinking, gambling, and womanizing. Gussie's definition of male marital fidelity could be summed up as: No mistresses, no emotional affairs, but casual, no-strings-attached coupling was okay so long as it was by mutual consent, in which case it was perfectly natural, like rutting, the male prerogative. Female fidelity, of course, was a different story.

All in all, Gussie was living a life that Louis XIV would have loved. Everything he touched had turned to gold, with the exception of his baseball team.

In ten years under A-B ownership, the Cardinals had not won a pennant. Gussie had burned through five managers and was planning to fire his sixth, Johnny Keane, who had guided the team to a second-place finish in 1963. The '63 team had ended the season winning nineteen of its last twenty games, yes, but everyone knew how Gussie felt about being second. The city was marking its bicentennial in 1964, and Gussie had been named by the mayor to head a committee of civic leaders tasked with planning the year-long celebration. A new 50,000-seat stadium was under construction near the downtown riverfront, rising in the shadow of the Gateway Arch, which was also nearing completion. Gussie had been a prime mover in both projects. In the case of the new Busch stadium, he had pledged $5 million toward the original $20 million financing package. His board pushed back, first suggesting a contribution of $1 million, then $2 million, until he beat them into submission by banging his fist on the conference table and bellowing, "No, goddammit, no! I said five million!"

All of which explained why he considered it do-or-die time for the Redbirds: If they didn't do it this year, then someone was going to die. His general manager, Bing Devine, took the first bullet. The team was in seventh place, trailing the league-leading Philadelphia Phillies by eleven games on June 15, when Devine and manager Keane made a controversial trade, sending star pitcher Ernie Broglio (18 and 9 in 1963) to the Chicago Cubs in exchange for the Cubs' .251-hitting outfielder Lou Brock. In his first fifteen games with the Cardinals, Brock batted .398 and stole nine bases. But the team still trailed the Phillies by nine and a half games on August 16, when Gussie pulled the trigger on Devine, who'd been the architect of the team that included likely Hall-of-Famers Curt Flood, Bob Gibson, and now Brock himself. Then word leaked to the press that Gussie was negotiating with former New York Giants manager Leo Durocher to take over as manager of the Cardinals, which embarrassed Keane and angered many of the players. With the Cardinals eleven games behind the Phillies again a week after Devine's firing, Gussie was so frustrated that he kicked a hole in the wall of the Red Bird Roost, his private viewing suite atop the stadium.

Then, suddenly, the Cardinals took flight. In what is regarded as the wildest pennant race in the history of major league ball, the Cardinals won twenty-one of their last twenty-nine games, including a three-game sweep of the Phillies, who lost ten games in a row. The Cardinals won the pennant in St. Louis on the last day of the season. The city went crazy. There hadn't been such an orgy of beer guzzling since the morning of April 7, 1933, and this time the beer didn't run out.

The Cardinals went on to beat the Yankees in seven games in the World Series. The very next day, Johnny Keane, still smarting from Gussie's Bing Devine–Leo Durocher debacle, announced that he was resigning as manager of the Cardinals to become manager of the Yankees. Devine and Keane were popular with the sportswriters, players, and fans, so Gussie found himself vilified in the newspapers and on radio and TV, accused of "destroying" the team he once was lionized for saving. As if that weren't enough, for the second year in a row, the respected St. Louis-based *Sporting News* magazine named Bing Devine baseball's "Executive of the Year."

It was easier running a brewery. During the first week of December, Gussie was informed that new computers used to measure production indicated that a record-setting ten millionth barrel would pour out of the pipes at the Pestalozzi Street plant the following week. Elated, Gussie pressed to find out exactly when the milestone would be hit. At 10:34 am on Tuesday, December 15, he was told.

At 10:15 on the designated day, Gussie and a group of company officers walked out of the administration building at 721 Pestalozzi Street and marched up the block to the bottling plant, where eight Clydesdales were hitched to a bright red wagon fully loaded with cases of beer. Employees lined the street, and a brass band began to play as Gussie led a parade into the plant and along the corridors to the racking room, where filled barrels were sealed with rubber plugs in a process called "bunging." At exactly 10:34, he was handed a silver mallet and a plug, and in two attempts he managed to bung the ten millionth barrel. The band then led the way out of the building, and he climbed aboard the beer wagon with the historic barrel on the seat next to him. "Here we go; give me room," he said as he flicked the reins and the giant horses responded as one. He drove the team up the street and stopped in front of the administration building, where the mayor and other civic leaders now waited. The sun was shining, the plant whistles screeched, and the employees cheered. A few people were even crying as he stood up in the wagon to address them. "This is a great day in the history of Anheuser-Busch," he said. "Our employees as well as our many consumers have played a very important part in this event. We use the best ingredients and machinery available, but without the loyal support of our employees we could not have accomplished this. They should all be proud."

He had reason to be proud as well. In the thirty-one years since that April night when he first spoke to the country on behalf of beer and Anheuser-Busch, he had accomplished everything his father and grandfather ever dreamed of, and more. Now, at age sixty-five, he was, indisputably, the king of beer.

Asked by a reporter what he hoped for in the future, he replied, "Another world championship baseball team and another world beer production record, I hope, I hope."

He would get what he hoped for, and then some. But he would pay a terrible price for it all in the years to come. In some ways, on this day, standing on a beer wagon in the sun congratulating his employees for a job well done, he had reached his peak.

THE PRUSSIAN LIEUTENANT

As Gussie Busch's firstborn son and the anointed heir to the Anheuser-Busch kingdom, August III might well have expected to occupy a special place in the Busch family. Instead, he became an outlier.

From the beginning, there was little love lost between August and Trudy. Out of loyalty to his mother, August resented his father's new wife. And it didn't help that his stepmother was just ten years his senior, the same age as his sister Lotsie. But what bothered him most about Trudy was that she monopolized his father's free time. Whenever Gussie wasn't at work, he wanted to be with her. And that was not what August had in mind when he moved into the Bauernhof with Gussie and Lotsie in 1947; he was hoping to spend more time with his father and get to know him better.

They'd made a good start of it, with Gussie taking him to work at the brewery and proudly introducing him around, letting him sit in on executive meetings and hang out with the workers in the Brew House to see how beer was made. At night over dinner,

Gussie schooled him in the traditions and principles of the family and company. Gussie also taught him how to handle firearms, and the two regularly went out into the deer park to thin the herds. August particularly enjoyed the time they spent together at Belleau Farm, which the family called the Shooting Grounds because that's primarily what went on there. Located thirty miles west of St. Louis near the confluence of three major rivers—the Mississippi, the Missouri, and the Illinois—the farm's 1,500 acres of floodplain and marshland sat smack in the middle of the Mississippi Flyway, the flight path favored by about two-thirds of the migrating birds in America, which made the Shooting Grounds a duck hunter's heaven. August took to it like nothing he'd experienced before; duck hunting became a lifelong passion.

August did not share his father's love of horses. His sister Lotsie recalls a day at Grant's Farm when a teenage August watched her guide a horse through a series of jumps. She teased him about his lack of equestrian skill, and he responded with a shrug, "Anybody can ride a horse."

"Then get on one and jump those fences," she challenged. To her astonishment, he did. Afterward, he deadpanned, "I just don't think there is any fun in that."

The bonding between August and Gussie was cut short by Trudy's arrival on the scene. August soon moved back to the Lindell mansion with his mother, and he never again lived under the same roof with his father. For her part, Trudy was keenly aware of August's resentment toward her. Wary of him, she invited him to all family gatherings nonetheless. He never became part of the new family, however. As her children grew, they came to view their much older half brother as an uncle figure, a relative who showed up for big family events a few times a year but always remained in the background, pleasant but reserved. None of them formed a bond with him. Billy Busch remembers a single one-on-one encounter with August when he was a little boy: "I played catch with him one day and he threw the ball back at me really hard."

As a teenager, attending Ladue High School in one of St. Louis's most exclusive suburbs, August acquired the hated nickname "Augie," made only a few friends, and was, once again, frequently absent. He was a good athlete who didn't play team sports. He had a very bright mind but posted poor grades. His biggest accomplishment during his high school years was earning a pilot's license. "He wanted to fly so badly that my sister and I paid a guy out of our own pockets to teach him," said Lotsie. "He was fifteen or sixteen, and we did it without Daddy knowing, because Daddy didn't like to fly; he said it was for the birds." Flying became August's second abiding passion, and by all accounts he was a careful, crack pilot. The same could not be said of his performance behind the wheel of a car.

On November 21, 1954, seventeen-year-old August was driving several guests home from a party at Grant's Farm when he lost control of the car and "sheared off" a telephone pole, injuring two passengers in the process, including Trudy's brother, William Buholzer, who suffered a broken ankle. A year later, August was ticketed for driving eighty miles an hour on a rural highway near Belleau Farm. He pleaded guilty to careless driving and was fined $35. As with the Halloween-night fracas a few years earlier, both driving incidents were fully reported in the newspapers, deepening his dislike for the media.

In his senior yearbook, August was quoted as saying his ambition was to become a "baby brewer," and his pet peeve was "Falstaff." Thus, when his fellow seniors named him "Most Likely to Succeed," it may have been more an ironic comment on his inherited privilege than a testament to his intelligence, industriousness, or talent, none of which had yet to manifest themselves.

In 1956 he enrolled at the University of Arizona in Tucson, a well-known party school. He'd grown into a good-looking young man—lean and muscled, with piercing blue eyes and dark brown hair that he wore sharply parted and slicked down in the classic "wet look." He was five ten but added a good two inches to his stature by wearing dress boots with lifts. Armed with mounds of spending money, a series of fast, expensive cars, and a surname that worked magic at every bar, restaurant, and nightclub in town, he had no trouble attracting attractive women. For two years, he practically majored in them.

The summer after his freshman year, August began working part time at the brewery. He joined Brewers and Maltsters Local Union No. 6 and, in accordance with family tradition, was assigned the bottom-rung job of shoveling used beech wood chips and spent grain out of the vats, a physically demanding, sweaty, and smelly task. Luckily, he didn't have to do it for long, just enough that he could say to *Fortune* magazine years later, "When you finished a shift there, you knew you were a man."

On May 4, 1958, August's mother, Elizabeth Overton Busch, suffered a cerebral hemorrhage and died at her home. She was sixty-three and had been diagnosed with hypertension. August was away at school and rushed home when he got the news. "He insisted on seeing her [body at the funeral home] even though I begged him not to," said Lotsie. "It broke his heart." Her death barely got a mention in the two local newspapers. Gussie and Lotsie attended the private memorial service at the Lindell mansion and the burial. Years later, Lotsie recalled her stepmother once telling her, "Always walk the straight line and never fall off, because if you do, it is very hard to get back on."

August did not return to college for his junior year. Instead, he joined the U.S. Army Reserves, thereby avoiding the draft. After six months of basic training at Fort Leonard Wood in Waynesville, Missouri, about 120 miles from St. Louis, he embarked on a life that seemed dedicated to the pursuit of princely pleasures, whether on European ski slopes, Caribbean beaches, or Wyoming dude ranches. This, too, was in keeping with a family tradition—young Busch males traditionally took some well-funded time off to sow their wild oats before settling down to career and family.

August would complain bitterly in later years that he "never had a daddy" when he was a boy, but it was Gussie who marked his passage into manhood with a stunningly thoughtful gift—a two-hundred-acre farm that abutted the Shooting Grounds, complete with a comfortable, rustic residence. August named it Waldmeister, after a fragrant European forest herb also called sweet woodruff, and he turned it into his private preserve, where he could party out of the eye of the despised media, enjoy some of the best duck hunting in North America, and hangar his twin-engine plane at a rural landing strip called the Spirit of St. Louis Airport a few miles down the road in the tiny town of Gumbo, Mo. He eventually expanded Waldmeister to more than a thousand acres and made it his principal residence for the next fifty years. During that time, the Spirit of St. Louis Airport grew into a lavish base for Anheuser-Busch's fleet of globe-hopping aircraft.

August returned to school in 1960, enrolling at the Siebel Institute of Technology in Chicago, the country's oldest college of brewing. Various biographical accounts have suggested that he went away to the school and returned to St. Louis a year later having "graduated" with a diploma as a "certified brew master." In truth, he completed a twelve-week course of study without really leaving home, flying his plane to Chicago each Tuesday morning to attend classes and usually returning on Thursday.

Whatever the depth of his brewing education, August's experience at Siebel seemed to change something in him. Rewarded by Gussie with a job as sales manager of the company's low-priced brand, Busch Bavarian, he threw himself into the task with monomaniacal zeal, putting in seventy-hour weeks, driving himself mercilessly, as if on a mission to make sure that no one, not even his father, knew more than he did about beer and the business of it.

Denny Long, the company's twenty-five-year-old head of pricing when August moved up from the Brew House into management, remembers his first impression of his future boss. "He didn't trust anyone, he needed to be in control, he had zero sense of humor, and he didn't want you to be his friend."

Long, the son of a construction laborer, started working for Anheuser-Busch in 1953 at the age of seventeen, immediately after he graduated from high school. He'd been offered an academic scholarship to Quincy College, but his family was "working class poor" and couldn't even afford the incidental costs. For such young men, Anheuser-Busch proved a godsend, offering a potential lifetime of employment at a fair wage, with good benefits and plenty of opportunity for advancement because the company had a long tradition of promoting from within. A-B even maintained the old German brewing tradition of *der Sternewirth*, which granted all employees a thirty-minute free beer break every day. Among the working class in St. Louis, it was believed that if you had a job at "the Brewery," you were blessed.

Denny Long felt doubly so. He had risen rapidly from office boy to middle management on the strength of "an incredibly simple pricing process" he'd perfected, which the company adopted nationwide. That caught the attention of the new Busch Bavarian brand manager. "August asked me to be his assistant," Long recalled fifty years later. "He said, 'I don't want any yes men around me; I want you to tell me what you think.' He told me that he was going places, and I was going with him."

Long soon learned August meant that literally, as he was dragooned into traveling with him constantly, hopscotching the country in August's plane to meet with distributors, usually accompanied by a pair of A-B's top marketing executives, George Couch and Charlie Aulbert, former Army Rangers and World War II vets who liked to let off steam after work.

"I was a poor kid from South Broadway and suddenly I am with a Busch and a very fast-moving crowd of hard drinkers. They'd work all day, then walk into a bar, and it was 'Bring on the wild horses and the wild, wild women.'"

Even though August never exhibited any effects from the alcohol, the whole scene was a bit too much for Long, a devout Catholic and devoted husband. He quickly figured out that he could join in the revelry for a short time and then slip away back to the hotel without them noticing, or at least saying anything. He eventually came up with a way to serve the boss without having to leave St. Louis, gradually taking over all the administrative aspects of the brand manager job—the home-office minutiae that bored August to death. "Everything that came across his desk, I read and summarized for him."

The process provided a terrific education for Long and freed August to continue crisscrossing the county to observe and absorb the field operations of the beer behemoth he would one day be called upon to run. By his own estimate, August spent 75 percent of his time on the road in the early years, and it was during this period that he began building a reputation as a fearsome drill sergeant whose white-glove inspections and impromptu interrogations could cause otherwise brave men to lose control of their bowels. Wherever his plane touched down, local sales reps and wholesalers went scurrying to make sure everything was in order. This wasn't just another brand manager, after all; this was the future king, baptized in Budweiser, for God's sake. He'd better not find a single bottle of out-of-date beer in any bar, restaurant, or package store he walked into, or there would be hell to pay. August seemed to relish the fear he engendered in the troops. He thought it was good for them. Kept them on their toes, competitive. Long likened him to "a Prussian lieutenant." They were an odd couple—the self-consciously poor kid from the rough-and-tumble Patch and the entitled brewing scion from the pampered country club suburbs—but they formed a partnership that would last twenty-seven years.

August's "playboy" period officially came to an end in the summer of 1963 when, at the age of twenty-six, he was promoted to vice president of marketing, one of the key jobs in the company, and elected to the board of directors, filling a vacancy created by the death of Eberhard Anheuser, the grandson of the brewery's co-founder. A few weeks later he married Susan Hornibrook, a beautiful, athletic blonde from a prominent Brentwood, California, family whom he'd met in his travels for the company. The wedding took place at All Saints Episcopal Church in Beverly Hills. August's best friend, John Krey, served as best man and Gussie picked up the tab for a dinner party the night before at Chasen's restaurant in Beverly Hills, a favorite hangout of the Hollywood crowd. The Busches of St. Louis did their boisterous best to make sure the Beverly Hills bunch would never forget them. During her toast to her little brother and his bride, Lotsie told Susie she "was going to have to learn to shoot" as she loosed a pair of flapping, quacking ducks among the startled guests. Nobody rode a horse through the banquet room, but the Busch party included a miniature Sicilian donkey that trotted around the restaurant and caused such a sensation that Jackie Gleason, who was hosting a party upstairs, insisted it be brought into his gathering.

After a European honeymoon, the newlyweds settled into domestic life at Waldmeister. On June 15, 1964, Susan gave birth to August Anheuser Busch IV, and dutifully fed him a thimbleful of Budweiser when he was a day old. Another child—Susan—followed two years later. A family man now, August slowed the pace of his traveling, cutting it back to about 50 percent of the time, while continuing his rapid rise in the company with a promotion to vice president and general manager of the brewery in 1965. His father had approved the promotion and thought he had earned it with his performance as marketing VP. But Gussie didn't want anyone to get the impression that his son's ascension to the top spot was guaranteed or imminent. "If I've told him once, I've told him a thousand times that the board of directors does the electing," he told *Business Week* magazine. "In my book, you rise or fall on your own."

Of course, no one believed that. When August sat down for an interview with a reporter from the *Post-Dispatch* in April 1967, the resultant headline read, "August Busch III Prepares for Job of Keeping Anheuser-Busch on Top." Al Fleishman had arranged the interview, with Gussie's approval. It couldn't have happened otherwise, because Fleishman tightly controlled all publicity for A-B, which didn't have its own PR department, just Fleishman's firm, Fleishman & Hillard, which devoted about 75 percent of its billing hours to telling the A-B story the way Gussie wanted it told. Apparently, he had decided it was time to introduce his heir apparent to the public.

August's official media debut was what's known in the publishing trade as a "puff piece." The article presented the picture of a handsome twenty-nine-year-old prince in waiting, "an intense young man . . . who has become a well-grounded specialist in the beer and is an articulate student of the brewing industry."

Crediting August with "a philosophy that shows both an understanding of corporate teamwork and a feeling for the pitfalls of nepotism," the article quoted him as saying, "Family members in the corporate executive structure of a company like Anheuser-Busch can either be a great asset or a great liability. . . . There are some very definite advantages to having people around who have grown up in a business, who have lived with the company around the dinner table in the evening, who have learned the personalities involved."

The article closed with a quote that now seems eerily prescient. "If you get a bad apple anywhere in the lower executive levels, you've got trouble," August said. "But get a bad apple at the top, and you've got super trouble."

THE OLD MAN AND
THE KID

In his late sixties, suffering from a number of age-related ailments, including a painful spinal disc problem that required him to wear a corset and sometimes walk with the aid of two canes, Gussie Busch had no intention of retiring any time soon, or maybe ever. Why would he?

His company had doubled its market share in the decade since he pushed it back into first place, and now it was pulling away from Schlitz and Pabst on the way to becoming the dominant brewery in America. Budweiser was practically selling itself.

His baseball team, too, was going gangbusters. Playing their first full season in the new Busch Memorial Stadium, and with newly acquired home run king Roger Maris in the lineup, the Cardinals set an attendance record of 2.09 million in the course of winning the National League pennant in 1967. They then went on to beat the Boston Red Sox in the World Series behind the pitching of Bob Gibson, who threw three complete games while striking out twenty-six batters and allowing only fourteen hits, and the base-running of Lou Brock, who stole a Series-record seven bases.

Gussie and Trudy and a large contingent of family members and friends descended on Boston in a flotilla of corporate and private aircraft for the final two games. Gussie was miffed when Boston owner Tom Yawkey failed to host a party in their honor (as he had done for Yawkey in St. Louis), so he threw his own extended party at the staid Ritz-Carlton Hotel. After watching the Cardinals lose 8–4 in the sixth game, he hosted Massachusetts governor John Volpe and his wife at a banquet that ended in a traditional Busch-family food fight, during which Gussie's oldest daughter, Lilly, hurled a dinner roll at her father that went wide and hit Mrs. Volpe instead. Watching people diving under the table to dodge flung food, one shocked waiter blurted out, "I'm wondering, Mr. Busch, what you do when you *win*."

He found out after the Cardinals' 7–2 victory in the seventh game, in which Series MVP Gibson struck out ten and hit a home run and Brock stole two bases in a single inning. Back at the hotel, Gussie and Trudy celebrated by taking fire extinguishers off the wall in the hallway and blasting other members of their group as they got off the elevators. (The hotel sent Gussie a bill for $50,000 for damages and cleanup, which was paid out of the advertising budget.) The Busch entourage then partied on the planes all the way back to St. Louis, where Gussie was hailed by the local press as the architect of the greatest Cardinal team in history.

The Cardinals won the pennant again in 1968, thanks in large part to the spectacular performance of Bob Gibson, who logged a (still) record 1.12 ERA, threw twenty-eight complete games, and struck out 268 batters. In one stretch, he won fifteen games in a row, ten of them shutouts. During June and July, he pitched ninety-six and two-thirds innings and allowed only two earned runs. He topped himself in the opening game of the World Series against the Detroit Tigers.

With a shutout going, Gibson struck out the first batter up in the ninth inning. Catcher Tim McCarver stood up, stepped across the plate, and with the ball in his hand, pointed to the scoreboard.

Known for his rapid-fire rhythm, an irritated Gibson hollered at McCarver, "Throw the fucking ball back, will you? C'mon, c'mon, let's go!"

But McCarver kept pointing, and the sold-out Busch Stadium crowd stood and cheered as the scoreboard reported that the Cardinals' right-hander had just struck out his fifteenth batter, tying the all-time record set by Sandy Koufax. It made for one of the most joyous moments ever in Gussie's Red Bird Roost. Gibson tipped his cap to the stands and quickly went back to work, striking out the next two batters to end the game.

The future Hall-of-Famer followed up with a complete-game one-hitter in the fourth game to put the Cardinals ahead 3–1 in the series. Leading in the seventh inning of game five—just two innings away from a second straight world title—the Cardinals collapsed and lost. That put a tired Gibson back on the mound for the seventh game. He pitched a shutout through six innings, but with two outs at the top of the seventh, he finally proved human, giving up back-to-back singles. Then, as Gussie and Cardinals fans everywhere watched in disbelief, the Tigers' Jim Northrup drove a Gibson fastball into deep center field, where multiple Gold Glove winner Curt Flood made a rare error and the ball sailed over his head for a two-run triple. Gibson completed the game, but the Cardinals lost 4–1.

It was a bitter defeat, but it did nothing to diminish St. Louis's enthusiasm for the team and its colorful president. St. Louis sportswriters ballyhooed the birth of a new sports dynasty and celebrated Gussie as a bona fide baseball genius. Not coincidentally,

Anheuser-Busch bunged 18.5 million barrels in 1968, another industry record.

The hoopla surrounding the Cardinals' ascendance distracted Gussie from the day-to-day operations of the brewery, as did his increasing involvement in civic and charitable endeavors. Still, his every move seemed tailored toward promoting the Busch brand. As general chairman of St. Louis University's 150th-anniversary fundraising effort, for example, he personally raised two-thirds of the $3.25 million needed to build a new student union in the middle of the campus, for which he was duly celebrated as the guest of honor at the 1967 dedication ceremony for the Busch Memorial Center. As much as he loved basking in the accolades that day, he would argue that his act of philanthropy was another example of "very good business" because it built goodwill among the fastest growing group of beer drinkers—baby-boomer college students. Wasn't that the American business system operating at its best—private industry, motivated by self-interest, acting in the public interest?

That was his view of it anyway, and few ever worked the system better than Gussie Busch, who could justify his most self-indulgent excesses as legitimate corporate expenditures. He once defended his favorite toy, the million-dollar yacht *A & Eagle,* to a newspaper reporter, saying, "You look at this here and say, 'Isn't that an extravagance?' Sure, it is. But in business benefits, it is tremendous. Just a week ago, we landed an important new yeast customer, one we probably couldn't have gotten without that cruise." Indeed, Gussie regularly used the *A & Eagle* and the smaller (fifty-one-foot) Rybovich sports fishing boat *Miss Budweiser* to entertain customers and cronies on lavishly provisioned "booze-and-broads" cruises to the Florida Keys, the Bahamas, and Cozumel, Mexico. When your corporate motto is "Making friends is our business," it forgives a lot of sins.

In a way, it was the perks and extracurricular opportunities his work provided that kept Gussie on the job long past normal retirement age. Though he was invariably described as the "owner" of the Cardinals, the team belonged to the company. So did the private rail car and the chauffeur-driven automobiles. The charitable donations he was applauded for making came from Anheuser-Busch accounts, not his. The brewery paid for the parties and the boats and the beach houses and the broads and most of the cost of Grant's Farm, including the Clydesdales and Cocky the cockatoo. If he retired, then he might have to pay for his grand lifestyle out of his own pocket, and he was not about to do that.

He did, however, begin scaling back his work schedule as he approached seventy, adopting bankers' hours at the Pestalozzi Street offices, usually arriving between 10:30 and 11:00 in the morning and leaving by 2:30 or 3:00 in the afternoon, on the days that he came in at all. Which was just fine with August III, who was increasingly at odds with his father about how the company should be run. They could not have been more different in their approach. Gussie responded to opportunity, usually decisively, but with no grand plan or strategy beyond maintaining first place among American brewers and avoiding anything that would dishonor the legacy of his father and grandfather. August, on the other hand, was an inveterate, even compulsive planner who carefully thought out his every action in advance. As one longtime family friend put it, "I've never once seen him do anything spontaneous."

August wanted to reorganize and modernize the company, which he thought was mired in the past, as evidenced by the fact that the executive offices were still in the hundred-year-old former schoolhouse around which the brewery had been built. The children of Adolphus and August A. had attended the school there. Gussie's office was in his old classroom.

It wasn't that August disdained tradition. He venerated his grandfather and great-grandfather, even kept their letters to one another in his desk drawer, often pulling them out and reading them for inspiration and guidance. He respected his father's accomplishments, too, but he worried that Gussie was no longer up to the task of leading the company, which had become hidebound by the old man's insistence that everything go through him. If August gave an order as general manager of the brewery while his father was out of town, Gussie was likely to loudly countermand it or quietly undermine it when he returned. There had to be a better, more professional way to manage the company, August was convinced.

Around the brewery and out in the field, August was referred to as "the Third," or "Three Sticks" or "young August," but on the third floor of the administration building, where Gussie held sway with his longtime right-hand man Richard Meyer, he was called "the kid," and it was not a term of affection. "They were all Gussie's boys up there," said Denny Long. "August and Dick [Meyer] would get into knockdown, drag-out disagreements, and the old man would always take Dick's side." As A-B's executive vice president, Meyer was officially the No. 2 ranked corporate officer, and it galled him that August didn't acknowledge that. But deference and humility were not in August's toolbox, and he made it clear to the rest of his father's executive team that he believed he was fully capable of running the company and intended to do it at his earliest opportunity. They thought he was cold, arrogant, and abrasive.

August sought to counterbalance Gussie's boys by hiring a cadre of young executives who were the antithesis of Gussie. He recruited them at some of the best business colleges in the country—Harvard, Stanford, Columbia University, and the Wharton School at the University of Pennsylvania—flying into town to interview recent or soon-to-be graduates of the MBA programs.

The Wharton School proved particularly fertile ground. It was there that August heard a speech by Robert S. Weinberg, a PhD in economics who was the director of analytical services at IBM. Weinberg's speech was on corporate planning, and it apparently knocked August out.

"He came to visit me in New York and took me out to lunch at the most expensive restaurant in town," Weinberg recalled later. "He said, 'I want to offer you a job,' and I told him I wasn't interested. He said, 'I'm disappointed; I want you to think about it.'"

Weinberg thought about it for several weeks and decided he didn't want to work for a beer company in St. Louis. So he sent August a letter asking for a salary so high he was sure it would be turned down. Six months later, out of the blue, August called and said, "You have a deal." He made Weinberg A-B's vice president of corporate planning.

At Wharton, August also met a professor named Russell Ackoff, who ran the school's Management and Behavioral Science Institute. "Management science was an area of study that was catching fire," Weinberg said. "Ackoff was a brilliant guy and a superb salesman, and he saw in August a willingness to take chances and look at complicated problems differently."

August saw in Ackoff a father figure with an intellect and education he envied. Theirs quickly became a mentor-protégé relationship. August was particularly taken with Ackoff's concept of "preactive" corporate management. Unlike inactive management, which ignored change in favor of tradition, and reactive management, which responded quickly to change when it occurred, Ackoff's preactive management sought through research and analysis to predict change and prepare for it. That's exactly what August wanted at Anheuser-Busch. But because Ackoff didn't want to leave academia for the beer business, August agreed instead to endow his institute, paying the university $200,000 to $300,000 a year for Ackoff's students to conduct computer-modeling studies of the company's advertising, marketing, and distribution practices.

"The various analyses had to be done in order for us to know if we were looking at something new or were just playing the same old game with new names," Weinberg explained.

Gussie and Dick Meyer rolled their eyes at the thought of computer-assisted planning, but they decided to give August his head as long as his little project didn't become too expensive or disruptive.

"Gussie had no interest in what we were doing," said Weinberg. "I think I kind of bamboozled him in the beginning. And, yes, I think there was an element of indulgence in his attitude."

Gussie might have been more concerned if he'd heard Weinberg's presentation, "The Philosophy of Planning," at the Super Market Institute in Chicago six months after he joined Anheuser-Busch: "Traditionally, getting smart is an evolutionary process. You have to wait for one level of management to die and a new level of management to come in. But now there is a means for changing quickly."

One of the planning department's first major projects was an analysis of A-B's production capacity versus the demand for its product. The result was a model that called for the construction of new plants strategically located to minimize freight costs. Gussie had been the first American brewer to build a plant outside his company's home city. But after boldly launching operations in Newark, Los Angeles, and Tampa in the 1950s, he'd grown cautious. A new plant was now a $100 million proposition. He worried about moving too fast, committing too many resources. The previous plants had been financed largely out of revenue. He didn't want to incur a big debt to the banks; his father and grandfather always tried to avoid that. But with both Dick Meyer and the board uncharacteristically supporting the planning department's model, he reluctantly agreed to build three new plants—in Houston; Columbus, Ohio; and Jacksonville, Florida. Of course, once he'd signed on to the plan, you would have thought it was his idea in the first place. At the groundbreaking ceremony for the Columbus plant, he hopped on a plow pulled by a team of eight Clydesdales and actually broke the first ground himself.

August pressed for even more expansion. In May 1969, during a state-of-the-company presentation to a gathering of financial analysts at Chase Park Plaza, he predicted that Anheuser-Busch would sell 21 million barrels that year, but the company suffered from an "efficiency problem due to its production capacity"—it still could not produce enough beer to meet demand. His proposed solution was to build more plants, beginning with one in Merrimack, New Hampshire, and another in Williamsburg, Virginia. Again, Gussie went along.

Two weeks later, on May 27, all seven operating Anheuser-Busch plants were shut down by a Teamsters strike. It began as a local action in Houston, where peaceful picketing had been going on for four weeks while management negotiated with the union over a number of issues, including the length of a new contract. A-B was seeking a three-year agreement similar to the one the Teamsters had signed with the Schlitz plant in Longview, Texas, but the union would agree to only one year. August had been acting as A-B's point man in the negotiations, with the approval of his father and Dick Meyer. As a former member of the Teamster-affiliated Brewers and Maltsters Local No. 6 in St. Louis, he believed his father gave up too much to the unions over the years in exchange for labor peace. So he was determined to take a tougher stand this time, and maybe show everyone there was a new sheriff in town. Unbeknownst to him, however, Gussie was playing good cop behind his back, indicating to Local 6 leaders that he thought his son was being needlessly hard-nosed. "Gussie just wanted everyone to love him," said Denny Long. "Everything August was asking for was correct. It was what we needed to grow, and Gussie knew that and backed it."

The Houston strike went national when the company—in the person of August—sought to have nonunion supervisors cross the picket line to make yeast brews prior to a settlement, arguing that it was necessary because yeast cultures had to be made several weeks in advance if the plant was to go into full production immediately after a settlement. The union responded by pulling its personnel from refrigeration and power departments, putting thousands of barrels of already produced beer at risk of spoilage. Then, in a calculated show of strength, the union dispatched pickets overnight to every Anheuser-Busch plant. More than 1,500 massed at the Pestalozzi Street facility, where Robert Lewis, the volatile business manager of Local 6, tore into August, saying he "lacked basic human understanding." In a statement to reporters, Lewis accused August of instituting a policy of worker harassment and abuse at the Houston and Jacksonville plants that had forced the labor action: "Foremen have been standing over [workers] like overseers, requiring them to obtain permission to even go to the bathroom," he said, adding that several workers were even denied treatment in the dispensary after they suffered burns from caustic fluid used in cleaning. "There has been a complete change of policy and attitude on the part of the company, and unless young Busch's activities are curbed there will be nothing left of this great company. He is directly responsible for the conditions that led to this strike."

Lewis even claimed that August had caused three of A-B's top managers to quit—the labor relations managers at the Houston and Newark plants, and the company's vice president of marketing, Harold Vogel. (Vogel later confirmed that he had resigned rather than report to August because, he said, "He instills fear and thinks it is respect.")

As the number of pickets grew to 2,000, preventing members of the plant's twenty-one other craft unions from entering the complex, the company enlisted the aid of the police department, which dispatched fifty patrol cars and officers armed with riot guns and nightsticks to protect the plant and the nonunion supervisors inside. August and some of his planning team used the dark-paneled boardroom on the third floor as a kind of control center. From there, they could peer through the blinds and monitor the movement of various union leaders as they walked back and forth in front of the Brew House. Listening to all the vitriol directed at August, they half expected to hear someone in the crowd holler, "Send out young Busch and we'll let the rest of you go."

With nearly 5,000 employees shut out in St. Louis, and more than 30,000 workers idled nationwide, Gussie and Dick Meyer quickly moved to settle the strike on terms that August considered far too lenient. Furious, he reportedly stomped into Gussie's office and handed him a letter of resignation. Gussie looked at it and said, "I'll give you another chance because you are a Busch, but if you ever do anything like this again, I'll see that the *Post-Dispatch* has your resignation letter within five minutes." Robert Lewis later boasted to reporters that Gussie told August, in his presence, "You are going to get along with Bob Lewis or you'll never become CEO of this company." On the third floor, Gussie's boys got a kick out of seeing "the kid" get a comeuppance.

August came away from the episode feeling he'd been sandbagged by his father, and more convinced than ever that Gussie's leadership, or lack thereof, was jeopardizing the company's future. He was troubled that his father didn't think it a big deal when cigarette manufacturer Philip Morris announced in June 1969 that it had purchased 53 percent of Miller Brewing Company. Miller had never been a threat. The eighth-ranked brewery, it had a 4 percent market share compared to A-B's 16 percent. But Philip Morris was a $1.14 billion company, bigger than A-B, with a record of building strong brands through sustained TV advertising. Marlboro was its Budweiser. August and Bob Weinberg thought Anheuser-Busch needed to develop a plan for dealing with Miller in the future. Gussie remained fixated on Schlitz, his archenemy of the past.

August had another family problem to deal in 1969: his marriage to Susie was on the rocks. Both of them would say later that the offending party was his work and the frequent absences it caused. For Susie, the transition from a bustling social life in Beverly Hills to the comparatively isolated rural setting of Waldmeister had been "overwhelming," leaving her feeling lonely and without friends when he was on the road. August eventually purchased an in-town home for them in Ladue, but he continued traveling extensively and liked to spend weekends at Waldmeister whenever he could. "I realized in about the fifth year that it just was not going to work," Susie told a local gossip columnist years later. "We tried for another year, but it just didn't get any better."

According to a former A-B executive who socialized with the couple, August's absences were not just physical but emotional as well. "She was the All-American girl who would brighten the mood in the room, and then he would knock it down. He treated her as if she were one of his possessions, as he treated us all."

The first public sign of trouble may have been an incident that occurred on May 9, 1968. According to newspaper reports, Susie was driving home around 11:30 p.m. after dropping off "a friend" with whom she'd spent the evening. On a straight stretch of Ladue Road just a few blocks from the Busch residence, she lost control of her car, ran off the road, took out a couple of small trees, and ended up in a ditch. She was treated at the hospital for facial cuts and bruises and then released, with no ticket issued or charges filed.

Not long after, a rumor began making the rounds in Anheuser-Busch social circles that Susie was having an affair with Harry Caray. It was a jaw-dropping, juicy tidbit that practically demanded retelling. Aside from the age difference (she was twenty-nine, and he was fifty-one) and the fact that both were married, Caray was the longtime voice of the Cardinals and one of her father-in-law's best buddies. That he and Susie would be an item seemed weirdly incestuous. The pair could not have been less discreet when they were seen dining together at St. Louis's only four-star restaurant, Tony's, just a few blocks from Busch Stadium, visibly under the influence and so physically affectionate that owner Vince Bommarito had to instruct his whispering waitstaff to stop staring at them. But it was hard not to. The sight of the florid, cartoon-faced sportscaster cavorting with the stunning young wife of August Busch III was not something a working-class St. Louisan ever expected to see, or would likely forget.

(To this day, Susie denies the affair ever happened. "We were a friendship item, but not a romance item by any means," she told the *Post-Dispatch* in her only interview on the subject. Caray, too, denied the affair rumors over the years, though less consistently than Susie, hinting on one occasion that it might have happened and admitting on another that he was flattered that people thought he was capable of attracting her.)

August moved out of the Ladue house and took an apartment on Lindell Boulevard across the street from the St. Louis Cathedral, but he said nothing to his colleagues about his marital situation. If he felt bad, he didn't show it, not even to Denny Long, who was pressed into service as his near nightly dinner companion in the Tenderloin Room at the Chase during the first few months of the separation. When the divorce came later that year, it was quick, clean, and quiet, with the newspapers devoting only a few terse lines to the fact that the couple had agreed to joint custody and no alimony (although Susie later revealed that August supported her "in the style to which I was accustomed"). August thus managed to spare his children, August IV and Susan, the embarrassment he had endured over his parents' prolonged and messy split.

Gussie was glad the episode had not developed into a public

scandal, but he still had to decide what to do about Harry. They were not only good friends, with a shared affection for booze, broads, and gin rummy, but also business partners, bound together by Caray's contract with the ball club and the brewery. Gussie could hardly condemn Harry on moral grounds—he'd been there and done that many times himself. And Caray was immensely popular among Cardinals fans and had become nationally recognized for his signature on-air catchphrases—"Hol-eeee cow!" and "It might be, it could be, it is—a home run!" In the public's mind, Caray was as much a part of the Cardinals/Budweiser family as Gussie, if not more. He'd been the Redbirds' most vocal booster for twenty-five years, since before Gussie bought the team. There had been a huge outpouring of public support for Caray when, a few weeks after the '68 World Series, he was struck by a car and nearly killed while crossing the street late one night, suffering two broken legs, a broken shoulder, and damaged lungs. Gussie responded by flying him aboard a company plane to the Anheuser-Busch beach compound in St. Petersburg, where he received round-the-clock nursing care during several months of recuperation and rehabilitation.

There was no question that Gussie loved Harry, and however mad he may have been at him for messing around in his family, he needed Caray in the Cardinals' broadcast booth in the spring of 1969. The winds of change were rustling through the well-manicured world of professional baseball, signaling the arrival of the 1960s nearly a decade behind schedule. Players were sprouting mustaches and sideburns; clumps of hair were starting to poke out from under their caps. Moreover, a new militancy was on the rise in the form of the Major League Baseball Players Association and its director, Marvin Miller. Deadlocked in negotiations with team owners over pension benefits, Miller had organized the first ever players' boycott of spring training in January. Confronted with the failure of four hundred players to report to camp, the league capitulated and ponied up more pension money, and spring training finally got under way three weeks late.

All of which was sticking in Gussie's craw on March 24, five days before his seventieth birthday, when he and Dick Meyer, the Cardinals' executive vice president, presided over an unprecedented meeting at the team's spring training facility in St. Petersburg. The players were surprised to find reporters present when they walked into the clubhouse at Al Lang Field, invited by Al Fleishman.

"I don't mean to give you a lecture," Gussie said, "but as president of this club I have a right to speak to you as men, frankly and straight from the shoulder." He then delivered what sounded a lot like a lecture. Pointedly mentioning that the team's $607,000 payroll was "the biggest in the entire history of baseball," he took the players to task for being greedy, rude, spoiled, and ungrateful. "I don't mind negotiations—that's how we get together—but ultimatums rub me the wrong way and I think they rub the fans the wrong way. . . . I am not suggesting that you should not have individual business managers or even press agents. That is your privilege . . . but too many fans are saying our players think of money more than the game itself. We are told too many players are refusing to sign autographs, pushing kids aside when they try to take pictures. . . . When the media people lose interest and when kids don't want your autographs, then we better begin to worry."

He didn't lose his temper and bang the table and shout, but in his rambling discourse he made quite a few intemperate remarks, including one that seemed to minimize their role in the organization: "It takes hundreds of people working every day to make it possible for 18 men to play a game of baseball that lasts for about two hours."

"This is no pep talk," he said in closing. "I haven't bawled you out. But I've tried to point out that baseball is at a serious point in its history."

He threw the meeting open to questions, but none were asked, except by the reporters, who queried the players about their reaction to the boss's comments as the boss looked on. "This is just another example of the first class way this club operates," gushed shortstop Dal Maxvill. "I bet there's not another club where the president and vice president would take so much time to talk to players, letting them know in the best possible way what the score is, without ruffling any feathers." Team captain Curt Flood's response was less complimentary. "It was something that helped clear the air," he said. Then, in a subtle dig at Gussie, he added that he agreed it was important "not to lose sight of who really pays your salary, and your pension—namely, the fan."

Privately, Flood was seething; he believed most of Gussie's comments were aimed directly at him, the result of their testy off-season contract negotiations. After Flood hit .301 in 1968, won his sixth straight Gold Glove award and was named "Best Centerfielder in Baseball" by *Sports Illustrated* magazine, Gussie offered him a raise of $5,000—from $72,500 to $77,500. Offended, Flood turned him down and held out for $90,000, which, he said, "is not $77,500 and is not $89,999." He suspected Gussie was punishing him for his costly error in the World Series.

Gussie ultimately gave in on the ninety grand, but held on to a grudge over Flood's comment, which he considered disrespectful. After all, he reasoned, he had championed the young man from the moment he first arrived in St. Louis in 1957, believed in him even when his manager and coaches didn't, insisting that they place him in the starting lineup, the only time he'd done that for a player. Flood didn't know it, but shortly after he joined the team, Dick Meyer had received a complaint about him from restaurateur Julius "Biggie" Garagnani, who was partnered with Stan Musial in one of St. Louis's most popular steak houses, Stan Musial and Biggie's.

Upset that the then-twenty-year-old ballplayer had shown up at his restaurant with a date, hoping to celebrate his signing with the team, Garagnani had refused to serve him and, in his complaint to the Cardinals front office, referred to Flood as a "fresh nigger" for even thinking it was a possibility. Gussie and Meyer ignored Garagnani's bigotry and focused instead on Flood's reaction to the incident. The young man had not said a word about it—neither to the Cardinals' management, to his teammates, including Musial, nor, more importantly, to the press. He had kept his mouth shut and played ball. Gussie respected him for that, at least until eleven years later, when he opened his mouth about his pay.

Flood wasn't the only veteran in the clubhouse that thought Gussie's spring training talk was patronizing and demeaning. But the reporters present apparently didn't pick up on the undercurrent and dutifully delivered the positive coverage Al Fleishman had promised his client: "Birds' Players Get Message, Applaud Busch," chirped the headline in the next day's *St. Louis Globe-Democrat*. "What Mr. Busch said was great, was thoughtful, had to be said, and should have been said by baseball executives long ago," said *Globe-Democrat* sportswriter Bob Burnes, calling Gussie "a remarkable man" who was "speaking up for the fans."

It turned out that the '69 Cardinals were not the team they were in 1968. The high point of the season might have been on opening day, when Harry Caray triumphantly returned to Busch Stadium, first hobbling onto the field with the aid of two canes, then dramatically flinging the canes aside and walking straight and tall as if he'd been struck by a miracle bolt of lightning from above. The crowd went wild.

It was downhill from there, however, with the Cardinals losing their first five games on the way to a dismal fourth-place finish in the Eastern Division. Gussie's reaction was swift and terrible. On the morning of October 7, Curt Flood got a phone call from a low-level executive in the Cardinals front office, telling him he had been traded to the Philadelphia Phillies. The next day, Anheuser-Busch announced it was not renewing Harry Caray's contract as the Cardinals' announcer. The actions belied all the talk about Gussie speaking up for Cardinal fans, who surely would have voted to keep Caray and Flood in their jobs.

Neither man went quietly. At an October 9 press conference to answer questions about his sudden ouster after a quarter century with the team, Caray drank dramatically from a sixteen-ounce can of Schlitz and disputed the company's assertion that he was let go on the recommendation of the marketing department. "That's a lot of crap," he said. "Nobody's a better beer salesman than me. No, I gotta believe the real reason was that somebody believed the rumor that I was involved with young Busch's wife. "

Curt Flood was shocked that Gussie had traded him. Over the years, he'd become close with Gussie and Trudy, or so he thought. An oil portrait he'd painted of Gussie—wearing his jaunty yacht captain's hat—hung in a stateroom on the *A & Eagle*. Flood's portraits of the seven younger Busch children were displayed prominently in the big house at Grant's Farm. (Cardinals manager Red Schoendienst had a Flood portrait of himself hanging above the mantel in his living room.) Flood had come to believe—as had Harry Caray—that he was part of a greater Redbirds-Budweiser-Busch family. And indeed they both were, but they were also, at the end of the day, Gussie's employees. And in his view, that made all the difference.

Flood didn't let it go, however. Refusing to report to Philadelphia, he challenged Gussie's right to trade him in a letter to baseball commissioner Bowie Kuhn, the opening line of which served as his own emancipation proclamation:

Dear Mr. Kuhn:

After 12 years in the major leagues, I do not feel that I am a piece of property to be bought and sold irrespective of my wishes.

He followed with a $4 million federal lawsuit seeking to have major league baseball's so-called reserve clause declared unconstitutional.* Gussie was not named in the suit, but Flood dealt his former patron a stinging rebuke when ABC sportscaster Howard Cosell said to him in a nationally televised interview, "What's wrong with a guy making $90,000 a year being traded from one team to another? Those aren't exactly slave wages." Flood's response remains one of the most memorable quotes in the annals of both baseball and American labor: "A well-paid slave is nonetheless a slave."

There is no record of Gussie's reaction to what must have seemed to him an unforgivable slur. But there's anecdotal evidence to suggest that the travails of 1969 took a toll on him emotionally. At Belleau Farm that fall, sixteen-year-old Adolphus Busch IV was awakened one night when his father came into his room in a state of agitation. "He had tears in his eyes," Adolphus recalled later. "He said he'd had a bad dream and he didn't know what was going to happen. Something had occurred that made him question whether he should stay on as CEO of the company or retire." Adolphus got up and talked to Gussie for a while, but his father could not articulate what happened in the dream that had shaken him so.

"It was a shock to me because Dad was always tough and sure of himself," Adolphus said. "I had never seen him like that before—in tears, vulnerable, doubtful."

---

* Flood failed in his lawsuit, which he appealed all the way to the U.S. Supreme Court. However, his action is credited with eventually pressuring major league baseball into doing away with the reserve clause in favor of free agency, thus ushering in an era of ever-escalating player salaries—exactly what Gussie feared.

GUSSIE'S LAST STAND

Thanks to the strike, Anheuser-Busch fell well short of August's 21-million-barrel prediction for 1969. But even with the five-week work stoppage, the company managed a record 18.7 million barrels. And ten months later, August stood in the racking room on Pestalozzi Street, smiling as he watched his father bung the year's twenty millionth barrel.

As Gussie proudly pointed out in his annual letter to shareholders, it had taken 118 years to reach the 10 million mark, and only six to more than double it. He didn't say so, but the stunning growth was a testament to the "preactive" management of August and the corporate planning department. Without the Houston, Columbus, and Jacksonville plants, A-B could not have hit that number, much less the 22.3 million barrels it wound up producing that year, a 19 percent increase over 1969.

The beer business as a whole did well in 1970. America's brewers produced a total of 122 million barrels, as per capita consumption reached 18.7 gallons, the highest level since before Prohibition.

According to the National Beer Wholesalers Association, however, 50 percent of the output flowed from the five largest companies—Anheuser-Busch, Schlitz, Pabst, Coors, and Schaefer—further proof that the future of the industry was going to be determined by a battle among a few superpowers. Smaller local and regional breweries were dying off, unable to compete with the national distributors and their big advertising budgets. Of the more than 700 breweries that were operating in the years immediately following Prohibition, only 157 remained. In two more years, there would be only 65.

A-B continued to widen its lead over No. 2 Schlitz in terms of barrelage, but industry experts noted that Schlitz was beginning to close the gap in two other important categories—production capacity and profitability. Schlitz was building new plants, too, and they were twice the size of A-B's plants, capable of producing four million barrels a year to A-B's two million. And Schlitz's new plants were employing a new brewing method the company called "agitated-batch fermentation." It involved adding artificial carbonation to the traditional brewing mix of barley malt, grain, and hops to speed up fermentation, thereby reducing the time it took to brew a batch of beer. Schlitz started calling its process "accelerated" batch fermentation, which sounded better than "agitated." Whatever it was called, ABF allowed Schlitz to cut its twenty-five-day brewing time to fifteen days—compared to Anheuser-Busch's forty-day brewing process for Budweiser.

At the same time, Schlitz was quietly beginning to cut the cost of its goods by partially replacing barley malt with corn syrup and by substituting cheaper hops extract and hops pellets for fresh hops. As a result of all the changes, Schlitz was producing its beer far more cheaply than A-B.

The man driving the changes at Schlitz was its CEO and chairman, Robert A. Uihlein (pronounced *Ee-line*) Jr., the scion of a hundred-year-old German-American brewing dynasty with a history almost as colorful as that of the Busch family. The Uihleins traced their stewardship of the company back to August Krug, who came to America from Bavaria in 1848 and established a namesake brewery in Milwaukee. After Krug died without heirs in 1856, his widow Anna Marie (née Uihlein) married the brewery's bookkeeper, Joseph Schlitz, who changed the company name to his own and ran it until he perished in a shipwreck in 1875. Schlitz, too, died without an heir, so the brewery passed into the hands of his closest relatives, stepnephews Alfred, August, Charles, and Edward Uihlein.

By the 1970s, the Uihlein family was one of the richest in America. Its members owned 82 percent of Schlitz stock and held fourteen of the seventeen seats on the company's board of directors. Robert Uihlein, August's grandson, had run the company for ten years, and during that time he and Gussie had become good friends. "Bobby" and his wife, Lorry, regularly joined Gussie and Trudy for weekends of duck hunting at Belleau Farm. Their son Jamie and Adolphus IV were pals; the boys even pledged the same fraternity at the University of Denver (the brothers of Phi Kappa Sigma thought they'd died and gone to beer heaven). So the traditional rivalry between Schlitz and Anheuser-Busch, while at times intense, had always been friendly and respectful. But that was about to change.

Gussie was becoming increasingly crotchety, and more and more, the focus of his irritation was August's corporate planning department, or "the MBAs," as they came to be called around the executive office building. It was part of the MBAs' jobs to question things, but some of their questions infuriated Gussie. Are the Clydesdales necessary? Do the beech wood chips in the Budweiser aging process really affect the taste? Does taste even matter to the average beer drinker?

"The old man started to see [the department] as a threat," said Denny Long. "He didn't want the company to be reorganized and modernized to a point where August was more comfortable but he wasn't. Weinberg would show him some computer model of something, and he couldn't follow it. He thought August was either trying to make him look foolish or push him out."

Gussie responded predictably. The week before the company's annual sales convention in St. Louis, "I was called into Dick Meyer's office and told that my services were no longer required," Weinberg recalled. "August felt compelled to accompany me to my home when I told my wife that I'd been fired."

Gussie also ordered Denny Long—in August's presence—to "go down there and get rid of that whole damn department." That provoked a loud argument between father and son behind closed doors in Gussie's office. After the shouting stopped, August walked into Long's office and stood staring out the window. His father had just demanded his letter of resignation, he said, turning from the window to face an astonished Long with tears in his eyes.

That night, Long and August's best friend, John Krey, drove out to Waldmeister Farm and begged him to give up his fight to reorganize the company for now and work things out with his dad. It wasn't the right time, they told him. Gussie was still too powerful. Think of another way. Wait for another chance.

August took their advice, and instead of tendering his resignation he wrote a conciliatory letter to his father that played up family ties and loyalty. In so doing, he managed to save not only his own job but most of the MBAs' as well. Only a few of the weaker staffers were let go, and Weinberg continued advising August on a consulting basis. Gussie seemed mollified by the sacrifice of Weinberg, boasting in an interview with *Forbes* magazine that he "recently cracked down on a computer expert" and had "slashed his million-dollar staff."

"When you try to run a company on a computer basis, I have to tell you no," he said. "Beer is a people business."

According to the magazine, when asked if August would succeed him, Gussie replied, "Not necessarily. I hope he can make it. I made it very clear that nothing would please me more than if he took over when I died. But he has to measure up and do the job."

There it was, as clear as he could make it: he intended to hold on to the reins of power until he dropped dead in the driver's seat.

And then came a backhanded, belittling compliment to the kid: "He is a grand, bright lad and he works very, very hard."

Gussie wasn't done yet. Several days after the *Forbes* interview, he announced at the annual A-B shareholders meeting in St. Louis that he was recommending to the board of directors that fifty-four-year-old Dick Meyer be promoted to president of the company. He said that he would remain chairman, and, oh yes, he also was recommending August for Meyer's job as executive vice president.

The announcement was nothing less than a public spanking. And it was all the more shocking because it marked the first time in A-B's history that someone outside the family was named president. The financial press jumped on the story, saying Gussie was "teaching his chilly, tough-minded son some humility," and that "growing speculation" favored Meyer to eventually succeed him in the top job.

August's reaction was stoic. If he felt humiliated, he didn't let on; he went about the business of the brewery as if nothing had happened. He did, however, ask Denny Long to start researching how boards of directors were constituted and elected, and how they governed in the modern business environment, as opposed to that of Anheuser-Busch, where they both had spent their entire professional lives.

Gussie soon was caught up in the hoopla surrounding the Memorial Day grand opening of the company's third brewery-adjacent theme park. Busch Gardens Houston was a $12 million, forty-acre Asian wildlife extravaganza that featured a monkey island, an elephant compound, a deer park, a Bengal tiger temple, a rhinoceros enclosure, a petting zoo, a free-flight bird cage where visitors could stroll among a hundred species of exotic birds, a miniature turn-of-the-century railroad called the Orient Express, and a canopied boat ride through the "Ceylon Channel." There was also an incongruous refrigerated geodesic dome called "The Ice Cave" that housed polar bears, penguins, and sea lions. Apparently, Gussie couldn't restrain himself. The company predicted that the Houston facility would draw between 700,000 and 800,000 paying visitors ($2.25 for adults, $1.25 for children) during the first year.

August made a public break with his father in November 1971, when he officially came out as a Republican. Appearing at a $500-a-plate fundraising dinner at the Greenbriar Country Club, he said he supported the GOP because he was "concerned about the success of this country over the next 10 years. I'm concerned about the will to do a day's work for a day's pay, which we've lost sight of. That's what made this country great, wasn't it?"

When a cheeky reporter asked him if his father knew where he was, August smiled and replied, "We have a great philosophy in our company: Everyone is encouraged to express his individual views."

Gussie's views had not changed since Prohibition—he remained a dyed-in-the-wool FDR Democrat. "I don't bite the hand that fed me," he liked to say. He was a close friend of former president Lyndon Johnson, who'd been aboard his yacht on more than one occasion, and he'd entertained Johnson's vice president, Hubert Humphrey, at Grant's Farm when Humphrey ran against Richard Nixon in 1968. There was one Democrat he couldn't abide, however: Bobby Kennedy. His animus stemmed from a meeting the two had while Bobby was serving as his brother John's attorney general in the early 1960s. According to the story Gussie told among friends and family, when he was escorted into the AG's office, "that arrogant little prick" didn't even stand up to greet him, but rather remained seated, leaning back in his chair with his feet up on the desk. Gussie took that as a sign of disrespect that bordered on contempt, and he never forgot it. When Bobby was assassinated in June 1968, his reaction was simply, "Serves him right."

Still, it was a stunner when Gussie announced in September 1972 that he was supporting a Republican for president. "I have examined the record of President Nixon and Senator George McGovern on the issues," he said, "and I feel that, all things considered, President's Nixon's re-election would be in the best interest of the nation and the future." Of course, the man who recruited him to the other side was Nixon's treasury secretary, former Texas governor John Connally, an old friend of Gussie's and a Democratic icon for having been wounded while riding in the open convertible with President Kennedy the day he was assassinated in Dallas.

McGovern's dumping of Missouri senator Tom Eagleton as his vice presidential running mate a few weeks earlier likewise may have had something to do with Gussie's sudden appreciation of Nixon. Eagleton was practically a member of the Busch family. His father Mark, a prominent St. Louis attorney, was a longtime Gussie confidant who had represented him in his divorce from Elizabeth. Tom Eagleton's first job out of Harvard Law School was as assistant general counsel at Anheuser-Busch, and Gussie had generously backed his subsequent political rise. McGovern picked Eagleton to be on the ticket with him on the last day of the Democratic National Convention. He asked him to withdraw eighteen days later when it was revealed that the first-term senator had once undergone electroshock therapy as a treatment for depression.

It's doubtful that Gussie took much joy in Richard Nixon's re-election, however; by that time he was fighting battles in every corner of his kingdom, with some embarrassing results.

It started with Cardinals pitcher Steve Carlton, who, after winning twenty games in 1971, held out for $10,000 more than Gussie wanted to pay him in 1972. When Carlton failed to show up for spring training in February, Gussie ordered him traded to the Phillies. "The sonofabitch is gonna go no matter how good he is," he bellowed.

Two weeks later, the Cardinal players voted 35–0 to join nine other teams in authorizing the Major League Baseball Players Association to call a strike unless the owners contributed more money to the players' pension fund. Gussie promptly blew his stack. "They can have a strike as far as I'm concerned," he told reporters. "I'm fed up to here [indicating his eyebrows]. They are going to ruin baseball the way they are going. I'm against knuckling under, and you can quote me."

The *St. Louis Post-Dispatch* did more than quote him. The newspaper published a baldly affectionate editorial titled "Gussie at the Bat":

> It looks extremely rocky
> For the Sudsville Nine today
> The players want more money,
> They may not get their way.
> The Mighty Gussie grumbles
> That he's fed up to here;
> Those who really know him say
> He's not talking through his beer
>
> "More!," cried the maddened players,
> And the echo answered "More!"
> But one scornful look from Gussie
> Showed them all that he was sore.
> They saw his face grow stern and cold,

They saw his muscles strain,
And they knew the Mighty Gussie
Wouldn't up their pay again.

Oh, somewhere in this favored land
The sun is shining bright.
The band is playing somewhere,
And somewhere hearts are light,
And somewhere men are laughing
And somewhere children shout.
But there is no joy in Sudsville
Mighty Gussie shut them out.

After an eleven-day strike, the first in the history of baseball, the two sides reached an agreement. But as the season finally got under way, Gussie continued to vent, accusing his players of ingratitude, disloyalty, and treachery, ordering them to travel in smaller planes and double up in hotel rooms, going so far as to cancel the free case of beer each player traditionally received during home stands. Al Fleishman could not spin the national media this time. A *Newsweek* article depicted Gussie as a petty, vindictive tyrant who "seemed chiefly intent on revenge."

"As a result, team morale is at its lowest ebb and the tense atmosphere in the Cardinals clubhouse is reflected on the field," the magazine reported. The article quoted several unnamed Cardinal players blaming the boss. Said one, "In all other cities the strike was forgotten right after the season started. Not in St. Louis. Busch kept talking about it, and the fans were all ready to boo when they got to the park—and that hurt us."

Indeed. The Cardinals finished the season in fourth place and posted a financial loss of nearly $600,000. Steve Carlton, on the other hand, finished his first Phillies season with 27 wins (including 15 in a row), 30 complete games, 8 shut outs, 310 strike outs, a 1.97 ERA, and a unanimous selection as the winner of the National League Cy Young Award. In sum, he made Gussie look like a chump.

It got worse. Four days before Christmas, Anheuser-Busch reported that Busch Gardens in Houston—Gussie's baby—was a bust, and the company was taking a $4 million write-off against fourth-quarter earnings. The company stock immediately dropped seven points. A week later, Gussie announced that the Houston gardens would be closed and converted into "a sales promotion facility." A local Houston newspaper, the *Baytown Sun*, declared the situation, with its loss of hundreds of jobs, "a disaster." When Denny Long was sent to Houston to oversee the closure, he found that someone had shot up the park's entrance sign.

At the annual shareholders meeting in April, Gussie, Dick Meyer, and August sought to play up the 26.5 million barrels A-B had produced in 1972 and the company's sixteenth consecutive year in first place. But questions about declining profitability, falling share prices, and the challenge from Schlitz put them on the defensive. They explained that the company was caught in a squeeze between the fast-rising cost of its "natural ingredients"— hops, barley, and rice—and President Nixon's Economic Stabilization Program, an anti-inflation effort better known as wage and price controls, which prohibited the company from passing the cost increases along to consumers. Schlitz looked better on paper for the moment, they claimed, only because the Milwaukee brewer used cheaper, non-natural ingredients in its brewing process.

"We are not going to trade cost efficiency for lower product quality," August vowed. "We are not going to trade solid long term growth for short term earnings gain." Gussie put it in a more personal context: "As long as I am in charge, I'm not going to lower quality." He believed in his bones that shortcuts and substitutions were the road to ruin in the brewing business and that his friend Bobby Uihlein was making a terrible mistake in playing around with his product formula, risking nothing less than the destruction of the company.

The Schlitz challenge was an underlying theme of A-B's 1973 national sales convention in Houston. The annual event was the company's most elaborate morale booster, bringing together several thousand wholesalers, wives, and sales and marketing managers from across the country for a few days of overindulgence and elbow-rubbing with the A-B brass and big-name Hollywood celebrities. No expense was spared. In addition to the ubiquitous MC Ed McMahon, the entertainment program for 1973 included pop duo the Carpenters and singer Tony Bennett.

"We are being challenged on all sides by those who would test our leadership," Gussie intoned in his opening remarks as he introduced a film that featured McMahon in a comic turn as the brew master of a faux Schlitz plant. In the slickly produced film, a bum wanders into the plant from a waterfront dock, sets down his rucksack, and begins pulling out dirty rags and throwing them into the brewing vat. "That ought to give it some gusto," McMahon's brew master says. The crowd in Houston's Music Hall howled at the allusion to one of Schlitz's most famous catchphrases.

The company's upcoming advertising campaign, as revealed at the convention by marketing VP George Couch, was aimed directly at Schlitz: full-page newspaper ads offering a tutorial on the traditional brewing process; a TV commercial extolling the virtues of natural ingredients; another touting the benefits of A-B's larger (than Schlitz's) aging vats, "Where Budweiser will be brewed slowly, as only Budweiser is"; and a recurring tagline, "Brewing beer right does make a difference."

Couch gave his presentation sitting at a desk near the center of the stage rather than standing at the podium like every other presenter. Earlier that day the heavyset, hard-drinking executive had complained of not feeling well and asked August if he could deliver his comments seated. In the middle of his presentation, Couch suddenly went silent. His head fell forward, chin onto his chest, and he didn't move. It took a few moments for people to realize something had happened. The stage curtain was quickly closed, but the audience, which included his wife, could still see paramedics working on him frantically. While the show went on, Couch was rushed to the hospital, where doctors determined he had suffered a massive heart attack. He died a few days later.

It was a bad start to an awful year. During the first ten months of 1973, the American economy was hit by a double whammy of an inflationary spiral and a bear market on Wall Street. Overall, wholesale prices jumped 17 percent, but the price of A-B's vaunted "natural ingredients"—barley, hops, and rice—shot up 34 percent. As the same time, the price of its stock plummeted, at one point dropping from $55 a share to $28. Schlitz stock fell, too, but not by nearly as much. Its per-share price remained above $40.

Then came an even worse turn of events. On October 17, the Organization of Petroleum Exporting Countries (OPEC) retaliated against the United States and its Western European allies for their support of Israel in its Yom Kippur War with Egypt. Overnight, OPEC raised the price of a barrel of oil to Western European countries by 70 percent and imposed a total oil embargo on the United States.

The result was catastrophic. With U.S. petroleum reserves already nearly depleted, President Nixon called for voluntary rationing of energy, asking homeowners to turn down their thermostats to 65 and for companies to trim work hours. Gas stations were asked to hold their sales to a maximum of ten gallons per customer and to shut down on Sunday. In California, drivers were restricted to buying gas on odd- or even-numbered days that conformed to the last digit of their license plates. Lines formed around nearly every gas station in the country, with waits of up to two hours in some places.

OPEC ended the embargo in January 1974, but held the price of a barrel of oil at triple what it had been before the embargo. Gas prices had quadrupled, from 25 cents a gallon to over a dollar. The Dow Jones average fell by a whopping 45 percent between 1973 and 1974. The price of A-B stock fell to $21 a share. The United States and most Western economies were thrown into a severe recession.

The economic crisis did not cause Americans to cut back on their beer drinking, however. Anheuser-Busch sold a record 28.9 million barrels in 1973, an increase of 3.7 million barrels over 1972, or 12.7 percent. But barrels didn't tell the story anymore. The financial press pointed out that A-B's profits had fallen by $11 million, and Schlitz was now the more profitable of the two. As *Forbes* magazine reported, Schlitz earned 21 percent on stockholders equity, compared to A-B's 13 percent. "This year [1974], the number will be more decisively in Schlitz's favor, the third year of declining profitability for Busch. . . . In beer, No. Two is No. One."

Schlitz quickly became Wall Street's new darling among brewers, with its stock trading above A-B's and its fifty-eight-year-old CEO, Bobby Uihlein, stepping forward to boast that thanks to his cost-cutting measures, "We are the company with momentum now." Gussie was infuriated by the comment, and Al Fleishman arranged an interview with *Business Week*, which put Gussie on the cover for a lengthy article about Anheuser-Busch's "struggle to stay first in brewing." The magazine quoted an unnamed A-B executive grousing about the competitive disadvantage inherent in Gussie's insistence on traditional methods. "We use five times as much labor as Schlitz does. We've got to import and store hops. We require larger aging facilities." Russell Ackoff was quoted as saying,

"I could cut production costs by 50 percent, but where quality is concerned, the subject is verboten." Even *Forbes*, which had celebrated Gussie in the past, took a swipe at him, depicting him as "slowing down" and out of touch with modernity in an article that ended on a smugly patronizing note: "It is hard not to sympathize with Gussie Busch, with his pride in tradition and in his products. Yet if the job of management is to make money for its stockholders and to assure the long-term health of the company, it is fair to ask whether Busch should be paying more attention to the dollar sign. Will Gus Busch's pride yield to economics?"

The answer was a resounding, table-pounding "No" from Gussie. There would be no change to the Budweiser brewing process as long as he was in charge, and he planned to be in charge as long as he was alive. As one A-B wholesaler put it, "The old man would burn the brewery first."

Of course, Gussie's refusal to cut brewing costs only increased the pressure to cut elsewhere. He had already ordered that the company cease paying for the helicopter that August used to fly back and forth between the brewery and Waldmeister every day. Now he suggested at a management committee meeting that all of the top executives give up their company-provided automobiles. It was not a popular idea to begin with, but when Gussie revealed that he wasn't including himself in the car giveback, Dick Meyer blew up. "You sonofabitch," he said. "You are going to keep all your four or five cars and your two drivers, but as president of this company I am to have no car? That's bullshit." And with that, he got up and walked out of the meeting.

The car privileges continued, but efforts were made to replace the egregious gas-guzzlers—including the big heavy station wagon used to ferry the Busch children—with more fuel-efficient vehicles. Gussie and Dick Meyer got into it again a few weeks later when Gussie demanded that he lay off more than a hundred people in the top and middle management ranks. Meyer thought Gussie was acting capriciously and unreasonably, so he refused. Gussie told him to either make the cuts or resign, and Meyer chose the latter, to the surprise of everyone except perhaps Gussie and August. Some executives believed that Gussie used the layoffs as a pretext to get Meyer to quit and thereby make room for August to finally take over the presidency. August had fully supported Gussie's stance on the brewing process, and the two had been getting along well since the Weinberg brouhaha. August's promotion was announced the same day as Meyer's resignation, and within ten days a handful of the young MBAs in August's corporate planning department were named vice presidents, prompting the *Post-Dispatch* to declare in a headline, "New Guard Takes Over the Reins of Anheuser-Busch." Denny Long was elevated to executive vice president and general manager of the brewery, becoming, in effect, August's No. 2.

It appeared to be an all-out triumph for August, but he was not fooled by his own publicity. He knew whose hands still held the reins, and how hard it was going to be to pry them loose. Even though his father was seventy-five, it might be years before he could claim his birthright. Once again, however, fate stepped in to speed up the Busch succession process.

It was cold and raining in St. Louis on December 6, 1974. The big house at Grant's Farm was bustling with preparations for the annual party celebrating the Feast of St. Nicholas, the Old World patron saint of children and precursor to the modern-day Santa Claus. It was one of the Busch family events that August usually attended. Trudy always made a big deal out of St. Nicholas Day, the highlight of which was a visit from an elaborately costumed St. Nick, who would suddenly emerge from the trees and enter the house carrying a bag full of fruits, nuts, and presents that he poured out onto the floor and distributed to the kids. The last thing St. Nick always pulled from the bag was the sapling whipping switches, which he held ominously in his hand while relating the naughty or nice things each child had done that year. St. Nick was usually Trudy's brother Willy, and the older kids were sworn not to tell the younger ones.

At 4:00 p.m. that afternoon, on Highway 244 a few miles from Grant's Farm, a tractor-trailer truck skidded off the pavement and hurtled across the grass median into the opposite traffic lanes, where it struck a car, jackknifed, and then collided head-on with a Volkswagen van carrying the two youngest Busch children— eleven-year-old Andrew and eight-year-old Christina—on their way home from school. The fifty-foot-long flatbed rig cut through the thin metal skin of the van like a can opener, severing the legs of the Busch family's longtime chauffeur, Nathan Mayes. Andrew Busch was thrown through the front window of the van and suffered serious injuries. Christina, who was sitting directly behind Mayes, suffered devastating head and abdominal injuries. Witnesses said the little girl made it to the hospital alive only because a car carrying five nurses happened by the accident, and they ministered to her and Andrew until the ambulances arrived.

Fifteen-year-old Billy Busch was waiting at his school for Nathan to pick him up. When the van didn't arrive by five, he called home and was told there had been an accident and someone else would come for him shortly. He was taken straight to St. John's Mercy Hospital, where much of the family was already gathered in a waiting room.

"I remember thinking, 'This can't be, this can't be,'" Billy said of the scene he encountered. "Christina was in the ICU, and Mom told me they had all these wires running in and out of her, and she couldn't breathe on her own. They told me that Andrew was going to be okay but that Nathan was dead, which really upset me because I was very close to him. But I thought Christina would get better because Dad would make it all right. He would get the best doctors and they would fix her."

The most shocking thing to Billy was the effect of the tragedy on his father, who was collapsed in a chair, sobbing uncontrollably, unable to take charge of anything. "I had never seen Dad like that," he said. "It was like everything had been taken out of him."

Gussie had doted on "Tina," his eleventh child, born when he was sixty-seven. Blond and blue-eyed like her mother, she was "the last of the Mohicans," he liked to say. He called her his little honey-bee, and allowed her to climb up on his lap at the dinner table and take out his false teeth and run away with them. He always danced with her at family parties, and the sight of the two of them, the oldest and youngest of the Busch clan delighting in one another, caused people to stop and watch.

Now they both were broken beyond fixing. "The doctors told us that if they turned off the ventilator, then Christina probably would not survive, and if she did she would be a vegetable anyway," recalled Adolphus IV. "But Mom and Dad kept her on it for eleven days to explore any possible scenario. They were looking for some expert somewhere who might say, 'There's a chance here.'"

There was no chance, however. On December 17, the ventilator finally was turned off and the baby of the Busch family died, along with a big part of her father, who would never fully recover.

"I understood why Dad felt so bad," said Billy, "but I thought he would come back. Instead, from what had been an incredibly happy family where everything went so wonderfully, it all began to fall apart."

CHOOSING SIDES

In the weeks following Christina's death, Gussie cried nearly nonstop and nursed his grief with copious amounts of alcohol, which only deepened his depression and further unnerved his children.

Trudy found comfort in the Catholic Church—the priests from Our Lady of Providence and the nuns at St. John's Hospital who had tended to the family during the eleven-day vigil outside Christina's room in the ICU, even Cardinal John Carberry, who said the funeral mass at Grant's Farm.*

The Christmas holidays at Grant's Farm—traditionally a time of constant parties with as many as fifty guests staying at the big house, the Cottage, and the Bauernhof—passed in sad silence, broken only by the sound of Gussie's sobbing.

"What kept Mom going was her belief that Christina was now

---

* Gussie showed his appreciation to St. John's by donating color televisions for every patient room in the hospital.

an angel in heaven and she would see her again," said Billy Busch, "but Dad didn't have that belief."

"I had six other children, so I couldn't go crazy," Trudy said years later. "I couldn't forsake them for my grief. I accepted in general that sad and terrible things are part of life. I was able to deal with it much better than Gussie. He couldn't handle sadness."

"He became like a child himself, and he didn't help her in that regard," said Adolphus. "He was another child for her to deal with."

On the days that he showed up at the brewery, Gussie was unfocused, erratic, and disruptive. His thoughts wandered in the middle of conversations; seemingly nonsensical statements popped out of his mouth. In a management committee discussion about the need for still more production capacity, for example, he said in apparent seriousness, "We don't need another brewery; we just need to keep raising the price until people stop buying it."

"August thought that Dad had lost his mind," said Adolphus. "Christina's death seemed to have speeded up his aging process, as if some form of dementia had kicked in."

Gussie brought twenty-two-year-old Adolphus with him to another meeting at the brewery. With his arm around Adolphus's shoulders, he said to the group of executives that included August, "I want you all to meet my son. He is the one who is going to be taking over for me; he will succeed me."

"Things like that went on constantly," said Denny Long. "August didn't react to it because he knew it wasn't reality. No one from the family was going to take his place. The old man didn't have his hands around the brewery. It was his way of fighting back, inflaming things, making August look bad or feel bad."

Gussie's sudden deterioration added urgency to secret meetings August held most Saturdays at Waldmeister Farm. The purpose of the meetings—which had been going on for more than a year—was to plan how the company would be organized and operated post-Gussie. The attendees were the core group of young executives—the MBAs and others like Denny Long—who owed their jobs and allegiance to August. They'd taken to calling themselves "the Dawn Patrol" due to the ungodly hour he imposed on the meeting—6:30 a.m., which meant they had to be on the road before 6:00 to traverse the thirty miles to Waldmeister. You did not want to be late for a meeting with August, or tired either, so they tried to be in bed early on Friday night. And this was in addition to the twelve-hour days they worked at the brewery and the calls they could expect from August at any hour on a Sunday or a holiday asking terse, pointed questions about their areas of expertise that they'd better be able to answer to his satisfaction. As much as they resented August's dominion over their lives, however, they were thrilled he'd chosen them to be on the team that would run Anheuser-Busch after Gussie either retired or expired.

In early 1975, August began considering a previously unthinkable option—forcing his father out. It would be a drastic move, to be sure, messy and emotional, but he saw no other way around the impediment that Gussie had become.

Miller provided the impetus. The Milwaukee brewery had doubled its market share and its production capacity since Philip Morris acquired it fully in 1971, jumping from seventh place to fifth, in terms of barrelage. Under CEO John Murphy, a savvy cigarette marketer, the company had reinvigorated its signature Miller High Life brand by repositioning it from "the champagne of bottled beers" to the working man's brew through a series of TV commercials that featured the tagline "If you've got the time, we've got the beer." The company further demonstrated its marketing chops in January 1975 when it introduced Miller Lite with a brilliant TV ad campaign that featured famous former athletes (including NY Yankees legends Whitey Ford and Mickey Mantle) comically debating the relative merits of great taste and fewer calories, along with the memorable tagline, "All you ever wanted in a beer. And less." It would prove to be the most successful new product launch in the history of the industry, propelling Miller into fourth place by the end of the year.

August didn't believe that a light, low-calorie beer would ever supplant his full-bodied Budweiser as America's favorite, but he saw Miller's rapid growth as a serious threat to A-B's industry dominance.

"August understood that we were at war with them," said Denny Long. "Gussie didn't."

So August set out to convince the board of directors that, for the good of the company, it was time for his father to go. He met with them individually over a period of months and found them surprisingly receptive to the idea. Even Gussie's closest friends on the board acknowledged that they were concerned about his mental acuity and the challenge from Miller.

August chose the May board meeting to make his official pitch to the directors. Gussie was alerted to the impending vote the night before, and Trudy was asked to accompany him to the brewery, where August had a doctor standing by in case the old man went into cardiac arrest. August entered the boardroom on the third floor armed with a detailed presentation and signed statements from all the members of the Dawn Patrol saying that they would resign if he was not named CEO. He was fairly certain he had the votes, but still he worried that some of the directors might lose their nerve in a face-to-face confrontation with Gussie, who doubtless went into the room thinking that he would prevail, as he always had.

This time, however, the board did not bend to Gussie's will. One by one, directors who had rubber-stamped his every whim for years went against him and voted him out as chief executive. As expected, Gussie flew into such a purple, vein-bulging rage that some people present wondered if his head might explode. Waiting in Gussie's office, Trudy heard him shouting over the commotion as he stormed down the hallway after the meeting had ended: "I thought you were my friend, goddammit," he hollered at someone.

"He was beside himself, screaming," Trudy recalled.

August walked directly into Denny Long's office and said simply, "It's done." He quickly called a meeting of all executives on the management committee. "There's been a change," he told them. "The board has put me in charge because the Chief has decided to retire." (He always called Gussie "Chief." Most people assumed it was out of respect, but Long suspected he was uncomfortable with the more intimate "Dad.")

The official story was, of course, a lie. Gussie hadn't decided anything. The terms August and the board had presented to him were nonnegotiable and, given his fifty years of service, brutal: He could retain the title of chairman, but it would be purely honorary. He would no longer have any say in running the company. Nor would he be entitled to the free use of company planes, automobiles, boats, or the Adolphus rail car or motorbus. Even the operations at Grant's Farm—the exotic animal enclosures, the deer park, the Bauernhof, and the Clydesdales—were no longer in his purview; the company had leased everything but the big house and the Cottage.

As an inducement for him to go quietly, they said he could stay on as president of the Cardinals, but only if he accepted the terms and stated publicly that he was stepping down voluntarily. He had twenty-four hours to decide before the offer was taken off the table.

Gussie arrived back at the big house that evening still raging. As he hollered for all the family to gather in the gun room, Trudy pulled Adolphus aside. "August has thrown out your father," she said. "Dad is not in charge of the company anymore." Adolphus was astounded. "What?" It was not something he ever imagined could happen. "I told you," Trudy said. "I always thought that little sonofabitch would do something like this, a sneak attack. It's the way he is."

As Gussie explained to the six kids what their half brother had done, his mood cycled from disbelief and despair one moment to vengeful resolve the next: "How could my own son do this to me?" . . . "That no-good goddamn bastard, I'll get him for this. . . . We are going to fight this thing."

By "we," he meant all of them. He made it clear that everyone in the family was going to have to choose—they stood either with him or with August. And if they sided with August, then they were dead to him, and disinherited, too.

Adolphus's mind reeled. He was about to graduate from college, and would be the first of the American Busch family to do so. His plan was to work at the brewery—starting at the bottom and, hopefully, climbing the management ladder to one day succeed August, who was seventeen years his senior. Gussie had always encouraged him in this regard, and was himself proof that the second-born son could become king. Adolphus had just filled out a pro forma job application at the brewery, but a routine entrance physical indicated he had a hernia that needed to be corrected through surgery before he could start. The surgery was two weeks away.

Adolphus knew he could never go against his father. The two had become increasingly close in the last few years. But he also knew that if he sided against August, and August prevailed, then he probably would never get to work for the company; August would see to that.

"There was no way any of us could avoid taking a side," he said. "You couldn't be neutral. Dad wouldn't allow it. You had to declare."

To Gussie's deep disappointment, three of his daughters by his previous marriages, Lotsie, Elizabeth, and, to a lesser degree, Lilly, supported August. "Daddy really needed to retire; he was exhausted," said Lotsie. "The board probably did what it had to do, even though it could have been done better."

Gussie quickly pressed Adolphus, Peter, Billy, and Andrew into service. "The four of you boys have to have a talk with your brother," he told them. "He owes the family an explanation."

Feeling "a mix of anger, sadness and disbelief," Adolphus put in the call to August and arranged a meeting at the fence that separated Waldmeister from Belleau Farm. "There was so much animosity right then that it couldn't have happened in either house," he said later. August brought along his twelve-year-old son, August IV, so all six of Gussie's male heirs were present for the face-off.

Adolphus did most of the talking for his side. "Why did you do this to our father?" he demanded to know.

"I had no choice," August responded. "Papa was slipping. The board of directors saw it, and you did, too. We all saw it."

"But why now, so soon after Christina? And why did you do it by surprise and humiliate him like that? Couldn't you have talked to him?"

"We tried," August said. "People went to him about some of the things that have been going on, and they advised him to step back and take some time off. But he didn't listen. If I had done it your way, then he would have fought it; he never would have gone along. You know how Papa is. He would have gotten rid of me." Adolphus couldn't argue with that; he knew it was exactly what Gussie would have done.

For fifteen minutes, August defended his action passionately but without emotion or apology, repeating that he'd done what had to be done for the good of the company, the family, and their father. Throughout the confrontation, August IV hung back about fifty yards, as if afraid to get too close. August turned to him several times, saying, "Come on up here, son. I want you to hear this." But the boy stayed where he was.

Adolphus didn't know what the meeting was supposed to accomplish, but he was sure it settled nothing. He walked away from the fence feeling the weight of his father leaning on him for support in a fight he feared they'd already lost.

The shock of the coup had the immediate effect of focusing Gussie. Now he had an enemy—his own son—and he was not without options, or friends. He owned about 15 percent of the company's stock, and through the trusts set up by his father he controlled another 15 percent. August, on the other hand, owned only about 1 percent of the shares. So it was not far-fetched for Gussie to think he might be able to use the imbalance to turn the tables on August. One of the first visitors to Grant's Farm after the board's vote was a politically connected attorney named Louis B. Susman. After conferring with Susman, Gussie tacitly agreed to the board's terms in order to avoid a public fight that would drive down the price of the company's stock. Susman, meanwhile, began secretly looking for a buyer for Gussie's shares.

On Thursday, May 8, Anheuser-Busch announced that the "Grand old man of the American brewing industry" was stepping aside as chief executive. In a press release written by Al Fleishman, Gussie was quoted as saying, "After more than 50 years of active association in the only job I ever had and the only company I have ever been associated with, I am stepping down as chief executive of Anheuser-Busch. This has been more than a company or a business to me, and it is not an easy decision.

"The fact is, I have had three love affairs in my life. First has been my wife and family; second, the company, which bears the proud name of Anheuser-Busch, and third, this great community of St. Louis." (Fleishman cleaned up Gussie's previous statement to a reporter that the company was first in his heart, followed by his family.)

The news coverage was as incurious as it was idolatrous. Every newspaper, magazine, and TV broadcast swallowed whole the fiction that Gussie had graciously stepped aside in favor of August III. Not one report connected his exit to recent events such as the death of his daughter, the management layoffs at the company, the resignation of Dick Meyer, lagging sales, or sagging stock performance. There wasn't a hint of his decline or of tensions with August and the board. Nowhere was it reported that Gussie's retention of the chairman title was purely honorary, leaving the public to assume that he still had the final say in things, even if August was now in charge of the day-to-day. Thanks to Al Fleishman and his public relations company, August's boardroom coup would remain a secret for nearly fifteen years.

Even as Gussie plotted revenge against August, he maintained the facade that all was well. When Fleishman managed to have him named to head a citizens' committee to raise funds for the completion of the St. Louis Convention Center and the mayor proclaimed him "the No. 1 Ambassador of the City St. Louis," Gussie posed for pictures with Trudy and the kids on the steps of City Hall, all of them dressed up as if they were going to church on Easter morning. "As long as I am alive, the citizens can count on me to do everything in my power to make St. Louis, our state and our nation the best place to live, raise a family and do business," he said.

Gussie took Adolphus along when he flew to Washington, D.C., with Lou Susman to confer with former defense secretary Clark Clifford. An adviser to Presidents Truman, Kennedy, and Johnson, and a former St. Louisan, Clifford was considered the wisest and wiliest honest broker in the nation's capital, and Susman wanted Gussie to get his advice on the various options available to him in the wake of the coup.

Clifford agreed with Susman that Gussie should avoid a big public battle with August, but said that through quiet negotiations, "we might be able to get back some of what you have lost." At the same time, Clifford said he thought Gussie stood a good chance of toppling August if he sold his shares to a potential buyer that Susman had lined up—RJ Reynolds Tobacco Company. Reynolds was enticed by the prospect of buying into the brewing business with a competitive advantage over its longtime rival, Philip Morris, which now owned Miller. So eager was Reynolds, in fact, that the company's CEO, Paul Sticht, flew to St. Louis to meet with Gussie at Belleau Farm, offering him $34 a share at a time when A-B stock was still trading in the low twenties. With Gussie's 30 percent stake in hand, and a willingness to pay a substantial premium over the trading price, Reynolds would have little trouble securing a controlling interest in A-B and placing its own people on the board. That wouldn't put Gussie back in charge, but it would mean good-bye to August, who would either leave on his own or be voted out by the new board.

While Gussie was mulling over the Reynolds offer, Susman managed to negotiate some face-saving concessions from A-B, including the continued use of his third-floor office and his full-time personal secretary, along with his company car and driver. Susman told him that he might even be able to arrange a deal to buy the Cardinals from the company. Gussie liked that idea so much that he called a press conference to talk about it, announcing with Adolphus at his side that the somewhat bewildered-looking twenty-two-year-old would be part of the Cardinals operation if a deal could be reached. Adolphus was praying that no one would ask him a question; for the life of him, he couldn't figure out why his father would want to buy the team. He'd been listening to Gussie complain for years about how the players association was ruining the game and making it impossible to turn a profit. The Cardinals had earned profits of less than $4 million over the entire twenty-two years A-B had owned the team. Who would want to own a business like that? You'd do better putting your money in a savings account.

Neither of the big deals came to fruition. After A-B placed an $11 to $13 million valuation on the baseball team, Gussie lost interest in being the real owner and chose to continue as its president. He would have August looking over his shoulder, but at least it wouldn't cost him any money, and he could continue to use the rail car and motorbus during spring training and the playing season. And after weeks of soul-searching, he decided that selling his shares to RJ Reynolds would be a betrayal of his father and grandfather. "I don't think they would ever go along with something like that," he told Trudy. August had dodged a bullet without even knowing it. The RJ Reynolds negotiations would remain a secret for more than a decade.

Though he said nothing publicly, in private Gussie continued to rage against August and the board, breaking off relations with everyone he thought had not supported him, including his daughters Lotsie and Elizabeth. "I tried to tell him to let it go," said Trudy. "I said, 'It's time. You have everything you could want. You have to deal with it. You have to move on and live.' But he was losing his empire and he couldn't accept it. He took out all his frustration on the people around him, yelling and screaming at everyone. He was like a wounded buck dying."

The saddest chapter in Gussie Busch's life ended with a vindication of sorts. Beginning in September 1975, reports began surfacing that Schlitz had secretly removed more than 500,000 cases of its beer from bars and stores in seventeen states based on customer complaints that it "tasted funny." CEO Robert Uihlein sought to blunt the impact of the stories, saying that only 3,685 cases had been pulled after a distributor reported an "off-taste" that may have been caused by "a very limited number of defective can-end lids supplied to Schlitz by a can company." But the company's problems were far more serious than that, and it all stemmed from Uihlein's corner cutting.

In the normal brewing process, a protein is produced that can cause a haze to form when the beer is chilled. Anheuser-Busch allowed the protein to settle out naturally during its longer aging process. Due to its shortened brewing process, however, Schlitz needed to add an artificial silica gel to counter the hazing effect. But Schlitz brewery managers feared the FDA would soon require brewers to list their ingredients on the label, exposing the company to attacks from Anheuser-Busch for using "unnatural" ingredients. So they began substituting another artificial antihaze additive called Chill-Garde, which could be filtered out prior to bottling and therefore didn't need to be listed on the label.

Schlitz's brewing technicians didn't realize that Chill-Garde would react in the bottles and cans with a commonly used (but not by A-B) foam stabilizer called Kelcoloid, forming tiny white flakes in the beer. The flakes got worse the longer the beer was on the shelf, eventually clumping together to form clots that resembled mucus or, according to one observer, "snot." In a rushed attempt to fix the problem, Schlitz executives in Milwaukee ordered their technicians to keep the Chill-Garde and lose the Kelcoloid, and the result was a headless beer that was "flat as apple cider," according to one distributor.

The shocking breakdown of quality controls culminated in the secret recall of more than 10 million bottles and cans of unacceptable beer that the company bulldozed into the ground at its Tampa and Memphis plants, a process that went on for months. But the damage was done. Schlitz sales fell more than 40 percent, its stock price plummeted to $5 a share, and its reputation as a quality brewer was irrevocably destroyed. Within a few years, the "beer that made Milwaukee famous" all but vanished from the marketplace (the brewery was purchased by Detroit-based Stroh Brewing Company in 1982).

Robert Uihlein died on November 12, 1976, just a few weeks

after he was diagnosed with a rare form of leukemia. Gussie refused to attend his funeral in Milwaukee, so Trudy and Adolphus IV went without him to pay their respects. They flew commercial.

The trade magazine *Advertising Age* summed up the whole sorry episode in an article that seemed aimed at the financial press that had so recently mocked Gussie for his "old fashioned" devotion to quality:

"A classic tale of human failing, the Schlitz saga now serves as a reminder for those who might lose sight of the fact that a company—no matter how modern its plants, how endowed its balance sheet or how lionized by Wall Street analysts—is really no stronger than the human beings who manage it."

Considering how the Anheuser-Busch saga ultimately played out, that passage now seems prophetic.

CAMELOT'S END

In the middle of the night, the big house at Grant's Farm can be a spooky place, cavernous and shadowy, with no neighboring homes for half a mile in any direction, and no sounds of civilization to compete with the rustling of the wind in the trees and the cries of myriad wild animals.

At 1:00 a.m. on February 8, 1976, the loud crack of a gunshot reverberated through the darkened house. Gunfire was not an unusual sound at Grant's Farm, where animals were hunted and harvested all the time. The property practically bristled with weaponry. Gussie had a collection of nearly one hundred rifles and pistols, many of which were on display in the aptly named gun room.

But this shot had been fired inside the house. The sound woke Adolphus IV, who was lying in his bed trying to figure out what he had just heard when his brother Peter burst into his room. "Please help me," Peter said. "Something terrible has happened."

Adolphus followed Peter through the bathroom that separated their bedrooms. He could smell the burned gunpowder as he entered the room, where he was stopped in his tracks by the sight of Peter's best friend, David Leeker, lying on his back on the floor, with a small bullet hole between his lip and nose and blood pooling on the carpet around his head. Adolphus's mind careened back nine years, to when he watched his best friend, Geoffery Meiers, die right in front of him after falling from a horse down by the lake at Grant's Farm, the blood pooling on the pavement around his head.

Adolphus wheeled and bolted out the door into the second-floor hallway, nearly colliding with Gussie, who had heard the shot, too, and was coming to see "what the hell's going on."

"Dad, don't go in there," Adolphus said, instinctively trying to shield the old man from another tragedy. Gussie pushed past him and knelt down next to the boy to feel for a pulse. He couldn't find one. "It was an accident," Peter said. "I didn't mean to shoot him. The gun just went off." The gun, a Colt .357-magnum revolver, lay on the floor. Gussie recognized it as the one his friend Robert Baskowitz Jr. had given Peter as a high school graduation present.

There was a time when Gussie would have taken charge and dealt decisively with the situation. But at age seventy-seven, he was no longer that man. With both his sons in a state of shock and Trudy visiting her family in Switzerland, he instructed the brothers to call the police and then went back into his bedroom and collapsed on the bed in tears. Peter phoned the police while Adolphus called Gussie's secretary, Margaret Snyder, who quickly contacted Lou Susman in Florida. Within minutes the police and paramedics arrived, followed shortly thereafter by Snyder, two lawyers from Susman's firm, and seventy-one-year-old Al Fleishman, who'd been rousted out of bed by Susman even though he had retired from his company.

David Leeker was rushed to the hospital, but Peter and Adolphus knew the caliber of the gun and the location of the wound pretty much guaranteed he was dead. While the police examined the scene in Peter's room, the Busch advisers gathered in Gussie's bedroom and listened to Peter sob out his description of the shooting.

After an evening of hanging out, watching TV and playing cards, David had decided to spend the night, and they were preparing a sleeping bag for him on the floor. Peter went out into the long hallway and, with the gun in his hand, got a pillow from the linen closet. He walked back into the bedroom, dropped the pillow on the sleeping bag, and started to toss the pistol onto his bed. That's when the weapon "somehow discharged," he said.

The police questioned Peter and Adolphus in the Blue Room, a parlor at the end of the second-floor hallway, and the brothers later went to the police station, where Peter gave detectives an official statement and took a lie detector test. At 3:15 a.m., detectives knocked on the door of the Leeker home less than a mile from Grant's Farm and gave his parents the awful news. At the same time, Al Fleishman faced a group of reporters gathered at the front gate of Grant's Farm and repeated Peter's version of events. When a reporter asked why the young man was carrying a loaded gun around his house, Fleishman explained awkwardly that all the Busch children were taught to handle firearms and used them for hunting and target practice. When he was finished, one of the reporters said to him, "I guess you know nobody is going to believe this."

There were problems with Peter's story. He told his lawyers and the police that David was standing across the room from him when the gun went off. But the powder burns on Leeker's face indicated that he'd been shot at point-blank range, with the muzzle of the gun inches away. Peter also said that the gun was not cocked before it discharged. But the county firearms examiner could find no reason why the gun would have fired so easily, and tests in the police laboratory showed that without the hammer cocked, it took eleven pounds of pressure to pull the trigger. All of which argued against an inadvertent discharge.

Nonetheless, the detective in charge of the case told reporters that Peter "has cooperated with us fully and we believe he is telling the truth." And by the end of the day, the chief investigator for the county medical examiner's office had ruled the shooting an accident, saying he "could find no evidence of reckless action that might prompt the lodging of a manslaughter charge" against Peter.

According to investigators, Peter told them he was carrying the gun around the house that night out of fear of kidnappers. "Apparently it was normal occurrence for this young man to walk around carrying a gun on the property and in his home," the chief detective told reporters. "Even though the family has security guards and other people around all the time, they always seem afraid something might happen."

It may have sounded like paranoia on Peter's part, or a convenient excuse for dangerous behavior, but a reasoned fear of kidnapping was in fact embedded in the Busch family psyche. It dated back to the Depression, when America experienced an epidemic of kidnappings for ransom, including that of August A. Busch's eleven-year-old grandson, Adolphus Orthwein, who was abducted at gunpoint on New Year's Eve in 1930 as he was being driven to Grant's Farm to have dinner with his grandparents. Young Dolph was rescued unharmed the next morning, but a shaken August A. from then on traveled with an arsenal in his Cadillac limousine—a pistol in the front seat for the driver, a pistol behind the backseat, another one in his suit pocket, and a double-barreled derringer in his hat. He went so far as to buy sixty .32-caliber pearl-handled Police Special revolvers, which he gave to friends and business associates as protection from kidnappers.

Indeed, brewers seemed particularly vulnerable. In 1933, the Ma Barker gang kidnapped William Hamm Jr., president of the Theodore Hamm Brewing Company, as he left his office in St. Paul, Minnesota. Hamm was held for four days and released only after a $100,000 ransom was paid. A year later Adolph Coors Jr., the son and successor to the Coors brewery founder, was targeted in a $50,000 kidnapping plot that was broken up by the police. His son was not so lucky. In 1960, forty-four-year-old Adolph Coors III, then president of the company, was shot to death in a botched kidnapping attempt on the road between his Colorado home and the brewery.

Over the years, Gussie received constant reminders of his family's vulnerability as various law enforcement agencies warned him about suspected kidnapping threats to his children, including Peter when he was a teenager and Christina in the week before her death.

If all that weren't enough to stoke Peter's fear, there was also the large oil painting by noted German artist Ferdinand Charles Wimar that hung on the wall in the dining room of the big house. A dramatic rendering of an actual event in America history, it was titled *The Abduction of Daniel Boone's Daughter by the Indians.** Intentionally or not, the fear of kidnapping was served up nightly with dinner at Grant's Farm.

The grieving Leeker family was angry that no one from the Busch family called or came to talk with them until more than twelve hours after the shooting, and that when Peter and Adolphus IV finally did come to the Leeker home, they were accompanied by family lawyers. "Why didn't you come get me? Why didn't you call me?" David's mother asked Peter. "They wouldn't let him," his older brother replied for him.

---

* Jemima Boone and two of her friends were captured by a Shawnee war party outside Boonesborough, Kentucky, on July 14, 1776. Her father and a group of men chased after them and rescued the girls three days later. The painting still hangs on the wall in the dining room at Grant's Farm, along with another Wimar epic, *The Attack on the Emigrant Train*. Billionaire Phillip Anschutz recently offered the Busch family $7 million for the pair.

At one point on the morning of the shooting, David's two sisters stormed over to Grant's Farm to try to find out what had happened. They were appalled when a member of the household staff ushered them into the gun room, with all its weaponry and animal heads on garish display, to wait for Gussie to come down from his room and talk to them. When he did, all he could do was weep and repeat over and over again, "It's a terrible tragedy."

By the time Trudy returned from Switzerland, the tragedy was being treated as a scandal by the media, which reported that police had found three other guns in Peter's room—two .45-caliber pistols and an M16 military rifle—and that Peter had a history of carelessness with firearms, once shooting himself in the leg while practicing quick draws with a revolver.

Over the next few weeks, the county prosecutor grew concerned about the discrepancies in Peter's story. The fact that the shooting had been ruled accidental did not eliminate the possibility that there had been criminal negligence on his part. So the prosecutor ordered investigators to reinterview all the witnesses, including Peter. He then presented the results of his inquiry to a grand jury, which returned an indictment charging Peter with manslaughter for handling a gun "in such a manner as to show a reckless disregard for human life."

(While Peter's case was moving through the court system, there was another shooting at Grant's Farm. On October 8, an unknown assailant with a .22 rifle fired into a herd of Clydesdale broodmares as they stood grazing by the light of a full moon. Four mares were wounded, and one them, an eighteen-year-old named Peggy Lyndale, had bled to death by the time a stablehand came upon the carnage the next morning. Peggy, who had produced fourteen foals and was carrying her fifteenth, was one of Gussie's most prized Clydesdales. "The fact that she is gone is just breaking my heart," he said.)

After first pleading not guilty in the Leeker case, Peter changed his plea to guilty on the eve of the trial. The prosecutor had refused to plea-bargain for no jail time, so he was taking a chance. "I am very sorry," he told the judge. "I know now that I had to have my finger on the trigger because there was no other way of the pistol going off. . . . I was very careless." He was sentenced to five years' probation, during which time he was forbidden to handle any kind of firearm.

Two weeks later, David Leeker's parents filed a $3 million wrongful death lawsuit,* naming Peter, Gussie, Trudy, Anheuser-Busch, and Colt, the manufacturer of the pistol. By that time, Gussie and Trudy were suing one another—for divorce.

By all accounts, life with Gussie had become unbearable, and the Leeker shooting and its aftermath were the last straw for Trudy. "Dad wasn't the same; he didn't have that vibrance anymore," said Billy. "He cried all the time, and she was mad at him for not being strong. They fought like cats and dogs."

When he drank, which was most of the time, "Dad got mean and was verbally abusive," said Adolphus. "All of a sudden, the twenty-seven-year difference in their age seemed like forty-seven years."

"Age had something to do with it," Trudy said later. "But I wanted my freedom. I couldn't stand a man crying over something that you couldn't do anything about. I wanted out."

Once again, the children were forced to choose. The girls, Beatrice and Trudy, sided with their mother, while all four boys stood by Gussie. "I was feeling very sorry for Dad," Billy said. "Mom became sort of bitter, and would say hard things to him, and he would break down crying. She got really cold."

"Why would you put him through all this?" Adolphus asked

---

* The case was settled out of court.

his mother. "Look what he's gone through already. He's seventy-seven years old. How much more can he take?"

Trudy moved into the Cottage in September 1977, and negotiations commenced, aimed at reaching an amicable divorce agreement. But the separation of only a few hundred yards quickly turned into a kind of "War of the Roses" when Gussie learned, through private investigators hired by Lou Susman, that Trudy had had a romantic fling during her trip to Europe. She'd never had an affair before, and it came on the eve of her fiftieth birthday, and on the heels of her finding out about Gussie's infidelities aboard the yacht in Florida. But Gussie's pride was hurt, and he instructed Lou Susman to take the gloves off.

Five days after they each filed for divorce, saying their marriage of twenty-five years was "irretrievably broken," Gussie moved to have Trudy evicted from the Cottage. In a letter addressed "Dear Trudy," he ordered her to "vacate the premises" within twenty-four hours. "No other living quarters will be available to you at Grant's Farm. At the time you move from the premises, please take only those personal items of clothing which you feel you will need immediately. I will make arrangements to have the balance of your personal clothing and effects delivered by appropriate means to the location you designate."

He told her that she could continue to drive the white Lincoln, but "you may not use any other Grant's Farm vehicles." Nor could she call upon the services of any member of the Grant's Farm staff, including the children's longtime nanny, Yolanda. "As of this date, I have terminated the employment of Yolanda Gloggner," Gussie wrote. "I am also advised that her lease for an apartment at the Bauernhof has been terminated." It was breathtakingly brutal. He was doing to Trudy exactly what August and the board had done to him.

Trudy obtained an injunction barring her eviction, and she remained in the Cottage while her lawyers and Gussie's slugged it out in court filings. But as lord of the manor, Gussie continued to torture her by, among other things, ordering his security guards at the front gate to search the trunk of her car whenever she drove off the estate, lest she attempt to remove any of his "personal property." At one point, when Trudy's brother Kurt traveled from Switzerland to visit her, the guards barred him from entering. Trudy was so incensed that she uncharacteristically complained to the press. "I think it's time this was exposed," she told a reporter from the *St. Louis Globe-Democrat*. "I was always hoping we could have an amicable reconciliation, and when that became impossible, an amicable divorce. But when it comes to my brother coming all the way from Switzerland for only three days. . . . I was horrified to understand when I came to the gate that my brother was not allowed in.

"He is the only uncle my children have, the only close relative my children have. I need someone from my family to help me. I cannot understand. To me, refusing him entrance is just totally diabolic."

Gussie's response to her public outburst was, "I have no comment."

A divorce was granted on February 28, 1978. Trudy came to court wearing a black dress and knee-high black boots, but Gussie didn't make an appearance. He was home recovering from a recent hip surgery. Under the terms of the settlement, Trudy received an undisclosed amount of cash and stock, and monthly maintenance for the rest of her life or until she remarried. The agreement also provided for a new home and a trust fund for her, in accordance with a prenuptial agreement.

On her way out of court that day, Trudy smiled for reporters and said graciously, "It is not a bitter divorce. I am glad we have had such great children, and I've had marvelous years with my husband."

Her children would not have agreed with her sunny assessment at that moment. In truth, the divorce had shattered the family. Divided by their loyalties, the six surviving siblings ceased functioning as a unit and began to scatter: Beatrice returned to college; Trudy moved into her mother's new home; Peter, Billy, and Andrew remained in the big house with Gussie; Adolphus had taken up residence at Belleau Farm.

"This became my sanctuary," he said, sitting in the rustic kitchen thirty-three years later. "I couldn't stand being at Grant's Farm anymore. And I was torn because Dad would always call and say, 'Please, you have to spend more time with me.' But it hurt me so badly to see him."

It would be seven years before he spoke to his mother again. "It was sad to see all of that crumble before your eyes," he said.

"WE ARE AT WAR"

The first real test of August's leadership came on March 1, 1976. The company's contract with its Teamster-affiliated bottlers expired at midnight, and picketers from bottling locals in Jacksonville, Florida, and Columbus, Ohio, appeared at the Pestalozzi Street plant just before dawn. Within hours, the Teamsters had shut down eight Anheuser-Busch breweries, idling eight thousand workers.

The issues in the strike had to do not with money but with the grievance and arbitration process and a demand by the Teamsters that they be given a say in any plant automation changes that might affect the number of union jobs. August sensed that the strike would be his crucible. He no longer had his father looking over his shoulder, second-guessing him, criticizing, interfering, undermining or countermanding his decisions. Now it was his photo on the first page of the annual report, his signature on the letter to shareholders. Newspapers and magazines could no longer refer to him as "young Busch." At long last, the kid had become the king, and it was up to him to rule.

When the picketers appeared, August was ready for them. A-B had built up its inventory in anticipation of the strike, and had a thirty-day supply of beer on hand. The company also had an unlikely ally.

The Brewers and Maltsters Local No. 6 was the second-largest union on the Pestalozzi Street premises, representing approximately 1,000 of the plant's 4,000 hourly employees (Bottlers Local 1187 represented 1,490 employees). Local 6 members had recently ratified a new three-year contract that gave them a wage increase of $2.25 an hour. It was "the best economic package in the history of the brewing industry," according to their business manager, Robert Lewis. As a result, Local 6 members honored the out-of-towners' picket line grudgingly.

"My people are bitter about being involved in this," said Lewis, who was furious at the leaders of his parent union, Teamsters International in Chicago, for calling a strike over such sidebar issues. In addition to the pay increase, Lewis had negotiated an employee stock-purchase plan that he believed "could be revolutionary" in the industry. "Now the average worker is going to be concerned with profit and loss because it will affect his investment," he said, noting that Anheuser-Busch had since incorporated the stock-purchase plan into eighteen of its thirty-three union contracts. The Teamsters' action threatened "everything we have gained," he said.

Lewis gave most of the credit for the stock-purchase plan to August, whom he had publicly blamed for the 1969 strike and once characterized to reporters as "biologically incapable of doing his job." In the intervening years, however, the two had taken Gussie's advice and learned to get along, to the point where they now considered themselves friends.

For the most part, Anheuser-Busch had a history of good relations with its craft unions, dating to the days before the turn of the century when the mostly German-born plant employees were part of the city's tight-knit German-American community, which made up the bulk of the local beer drinkers. Back then, if you angered your workers, you ran the risk of losing your customer base. As a result, labor disputes tended to be settled quickly. In June 1881, for example, five hundred workers at the Pestalozzi Street plant went on strike after management rejected their demand for shorter hours and higher pay. They labored from 4:00 a.m. to 7:00 p.m. seven days a week, at a salary of $55 to $75 a month, with free lunch furnished at 10:00 a.m. and 4:00 p.m., and a daily allowance of twenty free beers per man. They wanted $5 more per month, a company-furnished breakfast at 6:00 a.m., and three hours off on Sunday morning to go to church. (Apparently, they considered the beer ration sufficient.) After a short work stoppage, they got what they wanted.

Not this time. When the bottlers' strike reached its twenty-third day, Anheuser-Busch announced that it would begin making beer with the help of nonunion "supervisory" personnel. On August's order, the St. Louis facility transferred eight hundred office workers, accountants, and other salaried personnel to beer production and began brewing and bottling Budweiser, Busch, and Michelob for shipment.

August was especially eager to keep his St. Louis wholesalers supplied because Miller was taking advantage of the strike to flood the city with its product. One Milwaukee trucking company alone was bringing three 40,000-pound loads of Miller beer into St. Louis every day.

The Teamsters International in Chicago was stunned at August's audacity. The union's chief negotiator said it was the first time in more than eighty years that a brewer had attempted to make beer in the midst of a strike.

"This is nothing but scab beer," fumed Art Barhorst, the business manager for Local 1187, who claimed the brewery was forcing office workers, "including typists," to help break the strike by "threatening them with firing." A spokesman for the brewery countered that the employees were happy to be making the additional money that came from working twelve-hour shifts. In all, nearly three thousand salaried employees nationwide joined in the effort to keep the beer flowing.

Violence flared as strikers attempted to prevent trucks from leaving the plant and distributorships. A security guard fired a shot at strikers after an explosion blew a hole in a door at Lohr Distributing, the main A-B wholesaler in the city of St. Louis. The wife of Lohr's sales manager received a threatening phone call telling her, "We have your husband prisoner now." At Grey Eagle Distributing in St. Louis County, a fully loaded beer truck was overturned. Windows were broken at a liquor store. More than twenty strikers were arrested in the various incidents.

Art Barhorst defended the lawbreakers with some overblown rhetoric that seemed borrowed from the epic management-labor battles of the early 1900s. "When a man sees his job being jeopardized and his family going hungry, he reacts in other-than-normal manner," he said. "Any violence at the Anheuser-Busch plant is a direct result of the company's actions to destroy our union, and they must bear the weight of responsibility."

Despite the incidents, Anheuser-Busch managed to maintain 62 percent of normal production with its salaried employees, which prompted Robert Lewis to unleash an angry broadside at the Teamster leadership. "Teamsters International has brought on a situation that organized labor in various industries will have to live with from now on," he said in a lengthy interview with the *Post-Dispatch* that produced the front-page banner headline "Beer Strike May Have Broad Labor Impact."

"This strike has proved that unions no longer can effectively close down management," Lewis said. "Anheuser-Busch is producing beer as if the situation is normal, and because of that this strike may be an encouragement, an incentive, to management in other industries to take on organized labor. We feel at this point the strike has been lost."

And so it had. On June 4 the bottlers returned to work, having agreed to almost the same contract offer they'd walked away from at the end of February. The strike had lasted ninety-five days, making it by far the longest in A-B's history. It had cost the company a 4 percent drop in market share and an estimated $30 million in net profit. But August considered it an important victory, both for the company and himself.

"The union pushed us to the cliff," he said. "They wanted written into the contract that they would have the right to approve or disapprove any changes in production before we could implement them. They would manage our production, not us. It was a test of me. It was the first time they had to deal with me on the front line."

He showed his gratitude to the salaried workers who'd become temporary brewers and bottlers by giving them $1,000 bonuses, in the form of twenty-two shares of A-B stock and $356 in cash. This of course angered the union employees, who regarded it as an in-your-face payment to scab labor. It didn't help matters when, a few weeks later, August sent a letter to shareholders, executives, and administrative (nonunion) personnel, announcing that the company was forming a political action committee. Called AB-PAC, it would offer "you and me an effective, practical way to join forces and pool our financial support in a concerted effort to elect qualified candidates who will be willing to listen to the industry's point of view and support it."

While AB-PAC would be noncompulsory and nonpartisan, he made it clear that its "qualified candidates" were not likely to be union-loving Democrats:

"For years, labor and other special interests groups have been deeply involved in the electoral process by endorsing candidates and providing them with substantial financial support. American business has, however, been severely limited in the extent to which it could take part in this process. The result has been a gradual but constant erosion of the free enterprise system, a system we believe to be the basis for the future well being of this country and its citizens."

The unions took the announcement as a shot across the bow, signaling that A-B would be taking an even harder line in the years ahead. A company spokesman hurried to dispel that notion, saying August's statement had nothing to do with the strike and that labor was only mentioned "out of respect for the effective way some labor organizations have taken part in the political process."

August recognized that he had continuing problems with his labor force. "A strike leaves scars," he told shareholders at the company's annual meeting. "The attitudes of people are understandably affected by the tensions and ill will generated by picket lines and the operations of plants. It is important that these attitudes be replaced with feelings of mutual respect."

He began a concerted effort to bind up the wounds, launching a series of meetings at every brewery, inviting salaried and hourly employees and their spouses to hear executives present a comprehensive review of the state of the company and the brewing industry, and explain in detail A-B's financial and marketing strategies. He tapped Denny Long to help drive the effort, figuring that Long's working-class bona fides would play better with the rank and file than his own ruling-class résumé. "You are one of them," he said.

Long quickly saw that the union workers didn't consider themselves part of the company. During an employee meeting in Houston, a group of union workers still unhappy with the recent settlement stood together in the back of the large auditorium rather than sit with the nonunion workers. They weren't hostile, just wary, uncomfortable. So Long stepped away from the podium, and with the microphone in his hand walked to the back of the room and stood among them.

"Tell us what you need," he said.

"To be recognized," one bottler replied.

"Give me an example," said Long.

After a pause, another bottler said, "We need a place to play team softball."

Long knew they were testing him with a minor annoyance, but he turned to the plant manager and said, "Give them a field." Afterward, he said to August, "We have to get them working for us, and to do that we need a common enemy."

As it happened, there was one handy. Since 1972, Miller's annual output had gone from 5 million barrels to 18 million. The brewery had upped its production by 5 million barrels in the last year alone, the largest single-year increase in the history of the industry, and seemed certain to take over the No. 2 position behind A-B in the coming year. Funded by the deep pockets of Philip Morris, Miller was committed to a billion-dollar expansion program that included building a monster brewery in North Carolina capable of pumping out 10 million barrels a year. The company claimed its overall capacity would reach 40 million barrels a year by 1980. In Denny Long's view, "They were coming at us like a fast-moving freight train."

Which is why he thought Miller could be the unifying factor A-B needed. They just had to drive home the point to the union members: it wasn't management or their salaried coworkers that threatened their livelihood; it was Miller Brewing. "Let's not fight among ourselves," he urged at the employee meetings. "Let's fight them."

Long came up with the idea of distributing T-shirts to all St.

Louis plant employees, emblazoned with the declaration "I Am a Miller Killer." The white shirts with bright red lettering were so popular that workers in other plants began clamoring for them. Back in the days before August tapped him to be his assistant, Long had run what was known as the company's Standards Department, a group of young time-and-motion specialists that conducted studies aimed at making plants more efficient and productive. At the time, they were regarded suspiciously as management "tools," looking to reduce costs by eliminating jobs. Now, in the new "Miller Killer" environment, the standards people were seen in a new light, perceived as team members, partnered with the plants' industrial engineers in the battle against their common enemy, Miller.

The Miller Killers increased productivity by 20 percent nationwide, with minimal capital expenditures. August seized on the theme of teamwork as the hallmark of the new Anheuser-Busch. Under his father, the company often had been characterized as a "family," but never as a team. Like an overbearing parent, Gussie led by edict—"Because I said so, goddammit"—and August had seen the dysfunction that resulted. So *teamwork* became his favorite word, and a spontaneous display of esprit de corps could melt his normally frosty demeanor and make him go almost misty-eyed. (A psychologist might say this was connected to his being a loner as a kid and never participating in team sports.)

While Anheuser-Busch management was distracted by the strike, the American media fell in love with Miller Brewing. Business reporters were drawn to the story of the company's spectacular growth and its clever jock-filled TV commercials, and they invariably succumbed to the quotable Irish charm of Miller's CEO, John Murphy, whom the company PR department pitched as "the man who took Miller High Life from the champagne bucket to the lunch pail without spilling a drop." Murphy relished the spotlight, dropping bons mots such as, "Every Irishman dreams of going to heaven and running a brewery." He seemed to revel in taunting Anheuser-Busch and its prickly new boss, showing reporters the voodoo doll named August that he kept in his office and the foot rug under his desk displaying the A & Eagle logo. "Ours is a simple objective," he told *Newsweek*. "It's to be No. 1." He hinted that he had a specific date in mind when it would happen, but he just couldn't reveal it yet.

Naturally, reporters repeated Murphy's gibes to August, who was unable to resist the bait, responding testily (and memorably) to a *Business Week* reporter, "Tell Miller to come right along, but tell them to bring lots of money."

August didn't fully realize how tough the fight with Miller was going to be until he focused his attention on A-B's marketing effort. For the most part, the company had been doing the same thing for years—pitting its long-established brand (Budweiser) against another long-established brand (first Pabst, then Schlitz), with a familiar message (natural ingredients equal quality) aimed at a familiar customer (the monolithic male beer drinker). The formula had worked well enough to keep Anheuser-Busch in first place for twenty straight years.

But a lot had changed since Gussie's time. The latest research showed that 30 percent of beer drinkers actually consumed 80 percent of the beer. They were generally twenty-one- to thirty-four-year-old males, mostly blue collar, but including a growing number of college students. Unlike their forebears, they didn't down the bulk of their beer in bars; they bought it in liquor and grocery stores and consumed it at home at the rate of 10 million six-packs a night, usually while watching some sort of sports program on television. Their taste in beer varied according to their ethnicity. And, as the success of Miller Lite proved, they were not so brand-loyal that they wouldn't try a new product, even something as sissy-sounding as a "low calorie" beer.

Given the research, A-B's best marketing strategy going forward seemed a no-brainer: create ad campaigns that targeted those "heavy male users" and air them during nationally televised sporting events. So August convened a meeting of all the marketing executives on a Saturday morning in Denny Long's office. He wanted to know what sporting events A-B was sponsoring, and what else was available. The marketing guys sheepishly explained that the sponsorship rights to all the major network sporting events—the World Series, the Super Bowl, Monday Night Football, the College Football Game of the Week, the NBA playoffs, the Stanley Cup, Wimbledon, the Moscow Summer Olympics, the Indy 500—had been bought up by other brewers, including, um, Miller. The A-B marketing department had evaluated the cost of those sponsorships and decided they were too expensive.

August was astounded, and furious. He ordered the marketing people to contact each of the approximately 950 A-B wholesalers in the country and have them fill out a form that listed every sporting event that took place in their market, noting which ones were already sponsored and by whom, and which ones were still available at what price. He wanted all the information sent to St. Louis within a week.

The results of the frantic fact-gathering were presented during a four-day conference at the Quality Inn in Fort Magruder, Virginia, a few miles from the Busch Gardens resort in Williamsburg. In the hotel's ballroom, banquet tables were arranged in a square with August and Denny Long seated at the head table that transversed the front of the room. At each seat there was a note tablet emblazoned with a logo of an eagle swooping down on its prey with talons exposed, and the slogan "A Sense of Urgency." Next to each tablet was a baseball cap with the letters "ASU" stitched above the brim. The caps and the attacking eagle, which were Long's idea, gave the proceedings a military feel, as if they were about to embark on a dangerous mission. In a way, they were.

They went through the list of sporting events property by property as two media buyers from the ad agency D'Arcy, MacManus, Masius Advertising manned phones at a table in the corner. The NCAA basketball tournament was taken, but how about the National Catholic Basketball Tournament? "What's the cost?" August would ask. If the price were right, he'd bark, "Buy it!" Alabama football? Buy it! Notre Dame basketball? Buy it! And so it went. From the smallest college football game to the most obscure sport (hydroplane racing, hot air ballooning, water polo), he bought sponsorships by the barrel full, several hundred during the four-day conference and eventually thousands. He envisioned making Anheuser-Busch synonymous with American sport by planting the company flag at every competitive event in the country. If there was a three-legged sack race being cheered on somewhere, then, by God, there had better be a Budweiser sign at the finish line. And when the sponsorship rights for the major network sports contests became available again, he expected A-B to wrest them from Miller's grip no matter what the cost. Toward that end, he doubled the advertising budget, raising it to $100 million for 1978, matching what Miller claimed it was spending. "There is little choice for either of us," he said, "for we are at war."

Much of the burden for wrestling sports sponsorships away from Miller and other brewers, and for forging relationships with all teams in the major professional sports, fell on Michael Roarty, the vice president of marketing. Fortunately, he seemed ideally suited for the task. Exuding even more twinkly-eyed Celtic charisma than Miller's John Murphy, Roarty was A-B's designated MC and unofficial ambassador of bonhomie. Fellow Irishman Denny Long described him as a *shanachie*, a Gaelic word meaning "storyteller." He was an open tap of stories, jokes, and anecdotes, the guy everyone wanted to sit next to at dinner. "There is a charm about him that is almost hypnotic," a reporter once said.

Roarty turned that charm on the growing list of famous entertainers and sports figures A-B contracted to promote Bud and Bud Light, mixing easily with the likes of Paul Newman, Roger Maris, and Bob Hope, with whom he became particularly close. "He was in charge of intangibles," his good friend Long said many years later, chuckling. "I never cared for that stuff, and August couldn't bear it, but Michael loved it, and he was brilliant at it."

There was no question that the Miller Lite blitzkrieg had taken Anheuser-Busch by surprise. As Miller rolled out its new "less filling" beer in 1975 and 1976, August and some of the A-B brass scoffed at the very idea of light beer and claimed they had no intention of introducing their own low-calorie brand to compete. "We think our beer is light enough," said vice president of brewing Andrew Steinhubl, who repeated the company line that any weight gain among beer drinkers was probably due to the fact that beer enhanced people's appetite and had nothing to do with the calories in the beer itself. August predicted to his executive team that Miller ultimately would fail.

So it was doubly embarrassing when Miller Lite proved an unqualified success, with five million barrels shipped its first full year on the market. A-B responded by introducing two new brands in 1977—Natural Light and Michelob Light. But because of management's earlier scorn for the light beer category, the move was seen as a jumping-on-the-bandwagon act of desperation.

Miller said as much when it petitioned the Federal Trade Commission to halt the sale of Natural Light, claiming the new product's name infringed on its Lite trademark, which gave it the exclusive right to use the terms *lite* and *light* in marketing beer. According to Miller, A-B was attempting to "ride the coattails" of its multimillion-dollar investment in developing the Lite brand.

A-B struck back with its own FTC complaint, accusing Miller of fraudulently advertising its Lowenbrau brand. Miller had begun importing Lowenbrau (German for "lion's brew") from its six-hundred-year-old maker in Munich in 1974, positioning it as a premium-priced competitor to A-B's Michelob brand and playing up its Old World provenance. After two years, however, Miller quietly switched to brewing Lowenbrau under license in its Fort Worth, Texas, plant, while maintaining its premium, imported price. The Texas Lowenbrau was not the same as its Bavarian namesake. It contained corn grits and two chemical additives, ingredients that would put it in violation of Germany's so-called purity laws, which mandated that beer could contain only water, hops, barley, and yeast.

Sensing a delicious opportunity, A-B marketing executives enlisted their lawyers and their public relations reps at Fleishman-Hillard in a plan to use an FTC complaint as the linchpin in a media campaign aimed at embarrassing Miller and killing Lowenbrau as a competitor. In a presentation to August, they explained how they were going to provide every legitimate media outlet and every A-B distributor with a copy of the complaint, complete with nearly ninety pages of backup research and exhibits showing how Miller's advertising and package labeling were leading American consumers to believe they were buying a German import that had won six gold medallions in international taste competitions. Any reporters who needed more convincing would be sent six-packs of Lowenbrau so they could see for themselves that you needed a magnifying glass to find any reference to Texas on the labels or cardboard cartons. All in all, the executives believed the campaign would be so credible that it could not be ignored, and Lowenbrau drinkers would be livid, because they were educated, affluent, didn't like to be ripped off, and would not forget.

August was delighted. "We'll blow their doors off," he said. When he asked, "What do you think will happen with the complaint?" the lawyers told him, "Absolutely nothing; the FTC won't act on it."

But the media sure did. A-B's blitz mailing of several thousand thick packets—"I think we set a record for poundage," said a former Fleishman-Hillard executive—resulted in more than two hundred newspaper articles, the most damning of which was an Associated Press story that included a statement from a Lowenbrau executive in Munich saying the company was embarrassed by what its U.S. licensee had done. Within a year, the Lowenbrau brand was all but dead in America.

The two beer companies continued to pummel one another with seemingly petty legal complaints. Miller filed one with the U.S. Bureau of Alcohol, Tobacco, and Firearms, accusing A-B of falsely advertising Michelob Light as a low-calorie beer. The company pointed out that most light beers, its own included, contained about 100 calories, a third less than regular beers. But Michelob Light contained 134 calories, only 20 percent less than regular Michelob. In addition to asking the agency to stop A-B from promoting Michelob Light as a "light" beer, Miller's attorneys took a gratuitous—and inaccurate—slap at A-B's brewing process: "We understand that Anheuser-Busch produces Michelob Light by brewing a batch of Michelob and then diluting it with carbonated water. Although it has watered down its beer, Anheuser-Busch has not reduced the price."

A-B's attorneys replied drolly, "We find it hard to understand how we can be accused of misleading consumers [when] every can and bottle of the product prominently displays the statement: 'Contains 134 calories, approximately 20 percent fewer than Michelob.'"

Miller finally went with a nuclear option, asking the FTC to bar A-B from claiming that any of its beers were "natural products" or were "brewed naturally" or contained "all natural ingredients." According to the complaint, A-B used "800,000 pounds of tannic acid annually" in its brewing process, and its vaunted beech wood aging "consists of dumping chemically treated lumber" into its beer storage vats. "It is an affront to the American consumer that this industrial giant and major advertiser should be allowed to continue to resort to advertising claims that are false and misleading."

As schoolyard taunts go, it was the equivalent of telling little Johnny in front of all the other kids that his mother was a dirty whore. Miller compounded the insult by submitting "testimony" from three nutritionists who said that A-B's ad claims were deceptive based on a definition of a natural food as "one that has undergone only minimal processing after harvest, or contains no chemical preservatives," such as milk or washed fruit.

A-B called Miller's complaint "a publicity ploy without substance and deliberately misleading regarding our brewing process." It said the tannins used in makings its beer occurred naturally in many foods, including cereal grains, grapes, and tea, and its beech wood chips were not chemically treated, but rather washed in baking soda prior to being placed in the aging vats.

A-B filed one last patently silly complaint with the SEC, claiming that the labeling on Miller High Life, which still carried the slogan "The champagne of beer," was misleading because the product "contained none of the qualities of champagne." After the two companies had spent millions in the legal tit-for-tat, neither the FTC nor the ATF took action on any of their complaints.

Miller posted excellent numbers in 1978—31.3 million barrels shipped, 7 million more than the previous year, and an increase in market share to 19 percent. But the record came at great expense, as Miller reported that Philip Morris had invested $4 billion in its brewing operation since 1972.

Anheuser-Busch finished in first place for the twenty-first straight year, shipping 41 million barrels and increasing its market share to 24 percent. But despite its 10-million-barrel edge, the perception persisted in the financial press that Miller was winning the war.

In a caustic article illustrated with an antique Budweiser bottle covered with cobwebs, *Forbes* stated, "For six years now, Murphy's

Miller has been walking all over St. Louis' Anheuser-Busch." The article took August and his management team to task for "arrogance" and "complacency," saying they suffered a "classic case of self deception" and were "merely reacting" while Miller was "calling the shots." The magazine that once mocked Gussie for his stubborn insistence on quality now ridiculed August for his sports-sponsorship buying spree, saying it looked "like an overreaction."

Anyone who knew August could imagine him gagging on the humble pie when the reporter got him to admit, "We missed the boat." (Which the magazine turned into the article's headline.)

Denny Long, too, was forced make an embarrassing admission. "We didn't take Miller seriously, but we do now," he was quoted as saying. *Forbes* described him as almost shouting as he vented his frustration at the prevailing Miller-versus-Anheuser-Busch narrative: "They say Miller is innovative, that its ads are creative, that it brings out new products to create new market segments, that it's gaining market share. Aren't we doing all these things, too? In the last 12 months we have introduced more new products, more new ads, added more new marketing people and worked harder than in any similar time in Anheuser-Busch history."

(In the wake of the article, August issued an order to Fleishman-Hillard: "You are not to have anything to do with *Forbes* magazine again." The ban lasted eight years, and when one Fleishman-Hillard rep violated it by responding to a *Forbes* reporter's request for some publicly available A-B information, August had him fired from the account.)

August and the company received much more even-handed coverage in *Newsweek*, whose reporter pressed August about his new nemesis and captured the coiled warning in his response. "Miller is aggressive," he said. "They're fine marketers. We compliment them." Then, fixing the reporter with an icy stare and speaking very slowly, he added, "But we will remain No. 1."

REBIRTHING BUD

Four years after he was shown the door, Gussie still showed up at the brewery with some regularity. His office suite on the third floor of the administration building remained intact, with its large gilt-framed oil portraits of Adolphus and August A. and the dark mahogany roll-top desk from which he and his father had run the company for more than seven decades. He usually announced his arrival as he stepped off the elevator, either by sounding the familiar racetrack trumpet fanfare "The Call to the Post" on a battery-powered horn he carried, or by braying at an equal volume, "Awwwwwguuuust!" Which never failed to make people jump or set August's teeth on edge.

Their relationship was outwardly polite, and August went out of his way to praise his father's contribution to the company in public statements. But privately, each held deep resentments. Gussie did not attend August's wedding to Virginia Wiley in 1974 and, in August's opinion, was not a very attentive grandfather to their two children—Steven August, born in 1975, and Virginia

Marie, born in 1979. When a longtime A-B executive suggested to August, "Perhaps it's time you and your dad patch things up," August turned to him and said angrily, "That man to this day does not know the names of my children. He looks at them and he doesn't know who they are." On another occasion, when August sent word to Grant's Farm that the company would not approve some changes his father was planning to make at the Bauernhof, Gussie flew into a rage. "Who the fuck are you to tell us what we can do out here?" he hollered in a phone call to August. "If I ever see you again I will shoot you."

Fortunately for August, Gussie spent most of his time tending to his duties as chairman of the Cardinals. Unfortunately for baseball, he spent most of that time fighting with people—Marvin Miller and the players association, his fellow National League owners, the National League's president and its chief labor negotiator (both of whom he wanted fired), baseball commissioner Bowie Kuhn (him, too), and his own players.

The Cardinals were a shadow of the team they used to be. Only Lou Brock remained from the glory days of the 1960s. Gussie had been forced to remove his longtime friend and duck-hunting pal Red Schoendienst as manager. The fans still grumbled about his trading of Steve Carlton, who had gone on to become the undisputed best pitcher in baseball, winning four Cy Young awards. With Carlton in the lineup, the fans and local sportswriters agreed, the Redbirds could have won four division titles in the 1970s. Instead, the team was tied for last place with the New York Mets midway through the 1978 season, putting on its worst performance in fifty years.

Once again, Gussie blew his stack, but this time he didn't march into the dressing room with a retinue of reporters. In a published letter that sounded as if it had been dictated to his secretary, Margaret Snyder, rather than written by a PR man, he lit into the entire Cardinals organization, "down to the bat boys."

"I am getting damn mad," he said. "There is no way, and I repeat, no way, I am going to tolerate this type of performance for the most loyal fans in the world, and I mean this. . . . I want this message carried loud and clear: The Big Eagle, the Boss, Gussie—whatever they want to call me—IS NOT HAPPY! I am tired of excuses. Management does not pay salaries to supposedly quality players for constant mental errors. . . . I personally have not seen too many head-first slides, the opposition's second baseman being kicked into left field on double plays and people banging into walls to make plays. . . . My patience is getting thin. . . . I did not recommend the purchase of the Cardinals to the Anheuser-Busch board so that, 25 years later, the Cardinals would have the worst record in their history. I trust that I have made myself clear and for everyone's sake I am praying for the situation to improve." (It did, but only slightly; the Cardinals finished second-to-last, ahead of the Mets.)

It was a sign of the changing times that St. Louis sportswriters did not unanimously praise Gussie for his tirade. *Globe-Democrat* columnist Rich Koster called it a "cheap shot," and offered up a little sports relativism for the man who believed that second place wasn't worth shit. "[The Cardinals'] value is not that they win or lose; it's that they are here to enjoy," he wrote. "And while their owner is No. 1 in beer, his position in the community is perhaps misused by making failure out of mere defeat."

During Gussie's appearances at the office, he apparently didn't hear the heresy that was being bandied about, namely that Budweiser—the brand his grandfather had introduced to the world 103 years before, the cornerstone of the Anheuser-Busch empire, the lifeblood of the Busch heirs, and the guiding principle of his life—was finished. Budweiser sales were flat, and the future belonged to new brands like Natural Light and Michelob Light. The younger generation had no affinity for the beer of their fathers and grandfathers. The old warhorse was on its last legs.

At least, that's what Denny Long was being told by some of his young sales and marketing managers. Conventional wisdom in the beer business held that once a brand started to die, there was no reviving it. The younger executives believed that Bud was destined to go the way of Pabst Blue Ribbon and Schlitz, and the company should put its money and marketing effort into building new brands.

Long didn't buy it. It was true that both of A-B's new light beers had performed only moderately well, selling about 2.5 million barrels each in their first year on the market, and that Budweiser sales appeared to be stalled at 22 million barrels a year. But Bud was still the No. 1 selling beer in the world, and he suspected the lack of growth was the fault of the marketing, or the lack thereof, not the beer. The way he saw it, there were only a few brand names that had become part of the American fabric—Coca-Cola, Hershey, Levi's, Campbell Soup—and he believed that Budweiser could be one, too. So when one of his executives asked, "What are we going to do with Budweiser?" he responded, "We are going to breathe new life into it."

His idea was to saturate the public consciousness with print ads and TV commercials aimed at the blue-collar consumer. In addition to sporting events, "Every bus stop is going to say 'Budweiser,'" he told the marketing team. "You are not going to drink it there; it's not a place where you are going to spend your money. But Budweiser will be in your head, and you will have it with you all the time, to the point where asking for a 'Bud' becomes a habit."

The assignment went to D'Arcy, MacManus, Masius, the St. Louis–based ad agency that had handled the Budweiser account since 1915. D'Arcy and Anheuser-Busch had literally grown up together, bonded by business and blood. D'Arcy's CEO, James B. (for Busch) Orthwein, was August's first cousin and a longtime member of the A-B board. James's father, Percy Orthwein, had married Gussie's sister Clara, and served as D'Arcy's CEO and an A-B director before him. Over the years, D'Arcy had parlayed its Busch family connection and its high profile work for A-B into a national reputation as one of the most creative agencies in the world of advertising. D'Arcy was responsible for the enormously successful "When You Say Bud (You've Said It All)" campaign in 1970. More recently, "Jimmy" Orthwein had played a pivotal role in helping convince other board members to side with August in ousting Gussie.

Long wanted a new Budweiser campaign that would be "a salute to the American worker." He knew it would be criticized as jumping on the bandwagon again, because Miller was mining the blue-collar vein. But he thought Miller had the right idea, just the wrong beer. As he often said at the employee meetings, "We are not flashy. We are seldom the darlings of the industry. We just continue to meet and overcome challenges." D'Arcy was told that the new campaign—like its "When You Say Bud" campaign—needed to be "comprehensive," meaning it had to serve as the sole advertising message for Budweiser over a period of several years, not just for a few TV commercials.

August didn't get involved with ad campaigns until the agencies and the marketing department made their first storyboard presentations to him and Denny Long. He responded powerfully to this one, which proposed to show everyday folks working on the job and then rewarding themselves with a cold Bud at the end of the day. Thematically, it was derivative of the "Miller Time" campaign ("If you've got the time, we've got the beer"). But August fixed on one particular tagline from a list of a dozen or so suggestions— "For All You Do, This Bud's for You." He thought it was perfect: catchy, simple, and sustainable.

From then on, he practically dictated the elements he wanted to see in the ads and commercials, most importantly real people, not actors. Hence, the first commercial was shot with real factory workers on the job in a Houston meat-packing plant. Subsequent shoots featured real construction workers, truckdrivers, butchers, bartenders, and farmers. Per August, only twelve-ounce longneck bottles were shown, no cans. Even though cans were the real working man's preference, he thought the classic glass bottle looked better and was more in keeping with tradition, since his great-grandfather had established Budweiser as "the king of bottled beer." He also believed that bottles provided the consumer with a superior taste and tactile experience. To help insure blue-collar authenticity in the ads and commercials, he began inviting an ad hoc group of plant employees to D'Arcy's presentations, encouraging them to comment on what the agency was putting forward.

August's micromanagement at times rankled the D'Arcy creative team, but the collaboration ultimately resulted in one of the most effective and memorable ad campaigns of all time. "This Bud's for You" ran for more than a decade and, over the course of dozens of commercials, embedded itself in the American consciousness alongside the likes of Campbell Soup's "Mmm Mmm Good."

More importantly, the campaign paid off immediately as Budweiser sales roared back to life, increasing by more than 10 million barrels in the eighteen months following the airing of the first commercial.

D'Arcy also handled the Natural Light account, and the agency's campaign went at Miller head-on with a series of print ads and TV commercials "designed to drive them up the wall" in Milwaukee, according to Mike Roarty. A typical print ad showed a can of Natural Light with the caption, "Brewed with water, rice, hops, barley and yeast." Next to it was a can of Miller Lite with the caption, "Brewed with water, corn syrup (dextrose), modified hops extract, propylene glycol alginate, amyloglucosidase and potassium metabisulfite."

For the TV commercials, D'Arcy and Roarty's marketing team hit upon the idea of using Miller's own advertising against it by casting some of Miller's ex-jocks in spoofs of their famous "Tastes Great, Less Filling" spots. In addition to Mickey Mantle, they signed up former Miami Dolphin linebacker Nick Buoniconti, former heavyweight boxing champ Joe Frazier, former Yankees pitcher Catfish Hunter, and former NBA star Walt Frazier for a series of thirty-second spots that featured malaprop-prone comic Norm Crosby interviewing the "five athletic supporters" about why they had switched from Lite to Natural Light (they each signed a sworn affidavit that they picked it over Miller Lite in a blind taste test).

Roarty debuted the campaign during the broadcast of NCAA basketball finals, commercial high ground previously held by Miller but now captured at considerable cost by A-B, which also had acquired sponsorship rights for the 1984 Los Angeles Olympics and twenty of twenty-six major league baseball teams.

A spokesman for Philip Morris carped that the "Switch" ads were typical of A-B's copycat creativity: "What do you expect? The 'This Bud's For You' campaign was stolen from our 'Miller Time' spots. It violates every rule of marketing."

Roarty could barely contain his delight at the turnabout. "Sports figures are America's heroes, and [Miller] was wise enough to use ex-athletes," he told a reporter, smiling impishly. "But how long can you let them get away with that? You couldn't let them give the impression that they owned the franchise, could you now?"

In October 1980, August made good on his 1962 promise to Denny Long that they would rise to the top together, promoting his former assistant to president of the company. Two months later, A-B's two top dogs stood with Gussie as a group of plant employees and executives gathered in the racking room to witness the ritual bunging of the fifty millionth barrel of beer produced that year.

"This is the big one," Long said of the gold-plated barrel specially made for the occasion. "In the 128-year history of Anheuser-Busch there has never been a greater moment than this," said August, who had made sure his father was present for the ceremony. The old man smiled proudly as August used a gold mallet to pound the rubber plug into the commemorative barrel of Budweiser. It took him three tries, and he got a face full of foam in the process, but he wiped it off with a handkerchief and quipped, "Best thing in the world to take a bath in." Looking frail, Gussie didn't address the gathering, but he joined in enthusiastically when the crowd broke into in a ragged version of the old German drinking song "Ein Prosit" (A toast).

There was plenty to drink to. A-B's record 50 million barrels increased its lead over Miller to nearly 13 million barrels and brought its market share to 27.8 percent. Miller's operating profit dropped 20 percent, and after five years of gobbling up market share, the company posted a mere .03 percent gain, to 20.7. The fast-moving freight train had slowed to a crawl.

August already was looking past the war with Miller. He'd recently completed his long-desired corporate reorganization, which included making Anheuser-Busch, Inc., a wholly owned subsidiary of a Delaware-based holding company called Anheuser-Busch Companies, Inc. The new structure would "more clearly communicate the increasingly diversified nature of Anheuser-Busch business," he said. His plan had always been to diversify the company in much the same way his grandfather August A. had done during Prohibition, expanding further into related areas where A-B had developed expertise—theme parks, resorts, leisure-time activities, real estate, nonalcoholic beverages, snack foods, and baked products. The experience of competing with the much larger and more diversified Philip Morris made it all too clear that being the biggest brewer was not enough to guarantee the company's continued success and independence. With Denny Long and Mike Roarty in place, he felt it was now time to focus his full attention on a "diversification initiative," through which he hoped to lead the company to heights his ancestors never imagined.

Never one to be outdone, eighty-two-year-old Gussie announced an initiative of his own. On March 15, 1981, he revealed to forty guests at a private dinner party in St. Petersburg, Florida, that he had secretly married again. The fourth Mrs. Busch was Margaret Snyder, a sixty-four-year-old widow who was the first woman ever named to the A-B board of directors and who had been his secretary for sixteen years.

"TELL ME I'M A HORSE'S ASS"

In the early summer of 1981, Andy Steinhubl, A-B's vice president of brewing and chief brew master, was sitting in a meeting with the wholesalers' panel, a representative group of the company's distributors that conferred with home office executives several times a year. The panel was August's creation, and it was a good thing, but at times the meetings grew tedious. This was one of those times.

Steinhubl could tell that August was bored, too, because he'd left his seat and was pacing around in the back of room, his mind on something other than the presentation. Suddenly, August was standing next to him, leaning down and whispering. "I want you to make me up a recipe for something we will call Budweiser Light," he said, and immediately went back to pacing.

After more than five years of watching Miller dominate the light beer market, August finally was ready to commit the Budweiser name—with all of its prestige and tradition—to the fight. When the meeting ended, Steinhubl walked over to where August was sitting and placed a handwritten note on the desk in front of him.

"What's that?" August asked.

"It's your recipe."

"Already?"

"Yeah; it doesn't take long."

"When can I taste it?"

"I can have it for you by the first of September."

Steinhubl knew he was in for a rough few months. He may have written the recipe, but ultimately August was going to decide the taste of Budweiser Light. And until August tasted what he liked, he would make Steinhubl's life difficult.

Much of the company lived in constant fear of August's taste buds. He functioned as A-B's unofficial taster-in-chief, relentlessly sampling the output of all nine plants. "And if he tasted something he didn't like, then everyone down the line was definitely going to hear about it," said one longtime senior executive.

Each brewery had a tasting room where a panel of five to seven men from the brewing and malting operations sat at tables every afternoon and, along with the brew master and his staff, sampled and took notes on their plant's product, as well as that of other plants. Among other things, they tasted for the specific attributes of each brand, checking for any variations among the breweries. It was no easy task ensuring that 100 million barrels a year tasted consistent and uniform to the consumer.

Of course, a good taster could discern deviations that the average beer drinker would never notice. It was said that members of Andy Steinhubl's master tasting panel, which met in Room 220 of the Old Brew House, could sample a bottle of Budweiser and identify which plant it came from by the characteristics of the water that went into it.

August was considered one of the company's best tasters, if not the very best. He could tell whether a beer was five days old or fifteen. "There were very few who could taste like he could," said one former executive. "He was a genius at it," said Denny Long. "He set our standard."

He also enforced it. Plant managers outside St. Louis never knew when he might drop down out of the sky in one of the corporate jets, but whenever he did, they knew there would be a command performance in their tasting room that day. Gathering as many as twenty people, he would call for a particular batch from the cooler, say, Tuesday's Budweiser from the Newark brewery, and they would all take several sips and make notes. Then he'd ask what they had noticed. A wrong answer would be to have missed something he'd written down.

The tasting went on constantly wherever August went. At the end of a long day on the road meeting with wholesalers, he would press one or more associates into service in the hotel bar, announcing with almost childlike enthusiasm, "Let's taste some beer," and the sipping and quizzing would begin. If he happened to be in Denver, where there was no A-B plant, and he felt the need to taste that day's Budweiser from Houston, then samples would be flown to him.

"He truly enjoyed the process," said Mike Brooks, a former vice president of sales. "And by virtue of the fact that he did it with such commitment, it said to everyone in the company that quality was the most important dynamic of the business, because the chairman was on it like white on rice."

Serving as a roving one-man quality control department, August incessantly scanned bottles and cans for the "date codes" that identified not only where the beer had been brewed but also the date and the fifteen-minute interval during which it had come off the production line. Because the taste of beer deteriorates over time, A-B had a strict policy that any beer older than 105 days had to be pulled from distribution, removed from retail shelves, and destroyed. And woe betide the local wholesaler if August ever came upon an expired freshness date.

"Everyone knew that at any time they could get a phone call telling them that August had found a problem with their beer and they had to be available to discuss their involvement," said Brooks.

Andy Steinhubl remembers the call he got from August at home on a Saturday morning a few days before Christmas.

"I had some beer from St. Louis last night, and it was absolutely terrible," August said. "So I want you to come out here to the farm, and on the way I want you to stop at four different places and pick up a six-pack of Budweiser, and we will taste it together."

Steinhubl schlepped the beer thirty miles out to Waldmeister, but neither man could find anything wrong with it. "The beer I had the other night didn't taste like any of these," August said as Steinhubl began looking through the beer cooler under the bar. He pulled out a couple of bottles from the brewery in Columbus, Ohio. "Let me see that," August said, checking the date codes and finding, to his horror, that the beer was four months old. He turned to his wife in the kitchen and asked, "Ginny, where did this old beer come from?" Without even looking in his direction, she replied, "You know I never touch your beer, dear."

August knew then that he had allowed his own stock of beer to go beyond its expiration date. "You must think I'm a horse's ass," he said to Steinhubl.

"No, I don't."

"Yes, you do. I want you to tell me I'm a horse's ass."

"No, I am not going to do that."

"You can't leave here until you tell me I'm a horse's ass."

Realizing that August probably would not let him leave, and that this was his awkward way of apologizing for wasting three hours of his time on a weekend, Steinhubl gave in. "Okay, you're a horse's ass."

August smiled broadly and said, "Good."

Steinhubl and his brewing team set to work creating Budweiser

Light in a small pilot brewery behind the Brew House. They were shooting for a crisp, full-bodied beer with a "flavor impact" that built up quickly and then "finished clean," meaning it would leave no aftertaste in its wake. It would be brewed naturally and contain only five ingredients—water, rice, barley, hops and yeast. In other words, it would be pretty much like Budweiser, but with 60 fewer calories. And therein lay the difficulty.

To make a lower-calorie beer, it is necessary to reduce the amount of sugar produced in the mashing process, which in turn reduces the amount of alcohol produced in fermentation. Most beer drinkers are unaware of the direct correlation between calories and alcohol content. Steinhubl expected that naturally brewed Budweiser Light would have an alcohol content of 3 percent at best, compared to Miller Lite's 3.2 percent, which was achieved with the help of non-natural chemical additives. The disparity, though slight, could put Budweiser Light at a competitive disadvantage, since "less alcohol" was hardly a selling point to the college crowd.

Because alcohol enriches the combined flavors of hops and barley, less alcohol in the brewing process can result in less taste. Along with the entire A-B hierarchy, August thought Miller Lite tasted thin and watery, so Steinhubl's recipe for Budweiser Light increased the amount of hops in the mix to give it more flavor. Hops contribute a bitter taste that plays against the sweet taste of the barley malt. The relative bitterness, or "hoppiness," of beer is measured numerically by what are known as "international bitterness units." The higher the IBU number, the more bitter the brew. At the time, most European beers had an IBU between 20 and 45. Budweiser had an IBU of 15. For Budweiser Light, Steinhubl bumped the IBU to 17, which was potentially problematic because August didn't like bitter. In fact, he claimed that whenever he tasted Budweiser that contained a slightly elevated level of hops, he experienced a throbbing sensation in his forehead that he called "head feel."[*]

Veterans of tasting sessions with August had seen head feel. It registered on his face as he squinted his eyes, furrowed his brow, and began rubbing his forehead with his forefinger and thumb. But only one other person, Denny Long, ever felt the sensation. "Maybe it was because he trained me to taste," said Long, who described the feeling as "the onset of a sinus headache right above the eyebrows." Still, Long said he only experienced head feel once or twice. And most of August's fellow tasters thought head feel was a figment of his imagination. They'd roll their eyes and exchange looks whenever he brought it up, and joke behind his back: "Yeah, I've had head feel, boss. It's called a hangover."

After a month of tinkering with the Budweiser Light recipe, Steinhubl and his crew had the first sample brew ready for the tasting panel. The consensus in Room 220 was that it still needed a little tweaking, but they were close.

"Overall, pretty good," said August. "Nice body, smooth, with a good flavor impact that leaves nothing hanging in your mouth." Then came the note Steinhubl was expecting. "But it tastes a little bitter. What's the IBU?"

"Seventeen," Steinhubl admitted.

"How'd we get that?" August asked.

"We wanted to give it more flavor."

August didn't complain about head feel, and perhaps because no one else said the beer was too bitter, he didn't tell Steinhubl directly to reduce the hops. But in subsequent weeks, he pressured him in other ways. Mike Roarty let Steinhubl know that August was voicing misgivings about the IBUs. "He doesn't like a number

---

[*] August would eventually decide it wasn't hops that caused his head feel. Rather it was a certain grade of rice that included broken kernels.

that high," Roarty said. August sent samples to Professor Russell Ackoff's group at the Wharton School, and they conducted a taste test at a local tavern. Steinhubl only learned of the test when one of Ackoff's assistants came to St. Louis to present their findings in the conference room next to August's office. The studious-looking young man used a chalkboard to explain the methodology underlying the survey, which showed that a group of patrons at a bar in Philadelphia had found the beer to be "too bitter."

Irritated by what he saw as a put-up job, Steinhubl asked, "Did you taste the beer yourself?"

"No," the young man replied, adding, "I never drink beer."

"Did any of your research group taste it?" The young man shook his head.

Steinhubl turned to August in exasperation. "If we change it, then it will not taste the way you want it to. So please let us go ahead."

Once again, August gave no directive regarding the hops content. But several weeks later he called Steinhubl to Room 220, where he'd tasted the beer for the umpteenth time. "I just don't like it," he said. "We're not going to be able to sell it, and the board of directors is going to fire me. I'll be the first person to go."

Steinhubl didn't believe for a minute that the board would fire August, but he could tell that the boss was genuinely worried. After all, he was about to put tens of millions of dollars and the reputation of the company on the line. To him, Budweiser Light wasn't just another brand, more brightly colored packaging aimed at crowding competitors off the retail shelves. Budweiser was his great-grandfather's grandest achievement, his family's heritage. Nothing with the Budweiser name on it had ever failed, and he sure as hell didn't want it to happen on his watch.

Steinhubl was worn down from the months of pressure. "August, we are all good people trying to do our best, and we think this beer is right," he said. "But if you really disagree, just tell us what you want us to do, and then go away and leave us alone."

"I can't do that," August said heavily, as if history itself would not let him. Then, surprised at Steinhubl's uncharacteristic outburst, he asked, "Aren't you afraid I am going to fire you?" Steinhubl looked at him and said, "No, because Peter Stroh [the CEO of Detroit's Stroh Brewing]* told me they have a job for me anytime I want it."

Somewhere in that exchange, August apparently found the reassurance he was seeking. He believed in building a team of smart people, listening to what they had to say, and trusting their judgment. To a man, his team was telling him that Budweiser Light was good to go. Was he going to believe them, or some random bunch of barflies in Philadelphia?

The next thing Steinhubl knew, August was telling him, "I want to make this beer in Los Angeles, and I want to fly out there the day after New Year's to taste the first commercial packaging that comes off the line."

By the time Budweiser Light was ready for its debut, Denny Long and Mike Roarty had built a sales and marketing juggernaut geared toward servicing nearly a thousand hyperregional markets (roughly corresponding to wholesale distributorships) with made-to-order media plans. It was "the first comprehensive quantitative-qualitative marketing program in the industry," according to Long, who dubbed it Total Marketing in honor of the Dutch soccer team that came within a game of winning the World Cup in 1974 playing a style of game its legendary coach, Rinus Michels, called Total Football (Soccer) because it called for every member of the team, including the goalkeeper, to attack the opponent's goal. Long's Total Marketing recognized that beer drinkers in Dallas

---

* Stroh had just acquired the Schlitz brand.

were different not only from beer drinkers in Boston but also from beer drinkers in San Antonio, El Paso, and Houston. It subdivided Latino consumers into Puerto Ricans, Mexicans, and Cubans. It broke down geographical regions not just by states and cities but also by neighborhoods and even individual bars. And it designed a distinct plan for each, resulting in approximately ten thousand individual sales promotion programs nationwide.

Because beer drinkers everywhere seemed to have one thing in common, Denny Long created a sports division in the marketing department, and Mike Roarty put a young executive in charge of each major sport. Starting from scratch, the new division secured sponsorship rights with all the major league baseball teams, twenty-three of twenty-eight NFL teams, twenty-three of twenty-four NBA teams, and thirteen of fourteen NHL teams, in addition to three hundred college sponsorships. In most cases, A-B simply outbid Miller for the sponsorships (August had warned them to bring lots of money). The deal with the Washington Redskins was typical in that it guaranteed A-B signage placement at exit level in both end zones, so that the product was visible to TV viewers every time a touchdown, extra point, or field goal was scored. The product image then was reinforced when the network cut away for a commercial break that more often than not included an Anheuser-Busch commercial.

Budweiser Light hit the market in March 1982, backed by a multimillion-dollar ad campaign that was built around the slogan "Bring Out Your Best" and starred a young Clydesdale named Baron. The first TV commercial featured Baron, who had been born and raised at Grant's Farm, galloping in slow motion through the Pacific surf as a stentorian voice-over intoned, "Born of tradition . . . nurtured by pride . . . a light beer worthy of the Budweiser name." It was a powerful metaphor—the new brand imagined as a magnificent stallion, his muscles rippling in the sun, running as if to join his proud sire in some unseen paddock.

Subsequent commercials centered on season-appropriate sports—football, baseball, hockey, skiing—with a dissolve to Baron at the end, running slow-mo through season-appropriate scenery. The commercials were aired almost exclusively during sports programming.

The introduction of Budweiser Light marked the turning point in the Great Beer War. A-B and Miller would continue to skirmish for another decade, but there was no more talk of Miller taking over as No. 1. Unable to expand its market share beyond 22 percent, the Milwaukee brewer soon ceased to be a serious threat to A-B's dominance.

Anheuser-Busch closed out 1982 with sales of nearly $4 billion, a market share of 32 percent, and the highest unit profitability in the industry—$3.59 per barrel. The company's ten plants were running at 98 percent of capacity. Its stock was trading as high as $60 a share.

"The clear establishment of Anheuser-Busch as the undisputed ruler of the industry is a lesson in marketing," said *Business Week*. August didn't want to gloat, but he couldn't help himself, telling the magazine drolly, "We are working very hard to stay humble." At the same time, he boldly predicted that A-B would command a 40 percent market share by the end of the decade, a goal that competitor Peter Coors agreed was "attainable and reasonable." In fact, Coors said, "With all the money Anheuser-Busch has, there is almost nothing it can't do."

It sure seemed that way. In September 1982, after more than a decade out of the running, the St. Louis Cardinals won the National League pennant, and with a big assist from their eighty-three-year-old chairman. Gussie's contribution was hiring manager Whitey Herzog in 1980 and backing him over the next two years as he overhauled the team. In February 1982, Herzog acquired fleet-footed future Hall of Fame shortstop Ozzie Smith and made him the linchpin in what became known as Whiteyball, a crowd-pleasing style of play that relied more on speed than power. The Cardinals hit only sixty-seven home runs during the '82 season, the least in the major leagues, but they stole two hundred bases. Gussie and Whitey became genuine friends, bonded by a mutual admiration and a shared rough-edged sense of humor. It is said that when Gussie, in a fit of gratitude for the pennant win, offered Herzog a lifetime contract, the manager quipped, "Your life or mine?"

Gussie threw out the ceremonial first ball at the '82 World Series. A photograph of the moment captured "the Big Eagle," as St. Louisans will always remember him. No longer barrel-chested and vigorous, he looked shrunken and frail, almost swallowed up by his trademark Redbirds outfit of red ten-gallon Stetson and matching red western shirt, string tie, blazer, and cowboy boots. Yet his exuberance remained undimmed, as did his delight in being the center of attention. This was the elfin figure that never failed to bring the crowd to its feet as he waved from the red beer wagon drawn by eight Clydesdales around the perimeter of the field before a game, though he no longer drove the hitch himself, and the crowd could not see the brace that held him in place like El Cid.

Looking on in the photograph, August III beams with unmistakable pride and affection. He had publicly threatened to sell the team the year before, but now he stood applauding with the rest of the crowd, the headstrong young stallion bowing in homage to his ancient sire.

The Cardinals won their ninth world championship in the final game before a sold-out crowd at Busch Stadium. As in 1968, the city of St. Louis lost its mind in celebration. Happy days had come again.

The '82 contest is remembered as "the Suds Series" because the team the Cardinals defeated was—fittingly, it seems—the Milwaukee Brewers.

WARNING SIGN

Shortly after 1:00 a.m. on November 13, 1983, Michele Frederick made the mistake of her life: she got into a car driven by August Busch IV.

Michele was twenty-two and worked as a cocktail waitress at Dirtbag's, a raucous student hangout within stumbling distance of Fraternity Row on the University of Arizona campus in Tucson. She was a townie. A 1980 graduate of Sahaurita High School, she'd grown up in modest circumstances, living with her mother, younger brother, and stepfather in a series of rented homes in the semirural high-desert communities of Sahaurita and Rio Rico, which straddle Interstate 19 between Tucson and Nogales.

Whatever Michele lacked in socioeconomic status, she made up for with personality, energy, and good looks. "She was the most sought after girl at our high school," said a former neighbor in Rio Rico. "She could have any guy she wanted." She usually "dated up," preferring older guys with nice cars or tricked-out pickup trucks. Brown-eyed, blond, and athletic, "she could have been a model," said a schoolmate. "She was simply gorgeous, the most beautiful girl you ever saw. That's why Busch was interested."

Nineteen-year-old August IV was a regular at Dirtbag's. In his second year at U of A, ostensibly majoring in engineering, he still qualified as a freshman based on the courses he'd completed, indicating a casual attitude toward academics reminiscent of his father. He was a more serious participant in the local bar scene, where the Busch name had an even stronger cachet than during August III's time at the school, thanks to A-B's expanding promotional presence on campuses, particularly at party schools like U of A. On weekends, when Dirtbag's was so crowded that its 250-person occupancy limit required arriving patrons to stand in line out front until someone left, August IV was never made to wait; the doormen waved him in, along with anyone who was with him.

He wore his entitlement on his sleeve, casually revealing his family connection in the act of ordering rounds of Budweiser and Bud Light. He wasn't obnoxious about it. Picking up bar tabs was part of his heritage, after all. It was expected of him—promoting the family business. Good-looking and affable, he was basically a shy kid who'd learned growing up that being a Busch heir broke a lot of ice and drew people to him without much effort on his part. His car, a sleek black 1984 Corvette capable of hitting 145 miles an hour, added to the gravitational pull. Easily the flashiest set of wheels on the U of A campus, it helped attract hangers-on wherever he went. The general consensus among them was that for a spoiled rich kid, he wasn't an insufferable asshole.

On Saturday, November 12, August IV spent part of the afternoon drinking at Dirtbag's, and later that night turned up at another popular nightclub called Voila off Tanque Verde Road near Wilmot. Michele Frederick and her roommate, Deborah Harrold, arrived at the club sometime after he did. Michele knew August from Dirtbag's, of course, and it appears that they really hit it off at Voila. At closing time, they were part of a group that gathered in the parking lot to discuss moving the party to someone's apartment. Michele's younger brother Aaron was there, too, with a date. Separated by only a year, Michele and Aaron ran in the same social circle and sometimes even double-dated. "They were very close," said a friend. When the party destination was decided, Michele got into August IV's Corvette and told Deborah Harrold to follow them in her car. According to witnesses, August IV had downed as many as seven vodka Collins cocktails, while Michele had drunk two White Russians. Harrold tried to follow the Corvette, but August roared off at a high rate of speed, passing several cars in the process, and she was unable to keep up. Michele disappeared into the night.

Around 8:30 that Sunday morning, the Pima County Sheriff's Department received a call reporting a "collision with unknown injuries" on East River Road, a twisting, uneven thoroughfare that snaked along the Rillito River across north Tucson. Deputy Ron Benson, who was in charge of a unit that investigated all car accidents resulting in critical injuries and fatalities, arrived at the accident scene and found a black Corvette on its side about fifty feet off the pavement. Twenty feet behind the car lay the body of a young woman. She was cold to the touch, indicating that she had been dead for some hours. Benson noted several empty Bud Light cans lying near the car. He found a half-smoked joint in the woman's pocket and an expired driver's license identifying her as Michele C. Frederick.

Benson was familiar with the location, a particularly treacherous stretch of River Road west of Claycroft where the pavement dipped into a ravine and then rose sharply right in the middle of a tight S bend that the local kids called Dead Man's Curve. Despite the yellow warning sign and the posted 25 mph speed limit, the asphalt was periodically streaked with skid marks left behind by unmindful drivers.

In this instance, the lack of fresh skid marks told Deputy Benson that the driver of the Corvette had not even tried to slow down entering the curve, and it appeared that the vehicle had become airborne and then flipped when it came back down on the pavement, rolling over at least once. The woman had been thrown out through the detachable targa hardtop, which was lying by the road, and probably was crushed when the car rolled over her. She likely died almost on impact.

A man's sports coat was found in the car, with a sewn-in tag that said it had been "designed for August A. Busch IV." There was also a .44 Magnum revolver and a wallet containing two Missouri driver's licenses in Busch's name, one indicating that he was nineteen and the other saying he was twenty-three. A membership card to a local gun club listed a Tucson address for Busch. Benson sent two deputies to the address, which turned out to be a town house about four miles from the accident in the foothills of Catalina Heights, the most affluent section of the city.

The deputies could hear music playing inside as they knocked on the door. There was no response. After several more knocks, they tried the door and found it open. Inside, they called out and heard a voice answer from the bedroom, where they found August IV lying on his back in bed. He was naked and covered from head to midsection in dried blood. There was blood on the pillow, bloody clothes on the floor, a semi-automatic AR-16 rifle at the foot of the bed, and a loaded sawed-off shotgun on the kitchen table.

August IV told them he wasn't sure what had happened to him. He said he remembered driving his car, becoming tired, getting out of the car, and falling asleep by the road about 2:00 a.m. He wondered if he'd been hit by a car. The detectives wondered whether his glassy eyes and dazed demeanor were due to an apparent head injury or the consumption of alcohol or drugs. Did he understand that they were law enforcement officers, and he was potentially in a lot of trouble?

After conferring with Benson, the deputies read August IV his Miranda rights and had him taken by ambulance to Tucson General Hospital, where blood and urine samples were taken. All the while, August IV continued to answer questions. Yes, he was related to the Busch beer family, the eldest son of the chairman. No, he didn't think he'd had too much to drink the night before. He'd had a few drinks, yes, but he had a high tolerance for alcohol because, in accordance with family tradition, he'd begun drinking beer at an early age. At the same time, he suggested that perhaps he wasn't behind the wheel at the time of the accident, because sometimes when he had too much to drink he would let a friend drive his car. As for Michele Frederick, he didn't even remember being with her.

After an examination in the emergency room, August IV was admitted to the hospital for treatment of a possible skull fracture. The injury made his claim of amnesia more plausible, but Benson couldn't shake the suspicion that he was acting, that maybe his apparent lack of emotion over the fate of his passenger was due to the fact that he was just too cold to care. Benson was also unsettled by all of the weaponry in Busch's possession. Even in gun-loving Arizona, a sawed-off shotgun was not something you would expect to find in a college student's apartment.

From the outset, the investigators believed that it was highly possible, if not probable, that a felony had been committed in the death of Michele Frederick. If August IV was operating the vehicle in a reckless or negligent manner, under the influence of drugs or alcohol, or both, then he could be charged with involuntary man-slaughter and leaving the scene of an accident. The blood and urine samples taken at the hospital would tell the tale. Even though they were taken hours after the accident, any level of alcohol or drugs still present in his system could be used to scientifically estimate the level at the time of the accident.

The story hit the St. Louis newspapers the next morning. "Woman Killed, Busch Heir Hurt in Crash in Arizona," blared the headline in the *Post-Dispatch*. "Busch Heir May Be Charged in Fatal Car Crash," announced the *Globe-Democrat*. August III reacted to his son's predicament exactly the way his colleagues and competitors would have predicted—he promptly spent a lot of money assembling a formidable legal team to do battle with the Pima County prosecutor's office. Team Busch included one of the top law firms in Tucson, along with Norman London, the prominent St. Louis criminal defense attorney who had represented Peter Busch in the shooting death of David Leeker, and two local private investigation firms. One of the first things the lawyers did was get August IV out of town, telling the authorities that he needed to return home to St. Louis to be treated by his own doctors and spend Thanksgiving with his family. There wasn't much the prosecutor could do about it, since August IV had not been charged with any crime. The Busch attorneys promised to make him available in Tucson if the prosecutor needed further evidence from him.

As a matter of procedure, Ron Benson had to obtain search warrants from a judge in order to examine and test the two key pieces of evidence in the case, the smashed Corvette and the blood and urine taken from August IV at the hospital. The search warrant process took more than a week, and when Benson finally sent a deputy to the hospital to pick up the samples, he got a rude shock. "Bad news, boss," the deputy reported back. "They don't have it." The urine sample had been lost, and the blood sample had been run through a centrifuge and rendered useless for testing. No one on the hospital staff could explain how it happened.

Benson couldn't believe it. Never before had the hospital mishandled samples in one of his cases. It was a potentially devastating blow. Now the prosecution would not be able to prove scientifically that August IV was under the influence at the time of the accident.

They'd have to build a circumstantial case, relying on witnesses who could testify that he was impaired when he got behind the wheel.

Benson and his investigators conducted more than fifty interviews with August IV's friends and schoolmates, and with employees and patrons of Dirtbag's and Voila. One of August's closest friends on campus told them that August never let anyone else drive his car, contradicting the statement August gave to deputies at the hospital. Another student said in witness statement that August IV was a known "user of cocaine," which could have accounted for the cocaine residue the coroner found in Michele Frederick's nostrils. But no one said they had seen August using cocaine that night. Nor did anyone recall him behaving as if he'd had too much to drink.

It quickly became clear to Deputy Benson that August III's private investigators were bird-dogging his every move, sometimes arriving at the homes of witnesses just minutes after he had left. While investigators examined every inch of the Corvette, August III obtained an identical car and had it transported to Tucson, where a group of his hired experts blocked off River Road at the accident site and spent the better part of a day with cameras rolling as a driver ran the car through Dead Man's Curve at different speeds. The idea was to gather data that could rebut whatever the prosecution might present at a trial. "They told us what they were doing and invited us to watch," Benson recalled later. "But when we showed up at the time they told us, they were just finishing."

August IV's Corvette was equipped with a high-performance Z51 suspension that gave it the road-hugging capability of a Ferrari or Lamborghini, according to *Road & Track* magazine. Benson, who held a degree in automotive engineering, figured the car had to be going at least 55 miles per hour when it entered the S bend—more than twice the posted speed limit—for it to flip over the way it did. Investigators found hair and blood on the visor above the driver's seat. If they could match those to August IV, it would go a long way toward establishing that he was driving. Benson petitioned the Pima County Superior Court for an order requiring August IV to furnish blood, hair, and saliva samples, as well as fingerprints and palm prints. Despite their previous pledge to make August IV available, the Busch legal team fought the order all the way up to the Arizona Supreme Court, which in February confirmed the lower court ruling. The Busch attorneys then claimed their client's three-month-old head injury prevented him from traveling to Tucson. Pima County authorities accused them of "stonewalling," but agreed to send Ron Benson to St. Louis to gather the samples, provided that August III paid for all the costs.

Benson found himself in the first-class section on the flight to St. Louis. It was his first time. He was met at the airport by an ex-cop security officer from the brewery and was driven directly to St. John Mercy Hospital, where a conspicuous contingent of more than a dozen security men equipped with earphones and radio communications waved them through intersections and traffic barricades to a cordoned-off building with still more security men standing sentinel. With timing that could not have been accidental, August III arrived moments later, emerging from a limousine and striding into the building, where the waiting staff received him as if he were a visiting dignitary, which in a way he was—he sat on St. John's board of directors, and the Busch family and Anheuser-Busch were among the hospital's most generous benefactors.

"The bearing, the manner, the walk—it all conveyed a raging confidence," Benson recalled. "I think he was trying to show me that he was the man in charge."

On the plane, Benson had prepared himself mentally for just such an encounter. "I was determined to show that I was not there because he had *allowed* me to be there but rather because we had allowed *him* to do it this way. I wanted them to know that I was calling the shots. I would show tolerance, not deference. I was representing the victim. No one was going to speak for her but me."

"You will not be taking any statement from our client; we don't want you asking any questions," London said right off the bat. Benson bristled. "I'm going to ask whatever I need to ask," he replied, "and your client can answer or not, but I'm not taking orders from someone's defense attorney."

Despite the initial tension, the blood, hair, and saliva samples were taken without incident. Benson had not spoken to August IV before. He seemed nothing like his father—low-key, unassuming, and deferential to the hospital employees.

From the hospital, they drove in procession to the St. Louis County police headquarters for the fingerprinting. Once again, August III appeared to be in command, as uniformed cops and plainclothes detectives alike greeted him respectfully—"Good to see you, Mr. Busch." Benson didn't get the same reception: "The only person they stopped and asked for identification was me, a fellow officer looking into a possible manslaughter."

In the car on the way back to the airport, Benson wondered if the tiny Pima County prosecutor's office was overmatched. Evidence aside, did they even have the resources to go up against August Busch III in a trial? He suspected they didn't, and the thought left him feeling unsettled and vulnerable. It was a cold, gray day with remnants of snow on the ground as the Busch security man pulled the car into the dimly lit airport parking structure. "It was like a scene from a movie," Benson recalled. "And suddenly it struck me that I was all by myself, far from home and without backup. From what I had seen of their operation, it didn't seem all that far-fetched to think that they could easily do away with some lowly deputy sheriff from Arizona." The driver handed him his return ticket; it was coach.

Back in Tucson, Benson threw himself into the investigation with renewed zeal. For four consecutive weekends, he sat in his car near the crash site on River Road, writing down the license plate numbers of vehicles that passed by between 1:00 a.m. and 2:00 a.m. Then he traced the plates to the more than one hundred registered owners and called each one to see if they had driven by and seen anything the morning of November 12. He kept thinking about Mary Jo Kopechne, the young woman who was killed late one night in 1969 when Senator Ted Kennedy drove his car off a bridge on Chappaquiddick Island in Massachusetts and then left the scene without reporting the accident. Police found Kopechne's body in the senator's submerged vehicle the next morning. Kennedy received a two-month suspended jail sentence for leaving the scene after an inquiry found there was no evidence that he had been driving negligently.

Pima County faced a similar problem with August IV. Even though the blood and hair samples Benson collected in St. Louis turned out to match what was found on the visor above the driver's seat in the Corvette, it only proved that August IV was behind the wheel when the car rolled over, not that he was in any way impaired. There were no witnesses to testify that he was under the influence. No usable fingerprints were lifted from the empty Bud Light cans found by the car. All that could be proved beyond a reasonable doubt was that August IV was driving too fast to navigate a curve that local law enforcement had known for years was unduly dangerous.

The prosecutor's office concluded it was highly unlikely that a jury would return a felony conviction for negligent manslaughter. They felt they stood a better chance of a guilty verdict for leaving the scene, but at what cost to the county coffers? The Busch family was prepared to spend a fortune defending any charges, and it was only a misdemeanor.

So on July 3, 1984, Pima County authorities announced they were ending the investigation into the crash that took Michele Frederick's life and that no charges would be filed against August IV.

"I didn't feel good about it," Benson said recently. "My gut told me this guy was drunk and killed this girl, and I couldn't do my best for her because the evidence just disappeared. It didn't seem like we got justice done on this one, even though I'm confident that we did all we could."

In the course of the eight-month investigation, St. Louis press coverage was notable for what it did not contain. No details of Michele Frederick's life were reported beyond her age and occupation at the time of her death. To St. Louis readers, she was merely a "waitress" or a "passenger," and a faceless one at that. While the newspapers repeatedly published a yearbook photo of August IV looking choirboy innocent in a sports coat, white shirt, and tie, they never printed a picture of Michele, even though her high school yearbook photo was easily obtainable—a particularly surprising omission, given the media's long-standing love affair with stories involving pretty blonde victims. There were no published statements from grieving friends or family members either, not even a "no comment" indicating that a reporter had at least tried to get them on the record.

The family's low profile appeared to be due to a secret settlement agreement negotiated early on by Busch attorneys. A former neighbor noted that the family subsequently bought a Porsche and put in a pool, "in a neighborhood that previously had neither." Twenty-five years after the accident that claimed her daughter's life, Michele's mother, Greta Machado, declined to talk about it "because it is still so painful."

August IV didn't return to the University of Arizona, which was probably a wise decision, since the case had sparked bad feelings among his on- and off-campus peers, many of whom believed—incorrectly—that he had left Michele to die and that his family had bought off the authorities. As one high school friend of Michele's said recently, "I haven't had a Budweiser since."

The Busch family made no public statements about the Tucson case at the time, but years later August IV's mother, Susie Busch, offered a lofty perspective on the sad episode. "I was devastated, absolutely devastated for young August to have to go through something like that," she said during a conversation with a *Post-Dispatch* gossip columnist. Asked if she thought her son had been treated "justly," she reportedly replied, "No . . . because I feel there is no just treatment for families with a name and money."

"DO YOU KNOW WHO
I AM?"

After bailing his son out of trouble in Tucson, August III made sure the "Busch heir" had a soft landing back home in St. Louis.

He arranged for August IV to enroll at St. Louis University, where decades of Busch patronage guaranteed special privileges, including an electronic key that gave August IV access to the teachers' parking lot, which was a major perquisite on the parking-challenged urban campus. He replaced August IV's wrecked Corvette with a new Porsche and secured a town-house apartment for him on Lindell Boulevard, across the street from the place he'd rented when he split from August IV's mother.

If August IV had learned any life lessons from the Tucson tragedy, they weren't apparent as he jumped into the social scene in St. Louis's fashionably hip Central West End. His running mates usually included half a dozen other sons of prominent businessmen. The "millionaires' boys club," as some called them, might start the evening at Culpepper's Bar in Maryland Plaza, then move to Harry's Restaurant & Bar on Market Street and later caravan to Metropole downtown at Laclede's Landing. They all had fast cars, loads of money, and last names that rang a bell, but nothing could compete with the Busch aura, so August IV became the Big Dog and they functioned as his entourage, his protectors, even his advance men. Typically, one of them would be sent ahead to alert the proprietor of the next establishment: "August Busch IV is on his way here, and we will need a table for eight with iced buckets of Budweiser set up; he doesn't want to be bothered by the other customers, and he will not interact with you."

August IV thus let everyone know he was there and at the same time kept almost everyone away from him. If any strangers approached the table, one of his crew would block their way unless August gave the nod to let them pass. His boys ordered his drinks for him, paid the tab with his credit card, and fetched hot-looking girls he spotted in the crowd, either bringing them over to meet him or writing down their phone numbers for him.

From the bustling bar scene at Laclede's Landing, they would head across the Poplar Street Bridge to sample the after-hours pleasures of Sauget, Illinois.

Named for the French-descended family that had run it since the 1920s, Sauget (pronounced *So-zhjay*) was a kind of modern-day Deadwood, a four-square-mile industrial "village" that operated in the sweet spot between moral laxity and lawlessness. In Sauget, drugs were sold and consumed openly in numerous nightclubs and strip joints, and it was a lot easier to hire a hooker than buy a loaf of bread. In Sauget clubs, August IV and his friends would snort lines of coke right off the table, according to a compatriot who sometimes partied with them. "Those guys were out of control. They didn't do little lines of coke. They did foot-long lines. . . . I once saw August IV snort a line of coke as long as that table over there. I couldn't understand how a heart could take it."

On May 31, 1985, August IV was driving home from Sauget at 1:30 a.m. Barreling west on Highway 40 out of downtown at 75 to 80 miles per hour, he blew past the giant Anheuser-Busch "A & Eagle" animated neon sign at Chouteau Avenue and nearly sideswiped a car that was merging into the traffic lane from the Boyle Avenue entrance ramp. The car contained two undercover narcotics cops. "Motherfucker!" detective Nick Fredericksen yelled instinctively as his partner Bob Thomure swerved to avoid contact with the speeding silver Mercedes.

Fredericksen and Thomure were just coming off their shift after executing a search warrant with another undercover team, detectives Mike Wilhite and Junius Ranciville. It had been a long day, and the last thing they wanted was to chase after a speeder, which wasn't their job. But the Mercedes, with its dark tinted windows, looked an awful lot like a car that belonged to one Vernon Whitlock Jr., a former cop, federal marshal, and bail bondsman turned high-end drug dealer. The narcotics division had been trying to make a case against Whitlock for months.* Now, it seemed as if Providence had placed probable cause directly in their path. Armed with legal justification for stopping Whitlock and looking into his car, the two tired narcotics cops took off in pursuit.

Just east of the Kingshighway Boulevard exit, August IV slowed down, eased over onto the shoulder, and stopped. Thomure pulled the beat-up 1976 Buick Special sedan—a "covert vehicle," in police parlance—behind the Mercedes. Unshaven and dressed scruffily in jeans and T-shirts, the two detectives walked toward the Mercedes, but as Thomure approached the driver's window, August suddenly gunned the engine and roared up the exit ramp. Thomure had to

---

* Undercover narcotics officers arrested Whitlock at a St. Louis Steak & Shake later that year. He was convicted of drug trafficking and sentenced to twenty-four years in prison. Released after only three, he became a barber. He is the father of Kimora Lee Simmons, the ex-wife of hip-hop mogul Russell Simmons.

jump back from the car to avoid being hit. The detectives took up the chase again, but the Buick's six-cylinder engine was no match for the Mercedes, and they quickly lost sight of the vehicle. After a few more minutes of cruising the area, they gave up and headed for home, but not before broadcasting a description of the car and its last known location. Nine minutes later, a voice came over the radio. "Hey, he's here; we got him." It was Wilhite and Ranciville, who'd heard the radio transmission on their way home and turned back to help out. They'd happened upon the Mercedes at almost the exact spot where Fredericksen and Thomure had lost it. After another short chase, August IV pulled over again. Then, just as before, he took off when Wilhite approached the window. Again, the Mercedes narrowly missed hitting the detective.

Within a few minutes, a third narcotics team was converging on the area as Ranciville and Wilhite chased the Mercedes through the Central West End at speeds of up to 85 miles an hour. Thinking they were pursuing a known drug dealer who must have something very incriminating in his car, Ranciville pulled close enough to the Mercedes for Wilhite to lean out the right-side window and fire a bullet into the tread of the Mercedes' left rear tire. By the time the tire deflated, bringing the car to a stop, all three narcotics teams were on the scene, surrounding the car, blocking any possible avenue of escape. Detective Ron Kleier was the first to reach the Mercedes. Gun drawn, he flung open the door and ordered the driver out. When August IV emerged, they all knew right away that something was wrong. Instead of the flashy forty-something drug dealer they were expecting, the "suspect" was a nicely dressed, clean-cut college kid. "Why are you doing this to me?" August asked as they were cuffing him. "Do you know who I am?"

They found out quickly enough when they looked in his wallet. A check of the glove compartment revealed that the Mercedes was registered to August Busch III. The six detectives exchanged looks as it dawned on them they had just stepped in a steaming pile of trouble.

The chase, complete with the shot fired, had been broadcast over the police radio, where it no doubt had been picked up on scanners used by the news media. It was on tape. So that bell could not be unrung. August IV would have to be taken to police headquarters and booked for something. A report would have to be filed. All hell was going to break loose, a perfect shit storm of politics and publicity, with them caught in the middle.

As they transported August IV to the station, Fredericksen and Thomure were kicking themselves for not running the Mercedes' license plates prior to pulling the car over the first time. Had they known whom it belonged to, they might have backed off and gone home to bed, thereby giving August IV a break that the average Joe would likely never have gotten. In the car, they explained to a somewhat teary and shaken August IV what the process would be at the police station. "Just don't treat me like some little rich kid," he said from the backseat.

Word of the incident preceded them to headquarters, where the narcotics teams were greeted on arrival with sympathetic looks from their fellow officers, one of whom summed up the group sentiment by saying, "Boy, you guys are *done.*" The uncomfortable truth was that a sizable percentage of the department earned extra income from Anheuser-Busch and the Busch family, which together comprised the city's second largest employer of police officers, behind the department itself. Off-duty cops provided security for Busch family members and corporate officers, Busch homes and company facilities. Mike Wilhite was among the many who worked security details at Cardinals games. The Anheuser-Busch in-house security staff was rife with retired officers, as were numerous private investigation firms that derived significant income from myriad A-B and Busch family litigation.

If all that weren't enough to complicate matters, the narcotics cops who walked August IV into police headquarters that morning were acutely aware that the chief of detectives, their boss, had a son who worked at Anheuser-Busch in the advertising department. As *Post-Dispatch* columnist Bill McClellan drolly noted at the time, "Arresting a member of the Busch family is not the best way to get ahead in the St. Louis Police Department."

Indeed, the arrest of August IV prompted a huddle of nervous high-ranking officers, several of whom, the chief of detectives included, were awakened and called into headquarters that morning. They, too, were caught in the middle—between the media, which would be all over the story and looking for any signs of favoritism, and the power and temperament of August III, who could be expected to ruthlessly protect his errant son from any level of prosecution. They decided to proceed cautiously in releasing information about the arrest until the police report was fully vetted up the department chain of command.

Up in the fourth-floor office of the narcotics division, the arresting detectives went about the business of booking the suspect, writing up the arrest report, and processing evidence gathered at the scene. The latter included a .38-caliber revolver found on the floorboard of the car behind the driver's seat. There was one bullet in the chamber and five lying loose on the floor in the front, suggesting that August IV may have tried to unload the weapon during the chase. The detectives also brought in the tire that Mike Wilhite shot out. The media would report that they had "changed" the tire as a kind of mea culpa when they realized who August IV was, but in fact they were instructed by their sergeant to secure it as evidence because it contained the bullet that Wilhite fired.

August IV was not administered any form of sobriety test, a break that probably would not have been given to an August Smith under the same circumstances. He was allowed to make his one phone call, presumably to his father, and afterward sat dejectedly in the squad room. In an attempt to lighten the mood, detective Ron Kleier began teasing him. "Hey, kid, don't worry. When this is over you can go out to Grant's Farm, have a few beers and ride that little train. . . . I always loved that train." August replied that he had not been to Grant's Farm since he was twelve years old (about the time his father ousted Gussie) and added, morosely, "If you get me out of this, I'll fucking give you that train."

August IV was fingerprinted and booked on three misdemeanor counts of third-degree assault (with the car), one felony count of carrying a concealed weapon, and six traffic violations (running three stop signs and one traffic light, and speeding). Released on $8,000 bail within two hours, he was picked up at the station by A-B's head of security, Gary Prindiville, a former St. Louis cop. They were barely out of the building before the Busch family released a statement through Fleishman-Hillard: "Due to the unusual circumstances of the arrest, which involved undercover officers who were apparently impersonating criminal types driving an unmarked car, we are assessing the matter."

The headline in the *St. Louis Globe-Democrat* that morning must have seemed like déjà vu to August III: "Busch Heir Is Arrested after High Speed Chase." He reacted swiftly and decisively. While the police department was angering reporters by refusing to release the arrest report, which was supposed to be a public document, Fleishman-Hillard issued a statement depicting August IV as a victim of reckless cops:

"Mr. Busch was approached late at night by two persons who gave no indication of being police officers while his car was on the shoulder of the highway waiting for a friend traveling in a separate vehicle. The unkempt and unsavory appearance of these undercover narcotics officers, plus their life-threatening behavior, made it no more than prudent for a young man in Mr. Busch's position to escape."

The officers did not show badges, according to the statement, nor did they use flashing lights or sirens during the pursuit, thereby creating "a situation in which a terror-stricken young man had every reason to fear for his life and took evasive action against what he believed to be criminal elements."

The statement was clearly the handiwork of Norm London, who was fast becoming August III's on-call criminal defense attorney. The allegations immediately put the authorities on the defensive with reporters.

"I don't care how they were dressed or what kind of car they were driving," said one police department spokesman, "if he didn't think they were police officers then he should have driven to the police station and reported them."

"When somebody's got something the size of an automobile and you have to jump out of the way to avoid getting hit, that's considered assault," said the deputy commander of the narcotics division.

"No one is naive enough to believe there aren't undercover police officers around," said St. Louis circuit attorney George Peach.

Peach, whose office would prosecute the case, pointed out that even though there was a mobile phone in the Mercedes, August IV did not call the police to report that scary-looking men were chasing him. The prosecutor said he intended to subpoena the phone records to see if August had called anyone else during the chase. He defended the officers, calling Fredericksen and Thomure "two of the best," but he tore into the department brass for conferring the morning of the arrest and not providing his office with a copy of the official six-page arrest report until three days later. "If [August IV] was some normal everyday dope, we would have had that report by 2 a.m. . . . if the police do their job and they arrest Mr. Big, then why does the lieutenant colonel have to be called at home and told about it? I can't think of anything that justifies it."

The arrest report said the detectives showed their badges, sounded their sirens, and flashed their red lights during the pursuit. "We believe what the policemen have said happened," Peach said. "These are honorable men. The probable cause was the high rate of speed at which he was operating his car. If [the Busches] disagree, that's what we have courtrooms for."

For all his tough talk, Peach ended up pulling his punches. He dropped the felony weapons charge, saying it "did not meet the legal requirement" because the gun was not "on his person or within reach." He chose not to subpoena the mobile phone records after learning that August III sat on the board of the phone company, AT&T, feeling it wasn't worth the fight it would take to get them. And he assigned his least experienced attorney to the case—"a misdemeanor attorney who had never tried a misdemeanor case," according to Nick Fredericksen.

The detectives would have preferred that Peach drop the case altogether, but they knew he couldn't. Coming on the heels of Peter Busch getting probation in the shooting of David Leeker and August IV walking away scot-free in the death of Michele Frederick, it would be perceived by the public as whitewash, evidence that the Busch family routinely bought off the authorities. So the prosecution was going to trial because it was politically impossible not to. And the detectives were resigned to the fact that they were going to have to get up on the witness stand and take one in the teeth for the team.

Norm London, who'd begun his career as an attorney for the St. Louis Police Department, was considered the best criminal defense trial lawyer in town. No one was better versed in police procedures. And since the prosecution's case was based almost entirely on the arrest report—what the detectives said happened that morning—his defense narrative cast them as rogue cops who terrorized a young man into thinking he was about to be kidnapped or killed. He asked jurors to put themselves in August IV's shoes, to imagine if their son or daughter were caught in the same circumstances while driving home one night.

Most of the three-day trial was taken up with the testimony of the detectives, as London tried to trip them up, catch them in inconsistencies between what they said in the arrest report and what was on the recording of the chase.

"You claimed you were assaulted," he said to Fredericksen, "and yet you did not broadcast that?"

"I did not broadcast that because I didn't want the other officers taking an action more extreme than the situation warranted," Fredericksen responded.

Detective Mike Wilhite testified that near the end of the chase, his partner, Junius Ranciville, pulled their car up alongside the Mercedes, and he leaned out the right side window, displaying his badge and shouting at the driver, "Police officer." He said that August responded by swerving toward them, forcing them to swerve as well to avoid a collision. When London asked why he had not broadcast that information on the radio, Wilhite replied, "I was worried about our own safety. I was worried about the location where we were, and trying to stop the car."

Throughout the trial, August III sat in the back row of the courtroom with his wife, Ginny, and August IV's mother, Susie. His demeanor rarely varied from extremely pissed off. He glared at the prosecutor. He glared at the reporters who were scribbling down what was said. Most of all, he glared at the prosecution witnesses, his face at times reddening, the veins in his face and neck bulging. Nick Fredericksen would not have been surprised to see smoke coming out of his ears. During breaks in the proceedings, August III could be seen huddled with his legal team and his son in the corridor, talking and gesticulating animatedly as if giving orders: the man in charge. When reporters asked him for a comment, he responded with a baleful look. About the only time he smiled during the trial was when Norm London asked a defense witness, a waitress at a local restaurant, what August IV's favorite drink was, and she replied, "Bud Light."

As one of his key witnesses, London put Jim Sprick on the stand. Sprick identified himself as a friend of August IV's and testified that they were driving in separate cars to Jimmy's Cabaret at 4915 Delmar when he saw the Mercedes pulled over on Highway 40, but noticed no red lights flashing and heard no sirens.

Sprick had known August IV since high school and was the most devoted member of his bar-hopping entourage, the one usually sent ahead to prepare for August's arrival at the next stop. People who knew Sprick believed there was nothing he wouldn't do for August IV. The narcotics detectives recognized him as the individual who had approached them on Delmar Avenue as they were taking August IV into custody that morning and asked why they were arresting his friend. They wondered why—if he'd driven by the brief stop on Highway 40, as he testified—he hadn't pulled over and approached them at that point. And where was he during the subsequent fifteen-minute pursuit? How could he have followed them at the speed they were traveling? Did August call him? Without the phone records they would never know.

The detectives would have liked the prosecutor to press Sprick a lot harder than he did, and to raise the question of why August had pulled over in the first place. Something made him stop. If it wasn't their lights and sirens, then what was it? And why in the world would three teams of plainclothes police officers choose to chase down a suspect in a speeding car without establishing their authority by using their lights, sirens, or badges? Did that make any logical sense at all?

August IV did not take the stand in his own defense. In closing arguments, the young prosecutor called him "a man who plays by his own rules" and urged the jury to "send a signal that this type of reckless behavior will not be tolerated." In his summation, Norm London told jurors, "What you have seen in this courtroom is lies, perjury, and a police cover-up."

It took the jury less than two hours to return a verdict of not guilty. One juror told reporters that he was impressed by London's comment about putting themselves in August IV's shoes. "You have to walk in someone else's shoes," he said, "and sometimes those shoes are a little tight." Several said they were swayed to vote for acquittal by the fact that sirens could not be heard on the police recording of the pursuit.

Immediately after the verdict was read, August IV shook hands with the jurors and thanked them. "I am very, very happy," he told reporters. "Justice has been done." His father, too, thanked the jury, but had no comment for reporters. Several days later, however, he hand-delivered a statement to police headquarters demanding an investigation of the narcotics detectives:

"St. Louis Police Department officials should carefully review policies and management control over the undercover narcotics squad who disgrace the vast majority of good law abiding professional officers in the St. Louis Police Department by their unprofessional conduct and gross misstatement of facts, as documented in testimony in my son's trial."

Noting that he could afford good lawyers for his son, he said he was troubled by "the question of how persons of moderate to low income could defend themselves against a police unit that takes great liberties with citizens' rights and that obviously by their own testimony have taken liberty with the truth—which is what our whole system of justice is built upon. Therefore, I call upon the department to fully investigate the incident not only because it involved the safety of my son but because it brought to light action and attitudes that undermine the credibility of all police officers, and most important because such actions pose a threat to every resident of this community."

A police spokesman responded that neither the department nor the circuit attorney's office had any problem with the detectives' conduct the night of the arrest or their testimony at the trial. "We examined both the shooting and the pursuit and didn't find any violations of department rules or any other improprieties," said the commander of internal affairs, adding, "If he, Busch, wants to come forward and make [an official] complaint, we will be happy to entertain it."

If nothing else, the episode proved there was a limit to August III's power. Despite his wealth and connections, he was not able to get the charges dropped and prevent an embarrassing public trial. Perhaps that's what angered him the most as he listened to police officers testifying against his son. After all his family and company had paid to St. Louis police personnel for private security over the years, he didn't get his way when it really mattered.

To their surprise, the six narcotics officers never suffered any repercussions. There were no unwanted transfers, missed promotions, or derailed careers. Several years after the trial, in fact, Nick Fredericksen was given departmental approval for "secondary duty" working security at an Anheuser-Busch stockholders' dinner. The extra-pay, off-duty service apparently caused him to get a Christmas card that year from Anheuser-Busch, embossed with a picture of the Clydesdales and personally signed by August III.

Four months after the trial, August IV pleaded guilty to driving his Porsche at 65 miles an hour in a 35 mph zone, and was put on a year's probation. He'd gotten the ticket while he was awaiting trial, but his attorneys had managed to put off his traffic court appearance five times, until after the trial verdict was in. For all his vehicular transgressions, August IV never lost his driver's license.

Along with the Tucson crash, the high-speed chase would

become a public relations burden August IV would carry for the rest of his life, an obligatory paragraph in any newspaper or magazine profile of him. But he at least got the last laugh on city attorney George Peach, the only man who ever put him through a trial. In 1993, after earning a reputation for being particularly zealous in prosecuting pornography and prostitution cases, Peach was convicted of using city funds to pay for the services of prostitutes. August IV, then being heralded as a rising star and heir apparent at Anheuser-Busch, sent him a life-size blow-up sex doll.

16

"I PROBABLY FEEL WORSE
ABOUT THIS THAN YOU DO"

America's seemingly unquenchable thirst for beer finally began to slacken in the 1980s. Per capita consumption hit a historic high of 23.8 gallons in 1981, then sales went flat.

Experts blamed an aging population—baby boomers approaching forty—and rising public concern over alcohol abuse. Whatever the cause, the drop in demand left some formerly robust brewers—most notably Pabst—awash in red ink, and others—including Miller—saddled with excess production capacity.

August III had foreseen the development, which he termed a "growth gap." Beginning in the late 1970s, he moved to fill the gap. Leaving the day-to-day business of the brewing division to his two gregarious Irishmen, Denny Long and Mike Roarty, August turned his attention to expanding operations into related businesses to offset an expected slowing in beer sales. In 1981 A-B launched Eagle Snacks, distributing its own line of salty, thirst-inducing munchies—peanuts, pretzels, and potato chips—to bars, taverns, and convenience stores, placing itself in competition with junk food giant Frito-Lay and Planter's Peanuts.

A year later, in 1982, August acquired the second largest baking company in the United States, Dallas-based Campbell Taggart, Inc., which specialized in refrigerated-dough and frozen food products. The expansion wasn't as big a stretch as it seemed, considering that A-B was the country's No. 1 producer of baker's yeast and No. 2 producer of corn syrup. As with Eagle Snacks, the plan was to distribute Campbell Taggart products through A-B's existing beer wholesaler network, having the distributors warehouse and deliver the baked goods right alongside the beer. On paper, it made synergistic sense—the trucks were already delivering to every grocery store in the country.

A-B paid a whopping $570 million for Campbell Taggart, which represented a 20 percent premium over its market value. But August believed the acquisition would establish A-B as a major player in the food industry, a serious competitor to the big packaged goods firms he so admired—Procter & Gamble, Philip Morris, Nabisco, and General Mills. Among the new baked products A-B put on the beer trucks was a line of bread branded "Grant's Farm."

After bread, August took the company into wine, buying a California winery called Master Cellars that marketed bulk wine— also called "keg wine" or "wine on tap"—to bars and restaurants. Again, the plan was to ride piggyback on A-B's distributor network. August had wanted to move the company into the wine business back in the early 1970s; he even sent a group from his corporate planning department to Europe for six weeks to find a winemaker partner. When they presented the board with a detailed marketing plan, however, Gussie said no, and that was that. This time, August made Master Cellars Winery the cornerstone of a new division within the company that reported directly to him, and the

Anheuser-Busch Beverage Group soon introduced Baybry's Champagne Coolers and Dewey Stevens Premium Wine Coolers to compete with the popular Bartles and Jaymes wine coolers that were being marketed by the Gallo Winery.

From there, it was a short logical leap into the fastest-growing segment of the beverage industry—bottled water. In September 1984 Anheuser-Busch paid $900,000 for Saratoga Springs Mineral Water, a tiny, troubled 114-year-old company in Saratoga Springs, New York, with distribution on the East Coast from Washington, D.C., up through New England. A-B invested another $1.5 million in new equipment and renovations at the plant, making it capable of producing two million cases a year, and began marketing "Saratoga Naturally Sparkling Mineral Water." In April 1985, August approved the purchase of Sante Mineral Water in Santa Rosa, California, and the A-B beverage group introduced two brands of flavored water, aSante (Italian for "to health") and Zeltzer Seltzer. A-B also bought a controlling interest in Ireland's Ballygowan Spring Water Company (named for its source, an underground spring in County Limerick in southwestern Ireland). The plan was to distribute the Ballygowan brand of "pure Irish spring water" in the United States.

August III's timing could not have been better. Bottled water was exploding in popularity—sales more than tripled in the United States between 1980 and 1987, from $443 million to $1.5 billion—and A-B faced only one major competitor in the nation, Perrier, which controlled about 75 percent of the market. Despite Perrier's dominance, A-B management and beverage industry experts believed that the fearsome marketing and distributing machine that had vanquished Miller Brewing would have little trouble defeating the French. As one ad executive working on the Miller account told the *Los Angeles Times*, in grudging admiration, "Anheuser-Busch could drive the distribution of horse piss if they wanted to."

But things didn't work out the way August III had planned. A-B's new beverage group fizzled, producing nothing but losses between 1984 and 1987. According to Denny Long, the problem wasn't the products: "Wine and bottled water appeared to fit us like a glove, but we tried to load too many industries into the existing beer distribution system, and it was too many different items for the distributors to handle."

The bread didn't rise in the food products division either, as both Eagle Snacks and Campbell Taggart fell far short of expectations. As one investment banker sniped at the time, "Being superior planners and producers in the beer industry does not make [Anheuser-Busch] superior bakers."

"Actually, given our years in the production of baker's yeast, we were pretty damned good bakers," countered Long. "I think the biggest problem with Campbell Taggart was the age and condition of their plants and equipment." The overriding problem was that August III's great "diversification initiative" loaded too much onto the backs of A-B's distributors, many of whom who were either unwilling or unable to carry the weight.

Long was not responsible for the food products or beverage operations, but he felt the pressure nonetheless because beer supported it all. Every year, he had to sell tens of million of dollars' worth of beer just to offset the cost of the diversification. He was having trouble sleeping.

August didn't make it any easier for Long when he decided to expand the company's profitable theme park and resort operations to include a cruise ship company. A-B purchased a majority interest in the Seattle-based Exploration Cruise Lines, which operated a fleet of five smaller-size (five- to six-hundred-passenger) ships that specialized in "one-of-a-kind" travel adventures to out-of-the-way destinations in Panama, Tahiti, Alaska, and the Pacific Northwest. Some members of the board and the policy committee had misgivings about the venture. They fretted that cruise ships were expensive, profit margins were low, and the capital cost of growing the business was enormous, with each new ship costing anywhere from $50 million to $80 million to build. Their concerns were validated; Exploration Cruise Lines proceeded to lose $40 million over the next two years.

Fortunately, at the time Anheuser-Busch could absorb such losses. Americans may have been drinking less beer than in recent years, but more of what they were drinking was Budweiser and Bud Light. In 1985 they guzzled 46.5 million barrels of Budweiser alone, an increase of nearly 2 million barrels over 1984, and 25 percent of all beer sold in America. Bud Light sold 5.4 million barrels in 1985, an increase of 1.2 million. A-B's total output of 64 million barrels gave it a market share of 36 percent. The following year, the numbers increased to 72.3 million barrels and a 38 percent market share. It appeared that the company would hit a 40 percent market share by 1987, three years sooner than August had predicted. Now there was talk of reaching the milestone of 100 million barrels and 50 percent market share by the mid-1990s. "Is it arithmetically possible?" August responded to a reporter's question. "Yes."

Miller remained a distant No. 2. Its signature High Life brand had been beaten into submission by the booming sales of Budweiser, but its Lite brand accounted for 50 percent of all light beer sales, 18.5 million barrels in 1985, making it the second-best-selling beer in the country, behind Budweiser. Still, Bud Light was cutting into Miller's lead in the low-calorie category at a rate of more than a million barrels a year.

From the beginning, Bud Light had sold well among twenty-five- to forty-four-year-old professionals, the traditional drinkers of light beer. But in early 1987 A-B made a bold play for an even younger segment of the beer drinking population—twenty-one- to twenty-four-year-olds. When speaking for public consumption, industry executives referred to this group euphemistically as "contemporary adults." Among themselves, however, they described them more accurately as "heavy users." These were not the folks who stopped by the corner tavern at the end of a hard day's work to reward themselves for all they'd done. They were more the hard-partying college kids who liked to get hammered before a football game and drink themselves into a stupor on the beach during spring break. For them, Mike Roarty introduced a new ad campaign during the fourth quarter of Super Bowl XXI. It starred an English bull terrier named Spuds MacKenzie, riding a skateboard and wearing a Hawaiian shirt, sunglasses, and a God-given shit-eating grin while an adoring trio of beautiful girls in bikinis jiggled and sang his praises as "the original party animal."

The ad campaign was an instant sensation. Taken by the tongue-in-cheek idea of a "spokes-dog" for a beer company, the media jumped on the story like, well, a dog on a bone. Reporters, columnists, TV producers, and talk show bookers inundated A-B with so many calls about the studly Spuds (in real life a female named Honey Tree Evil Eye, or Evie for short) that Fleishman-Hillard assigned the pooch his own PR rep, who played along with the conceit by referring to his client as "Mr. MacKenzie" while scotching persistent rumors that Spuds had been killed either in a limo accident or a "hot tub mishap in California." One writer for the trade magazine *Adweek* raised concern about the campaign's underlying message, noting that Spuds was presented all too cleverly as "the embodiment, the visual equivalent of, a pleasantly inebriated state," which would have violated FCC regulations if Spuds were a human.

Spuds quickly became a pop culture icon. The dog traveled to public appearances accompanied by his three "Spud-ettes." He did a spot on *Late Night with David Letterman* and one with Joan Rivers on Fox's *Late Show*. He landed a role in a movie with Martin

Mull and made *People* magazine's annual "Best Dressed" list. He inspired a line of Spuds MacKenzie merchandise that grew to more than two hundred items—wall posters, beachwear, sunglasses, satin jackets, stuffed dolls, plastic toys—enough that Macy's opened twenty-two Spuds MacKenzie boutiques in its New York department stores. Most important for Anheuser-Busch, Spuds sparked a dramatic increase in Bud Light sales, a jump of 21 percent—to 8 million barrels—in the first year of the campaign, pushing the brand to the No. 3 position, just behind Miller Lite and gaining.

Like many celebrities before him, however, Spuds eventually was undone by his success. Over the course of some twenty national TV commercials, the character developed a following among a group of consumers with a particular affinity for goofy-looking dogs in silly outfits—kids. And when Spuds paraphernalia began showing up in toy stores, howls of protest went up from Mothers Against Drunk Driving, the National Parent Teacher Association, and even the U.S. Bureau of Alcohol, Tobacco, and Firearms, all of which accused Anheuser-Busch of cynically marketing to minors. Senator Strom Thurmond held a stuffed Spuds doll as a prop while delivering a stem-winder on the Senate floor attacking beer advertising aimed at youngsters.

A-B spokesmen responded that they were shocked, *shocked*, that anyone would think the company would "spend money and manpower and energy to advertise to a group that legally cannot consume beer." (In truth, the industry was well aware that "heavy users" tended to settle on their brand preferences while they were in high school and college, before they reached the age of twenty-one.)

"The company does not apologize for the Spuds character," an A-B spokesman told *Adweek*, which promptly busted the company for an egregiously inappropriate instance of target marketing that took place on the White Mountain Apache reservation in eastern Arizona.

"At the Apaches' annual Labor Day rodeo and tribal fair, life-size versions of Bud Man and Spuds MacKenzie rode an antique Model-A delivery truck down the parade route," the trade magazine reported. "As the familiar spokes-characters passed by, eager children rushed to the truck to gather handfuls of Budweiser can-shaped candies that showered down." Noting that the Native American community was predisposed to high rates of alcoholism, *Adweek* called the promotion by A-B's local distributor a case of "brand-building among minors, targeting vulnerable consumers and ignoring the issue of alcohol abuse."

Faced with increasing controversy and bad publicity, A-B finally agreed to put Spuds down figuratively, but not before the character had taken a crippling bite out of Miller Lite's market share. In the annals of A-B advertising, Spuds MacKenzie still ranks as the company's most effective spokes-mammal.

During the first rush of Spuds-mania in the spring of 1987, Denny Long had every reason to be proud of his thirty-five years with the company. In his rise from office boy to president, he had played a key role in transforming Anheuser-Busch from a $700 million brewery that was "run like a grocery store," in the words of former corporate planning VP Robert Weinberg, into a $7 billion conglomerate the *Los Angeles Times* described as "archetypical of the corporate giants Coca-Cola and Pepsico in soft drinks and Philip Morris and R. J. Reynolds in cigarettes." During Long's eight years in charge of the brewing division, sales had doubled and profits had quadrupled.

Every step of the way, Long had been with August; they'd grown up in the company together. August had gone out of his way to credit him with winning the great beer war, publicly presenting him with a bronzed sculpture of a soccer shoe delivering a crushing soccer-style kick to a Miller High Life can. August and Long weren't actually friends; Long knew that. Even though they'd talked practically every day and spent thousands of hours together on company planes, August always maintained a boss-employee distance. August didn't seem to make friends; he didn't have time. He'd only had two or three that Long knew of, and the closest of them, John Krey, the scion of a St. Louis meatpacking family and, thanks to August, the owner of an A-B distributorship in St. Charles, Missouri, had died of cancer recently. In the last few months of Krey's life, August had ordered one of the company planes retrofitted with a hospital bed and flown Krey and his wife to Europe. Long suspected that now, after Ginny and the kids, he was one of August's closest relationships. He was confident that whatever happened, August had his back.

Which is why he didn't see it coming.

A few months earlier, in December 1986, the A-B legal department had been contacted by a lawyer acting as the court-appointed trustee in the bankruptcy of a St. Louis–based advertising and promotions firm that had done a lot of work for the brewery. The lawyer said he had come across documents indicating that the firm's principals, one of them a convicted embezzler, may have engaged in a kickback scheme with several A-B executives. It appeared that the executives—Michael Orloff, the vice president of wholesale operations, and Joseph Martino, the vice president of sales—might have traded A-B business for cash and gifts. Since the bankruptcy was part of a court proceeding, the documents would become public at some point, and barring the discovery of some convincing mitigating evidence, the court would turn the matter over to the appropriate law enforcement agency for investigation.

August III was immediately briefed, and an internal investigation was quietly launched. Long was told about the investigation, but August decided to keep it out of his purview because Orloff and Martino worked for him; Martino was considered Long's protégé. The decision to exclude him didn't sit well with Long. He thought it created the appearance that August didn't trust him.

The next few weeks were difficult; as auditors brought in by the board of directors began going through thousands of invoices from outside suppliers, Long was not kept posted. Every now and then August would drop a little bombshell on him, telling him, for instance, that a no-name New York rock band managed by an old friend of Joe Martino's had been paid more than $200,000 by the company but had performed no services. Long was shocked that Martino could have been involved in something so sleazy. It didn't sound like the guy he knew. Martino had grown up working-class poor in the Bronx and went on to earn an MBA from the Wharton School of Business. At age thirty-four, he was a rising star in the company, regarded among his peers as a street-smart straight arrow. Which is why August's suspicions about Martino and drugs didn't ring true either.

Ever since his son's trouble in Tucson, August had been on a tear about drugs, especially cocaine, which he blamed for all manner of society's ills. Now he was convinced that Martino and maybe a few others were involved in cocaine, possibly to the point of distributing it throughout the company. "Did you know that 65 percent of the employees in the Bevo [bottling] plant are on drugs?" he said to Long one day. "How do you know that?" Long replied.

August responded vaguely that the investigators had said that to A-B's chief of security, Gary Prindiville.

Like August, Long was an old-school beer guy who knew next to nothing about drugs, but he was fairly certain you couldn't come up with a number like that unless you conducted extensive testing among the plant employees, which he knew had not been done. He thought the 65 percent was a wild exaggeration, and the idea that Martino was behind the distribution was completely out of line. Of course, it didn't matter what he thought. What mattered was that August believed it. The conversation left him unsettled, wondering if perhaps August's opening question—"Did you know that . . ."—wasn't entirely rhetorical, and what he really meant was, "How could you have let this happen?"

On February 28, August ordered Long to inform Martino about the existence of the internal investigation. Long and Martino were both in Chicago for a wholesaler presentation, so Long took the young vice president for a ride in the company-provided town car and, as August had instructed, gave him the bare bones of what he knew, mentioning the alleged band scam and the drug suspicions. Martino, apoplectic, said none of it was true.

Back in the office the following week, an A-B security detail searched the closet outside Martino's office where he kept promotional items—golf balls, T-shirts, and ball caps emblazoned with the Budweiser name or the company logo—that were routinely handed out by the marketing executives. Every marketing executive had such a closet, and the higher-ranking the exec, the better the goodies. Mike Roarty's closet was like Ali Baba's cave, crammed with treasure ranging from golf bags to high-end electronic equipment that he'd received as gifts from wholesalers and suppliers and in turn gave away to VIPs and favored employees in the great circle of corporate swag. Lavish gift giving and receiving was part of the A-B corporate culture dating back to the beginning, when Adolphus Busch established the practice of giving away sterling silver pocket knives engraved with the company logo. His son, August A., handed out guns, and his son, Gussie, awarded yacht cruises with booze and broads. Making friends was their business, after all. In more recent years, sales executives motivated sales reps and cemented business relationships with Rolex watches, which were purchased in quantity through the company. One newly appointed vice president once found boxes of Rolexes stashed in the back of a cabinet in his new office, apparently long forgotten by a previous occupant.

The "raid" on Martino's closet yielded nothing incriminating, but it blew the cover off the internal investigation and set people whispering in the hallways. Word quickly got around that security men were asking about drugs and Martino's possible involvement. One person who worked for Martino at the time said recently, "Joe wouldn't have known what cocaine was if it had walked up and bit him on the ass."

The subject of drugs was not brought up when A-B lawyers questioned Martino and Orloff later in the week. Both men vehemently denied receiving any improper gifts or payments, but on March 9, they were fired for "wrongful conduct." News of their dismissal played at the top of the local TV newscasts and on page one of the newspapers, but thanks to some skillful media management by Fleishman-Hillard reps—always quoted as "a spokesman for the company"—it appeared to be a one-day story, the gist of which was that several bad apples had been discovered in A-B middle management and tossed out. There was no mention of drugs.

A week went by with no new reports, and Denny Long was hoping the crisis had passed and he could get back to running the beer company without all the distraction. Then, on March 16—the day before St. Patrick's Day, he would always remember—August called him from the plane on the way home from Europe, agitated. "This Martino thing is heating up again," he said, rattling off a litany of developments—the internal investigation was expanding, the auditors were cooperating with the U.S. attorney's office, there was talk of presenting a case against the two former executives to a federal grand jury.

"Do you want me to resign?" Long asked, reflexively. "I'm willing to do that if it will take some of the pressure off you." He didn't really mean it, of course. He was trying to be a good soldier, demonstrating loyalty to his commander. He was relieved when August barked, "No, goddammit, I'm not asking you to resign." Another executive who was on the plane told Long later that night that

August had "erupted" over something—he didn't know what—and he quoted August as saying, ominously, "The shit is about to hit the fan."

The next day, August walked into Long's office and said flatly, "I need to talk to you." Long followed him into the adjoining conference room, where August took a seat an uncomfortable distance away from him. The space spoke volumes, as did the file folder, legal pad, and pen that August placed on the table: Long felt the ground moving under his feet. He was expecting questions about Martino, but instead August immediately pressed him about his two sons-in-law who worked for the company, one in branch sales and the other in marketing statistics. "How did that come about?" August wanted to know.

Nonplussed, Long replied that he had helped them obtain interviews for the clerk-level positions, which were posted, and he had vouched for their character when asked, but he insisted they had been hired on their own merit, not because of any directive from him.

"So you brought a bricklayer into the company?" August sneered, referring to the job one of the young men had held while working his way through college.

"Yes," Long replied, "a bricklayer with a master's degree. And what's wrong with bricklayers, anyway?"

His impertinence infuriated August, who instantly reverted to his worst self, slamming his hand on the table, spitting out questions, and glaring at Long as he answered. Long had seen it many times before, so he knew not to argue back but rather to keep his cool and respond calmly until the storm passed.

Reading from documents in the file folder, August asked about Long's brother, who was the local broker for Waterford crystal, another gift favorite among A-B executives, who sent out hundreds of A & Eagle–engraved items at Christmas. August said he'd "heard" that Long steered all the company business to his brother and may have even profited from it. Not true, said Long. He didn't direct the gift giving among the staff; the corporate promotions department handled that. He couldn't help it that his brother was the only Waterford broker in the area, and the arrangement had been reviewed and approved by the conflict-of-interest committee of the board of directors.

August said he'd also "been told" that Long's uncle had flown with him aboard a company plane on a company-paid trip to Ireland. True, said Long, explaining that his uncle was an A-B wholesaler in Joliet, Illinois, who, along with several other wholesalers, had won the trip as a prize in a company-sponsored sales contest. He added that August and the board had approved making his brother a wholesaler.

As August scowled and scribbled notes in his legal pad, Long asked, incredulous, "Am I being accused of nepotism?" The idea was absurd, considering that nepotism was almost a founding principle of the company. Busch cousins sat on the board and owned distributorships. August's half brother Peter was now working at the brewery, as were August's oldest daughter, Susie, and August IV, whose recent automotive adventures had not prevented him from landing a job as assistant to the brew master. Everyone knew that one of Long's daughters and his twenty-one-year-old son worked for the company, as did his cousin in Chicago. Nepotism had never been considered a breach of ethics at Anheuser-Busch; it was an honored tradition.

August railed on for more than half an hour, hurling accusations seemingly based on office gossip that ranged from exaggerated to fanciful. At one point, he asked if Long or any member of his family owned a storefront shop on Arsenal Street that sold A-B paraphernalia that had been pilfered from the warehouse. All Long could do was shake his head sadly and say, "No."

August's rage gradually subsided to the point where he sought to explain why he was subjecting Long to such an inquisition. "Because if you've done something wrong and we don't know about it or didn't ask you about it, then it puts me and the board in a bad position," he said. Again, Long offered to resign, but this time he felt more like he meant it. Again, August waved off the idea, but this time Long suspected he didn't mean it. The session ended with August tearing the pages of notes from the legal pad, folding them neatly, and slipping them into the inside pocket of his suit jacket. "I'm going to keep these in the safe," he said as he got up to go.

If August was trying to intimidate him, he succeeded. Long was traumatized and bewildered. Why were they investigating him? What did they think he had done? It was as if someone were shooting at him in the dark, and he couldn't see where the shots were coming from. This was not the August he knew, the one who always had his back. This was someone who was out to get him. But why?

August came back to Long's office later that day, closed the door quietly, and said in a soft voice, "I'm afraid the board of directors will now accept your resignation. I probably feel worse about this than you do." Long doubted that, but he said nothing as August walked to the window and stood staring down at the parking lot. Long was reminded of the day years before when August had done the same thing after his father asked for his resignation. After a full minute, August turned away from the window and, without looking at Long, left the room.

August came back later with a press release Fleishman-Hillard intended to put out, announcing his resignation. It quoted Long as saying, "As president of Anheuser-Busch Inc., I take full responsibility for the actions of its officers and employees and have chosen to resign in the best interest of the company." It was boilerplate bullshit. Long didn't think his resignation was in the best interest of the company. He was leaving only because August gave him no other viable choice. August had made it clear to him that if he stayed on, he would be held personally accountable for any future wrongdoing by any A-B employee. "You mean if some guy in the bottling plant kills somebody with his car while he is on drugs, then that would be on me?" Long had asked. "That's right," August replied. Long interpreted that to mean he could resign now or be fired later. He okayed the wording of the press release.

The next day, they flew to Tampa on separate corporate jets, August on his Dassault Falcon 50 and Long on the smaller Lear that was always at his disposal as president. Long could have begged off attending the meeting, but he didn't want it to seem as if he were slinking off with his tail between his legs. He wanted to tender his resignation directly to the board while looking them in the eyes. Given the circumstances, he didn't intend to deliver the sales performance report as he always did. He figured August would handle it. But five minutes before the meeting was to begin, August came to him and said, "You know I don't know how to do these things. Will you please do it?"

So he did, one last time. Fortunately, the numbers were all good: gross sales up 9.6 percent; net income up 18.6 percent; barrels up 7.7 percent; market share at 40.6 percent. When he finished, the board gave him a standing ovation, and every director came over to shake his hand. On the flight back to St. Louis, he felt nothing but numb.

The announcement of Long's resignation hit the city like a midwestern thunderclap. He was a well-known figure, enormously popular among A-B employees, and something of a folk hero in the Irish-American community, where he was celebrated as the scrappy South Side kid who'd sung tenor in the choir at St. Columbkille's and rose to head the brewery that loomed over their lives. Local soccer moms and dads knew him as the former parish grade-school coach who'd spearheaded the drive to raise nearly $1.5 million to develop the thirty-four-acre St. Louis Soccer Park for the Youth Soccer Association, and then persuaded his brewery to buy the park and turn it into the finest soccer facility in the nation. You couldn't get much more St. Louis than Dennis Patrick Long. That he would abruptly resign from Anheuser-Busch in connection with an alleged kickback investigation was unthinkable. "Scandal Cracks Anheuser-Busch," declared one headline in the *Post-Dispatch*. "Long's Quitting Is Sign of Split in His Friendship with Busch," said another, which was followed by "Further Upheaval Feared at Busch."

Coverage of the story quickly spread to the *New York Times*, the *Wall Street Journal*, and even the *Irish Times* in Dublin. Reporters swarmed Long's house, standing at the iron gate across his driveway and calling out, "Can you give us a comment, Mr. Long? Tell your side of the story."

Long didn't want to talk to anyone. He was in a deep funk, demoralized and dealing with lawyers in trying to work out some sort of severance package that would protect his family. He was fifty-one, with two kids in college and a wife with an incurable, debilitating illness. He was scared. A-B was offering him a contract as an "outside consultant" for five years at $375,000 a year, a good amount of money even if it was less than half his compensation as president. As part of the deal, he was told he could continue to oversee A-B's operations in Ireland, and the company would provide him with an office near his home and a secretary.

Long was torn. August had plucked him from working-class poverty and taken him on an amazing ride that carried him to places he might not have seen otherwise. He would always be grateful for that, and he didn't want to do anything that would hurt the company. August was now saying nice things about him to the media, calling him "my closest business associate and friend for the past 25 years . . . one of the finest business executives I know."

At the same time, August had made him the scapegoat in the scandal, issuing a statement saying, "The individuals involved were under Mr. Long's direct supervision and he has assumed full responsibility for their actions." It was a subtle twisting of the wording in the press release. And it wasn't true. He had not assumed responsibility for whatever Martino and Orloff had done, and to say they were under his direct supervision was an exaggeration that made it sound as if the scheme had been hatched right under his nose. Neither man reported directly to him. They were among dozens of executives who were technically under his supervision. He couldn't possibly have known what they all were doing in the field. The president of the corporation did not pore over billing statements from suppliers to make sure the company got the individual services it paid for.

Long believed that August had taken advantage of his loyalty, as evidenced by the fact that, shortly after he officially tendered his resignation at August's insistence, A-B lawyers coolly informed him that by resigning he had forfeited his options on 100,000 shares of stock, which would have been worth millions.

Long's family urged him to fight back, tell his story to the newspapers, sue if necessary, do something, anything, to counter the impression August was creating that he had done something wrong.

"To what end?" he responded. "They are not going to give me my job back. They are not going to pay me any more money. You don't know these people the way I do. I've seen the Busches when they get mad. I know what they are capable of. August knows no boundaries."

He'd seen August fire one executive because he stammered when he got nervous, another because he hated the way the man pronounced French words with a French accent, and still another because he showed up at a meeting with a beard after August had told him to shave it off. For that matter, he'd seen August fire his own father, who was perhaps the most powerful man in the city at the time. "What chance do you think a Long would have in a fight with a Busch?" he said to his son. "Why would I put our family through that?"

In a meeting with shareholders, August called the kickback allegations "a distasteful chapter in our company's proud history" and sought to reassure them that the worst was over and the company itself was not the subject of an FBI, U.S. attorney, or grand jury investigation. "Our pride has been hurt," he said. "Our performance has not been hurt. Your company behaved in an honorable and exemplary fashion in resolving this matter, in keeping with its reputation as one of the most admired companies in America."

Amid widespread speculation about who would be named to succeed Long, August issued a statement saying, "I have assumed Mr. Long's responsibilities as president of Anheuser-Busch Inc. and will remain in that position for at least two years."

To Long, that finally explained everything—the nepotism investigation, the table-slamming interrogation, the assignment of blame, and the insistence on their version of his resignation for the questionable conduct of a couple VPs. August's diversification initiative had proved an utter failure, costing the company hundreds of millions of dollars. The way Long saw it, August wanted to be back on the beer side of the company, and now the internal investigation into the kickback scheme provided him with the perfect pretext for riding in on a white horse to save the day. All he had to do was sacrifice his closest associate, who was, in the end, just an employee, not blood. He was his father's son, after all.

In the months that followed, Martino and Orloff were indicted on twelve counts of mail fraud and one count of filing a false tax return. Martino was also indicted for fraud in the alleged rock band scam, but the government eventually dismissed that indictment. Drugs never came up.

At the trial, Martino mounted a spirited defense that portrayed him and Orloff as having been singled out for doing what was common practice at the company. He admitted that an executive of the outside advertising firm had provided him with clothes, club memberships, airline tickets, and gifts for his parents, but he insisted they were gestures of friendship, not bribes. He testified that every year at Christmas so many gifts for executives arrived at A-B headquarters that they spilled out of the offices into the hallways. One Christmas, he said, Fleishman-Hillard sent A-B executives, himself included, beer-pouring robots that were valued at more than $600. Martino's lawyer called Denny Long as a defense witness. Long testified that he "frequently" gave gifts to motivate and reward wholesalers, employees, and "virtually anyone involved with Anheuser-Busch." Gifts were "part of the Anheuser-Busch style," Long said.

In the end, Martino and Orloff were convicted on only one of the original twelve counts of mail fraud, one count of conspiring to defraud the IRS, and one count of filing a false tax return (for failing to report the gifts they'd received). They were sentenced to three years in prison, a punishment that shot fear through the hearts of dozens of A-B executives whose homes and offices contained thousands of dollars' worth of similarly undeclared gifts.

Throughout the remainder of 1987, August and Fleishman-Hillard worked hard to spin the story of August's triumphant return to the brewery. Naturally, they turned to the always Busch-friendly *Fortune* magazine, inviting one of its reporters out to Waldmeister Farm for a rare and intimate sit-down with America's once-again-reigning king of beer. The result was a long and unabashedly celebratory article that contained only two sentences about the recent unpleasantness while describing August as "fanatical about the reputation of his company" and reporting that he was "personally" taking over the beer business for at least two years "lest anything impede its fearsome progress."

Adolphus Busch, the first King of Beer, was an immigrant from Germany who turned a struggling St. Louis brewery that made bad-tasting beer into the world's most successful brewing operation, and in the process became immensely wealthy. *Courtesy of the Missouri History Museum, St. Louis*

The historic Anheuser-Busch Brew House at the corner of Ninth and Pestalozzi Streets in St. Louis, where a crowd of 35,000 gathered to count down the minutes the night Prohibition ended. *Courtesy of the Missouri History Museum, St. Louis*

Anheuser-Busch workers gathered outside their rapidly growing brewery in the 1890s. They labored from 4:00 a.m. to 7:00 p.m. seven days a week, with three hours off on Sunday to go to church. Their salaries ranged from $55 to $75 a month, with meals furnished at 6:00 a.m., 10:00 a.m., and 4:00 p.m., and a daily allotment of twenty free beers per man. *Courtesy of the Missouri History Museum, St. Louis*

The "big house" at Grant's Farm, a twenty-six-room French Renaissance–style chateau built by August A. Busch in 1910, at a cost of $300,000, on land once owned by Ulysses S. Grant. Missouri's version of Hearst Castle, it has been the Busch family estate since the early 1900s. *Courtesy of the Busch family*

Adolphus III and August A. Busch Sr. pause to feed a large buck during a carriage ride through the deer park at Grant's Farm (circa 1930). Adolphus took over the brewery in 1934, when his father shot himself to death. *Courtesy of the Busch family*

Gussie Busch at age thirty-seven, a budding beer baron serving restlessly under his older brother. He took control of Anheuser-Busch in 1946, when Adolpus III died of stomach cancer, and led the company to heights his grandfather Adolphus had never imagined. *Courtesy of the Missouri History Museum, St. Louis*

August A. Busch Sr. *(center)* and his sons, Adolphus III *(left)* and August Jr. ("Gussie"), packing the first case of post-Prohibition Budweiser for shipment to President Franklin Delano Roosevelt. August A. took over the brewery when his father, Adolphus, died, and guided it through Prohibition and the Great Depression. *Courtesy of the Missouri History Museum, St. Louis*

August Busch Jr. and August Busch III raising a stein of beer in celebration of the 10 millionth barrel of beer from Anheuser-Busch, as captured by staff photographer David Glick on December 15, 1964. *Courtesy of the Missouri History Museum, St. Louis*

Gussie and Trudy Busch with their children in the great hall of the mansion at Grant's Farm in the early 1970s. *Standing, left to right*: Adolphus IV, Gussie, and Peter. *Seated*: Andrew, Trudy, Gertrude, Christina, Billy, and Beatrice. *Courtesy of the Busch family*

Trudy with Christina, the baby of the family, whose death following a car accident in 1974 marked the beginning of the end of the "Camelot" years at Grant's Farm. Gussie would never fully recover from the loss of the little girl he called "Honeybee," and neither would his marriage to Trudy. *Courtesy of the Busch family*

Octogenarian Gussie, "the Big Eagle," as St. Louis Cardinal fans would always remember him, urging on both the crowd and his beloved Clydesdales before a championship game. *David Glick, St. Louis Post-Dispatch*

August Busch IV in the spring of 2008, raising a bottle of Bud to mark the seventy-fifth anniversary of the end of Prohibition. Having finally completed his rise to CEO, he began his rapid descent. He would be the last King of Beer. *Courtesy of Whitney Curtis Photography*

At the same time, *Fortune* and the rest of the financial media took little or no notice as August's various diversification ventures—bread, wine, water, and cruise line—toppled like dominos over the next eighteen months.

Denny Long signed his consultancy agreement and settled into his new office in Sunset Hills, not far from Grant's Farm. It took him a few months to realize that the company wasn't going to give him anything to do. He was being paid to be, as he put it, "a silent consultant." August finally called about a year later and invited him to the farm for breakfast on a Saturday. Long resented being asked to drive the thirty miles to Waldmeister on a weekend after he'd been let go, but he went because he thought maybe August was going to offer him something.

The two men sat in August's kitchen while Ginny prepared breakfast. They talked casually about brewery business for a while before August got down to the reason for the meeting. "I have been wanting to thank you for your loyalty in not talking publicly about everything that happened," he said. "I know that wasn't easy for you."

"It sure wasn't," Long replied, "especially when all the reporters were at my gate, and—"

Flashing an irritated look, August cut him off. "I'm telling you that you did a good job, okay?" he said, as if that was all that needed to be said on the subject forever. Ginny said breakfast was ready, so they ate, engaged in more brewery small talk, shook hands, and never spoke to one another again.

Long would hold his tongue for twenty-three years.

17

"HEY, PAL, YOU GOT A QUARTER?"

In October 1987, Gussie Busch got to see his Redbirds play in one more World Series.

Facing the Minnesota Twins, the Cardinals performed horribly in the opener at the Hubert H. Humphrey Metrodome in Minneapolis, losing 10–1, and then suffered an 8–4 drubbing in game two.

Back home in the open air of Busch Memorial Stadium for game three, a crowd of 55,347 stood as Gussie threw out the ceremonial first ball. The eighty-eight-year-old "Big Eagle" had never appeared more frail or, judging by the thunderous applause, more beloved.

In a city with a population a fraction the size of New York and Los Angeles, the Cardinals had sold 3.07 million tickets in 1987, more than any other team. In the last twenty-three years under Gussie's "ownership," they had won six National League pennants and three World Championships. Great players had come and gone—Musial, Flood, Maris, Carlton, Gibson, Brock—but Gussie remained, wearing his goofy red Cowboy-Budweiser-Cardinal getup and waving happily to the crowd: the man who saved the Cardinals for St. Louis and gave the Clydesdales to the world. The fans in the stands cheered as if they suspected this might be their last chance to thank him.

The Cardinals won three straight games at home to take the lead in the series, but then lost the final two games in Minneapolis. They wouldn't appear in the World Series again for seventeen years.

Gussie's game-three appearance turned out to be one of his last. In the months that followed, his health deteriorated to the point that he was confined to a wheelchair and rarely left Grant's Farm except to travel to his beachfront winter home in St. Petersburg. No longer the king of beer, he remained the emperor of his St. Louis estate, however, with a household staff of seven and a round-the-clock team of nurses attending to his needs. His day usually began with a breakfast of two poached eggs and three pieces of low-sodium bacon and ended with two dry Beefeater gin martinis with three onions and three olives. He invariably pushed for a third martini, and the nurses often gave in, but no one acceded to his constant requests for a gun so he could shoot the sparrows that invaded his fifteen-foot-high faux castle pigeon roost. The prospect of a gin-fueled ninety-year-old blasting away at "those goddamn chippies" with a rifle was just too frightening.

Gussie spent most of his time in the gun room, where the weapons were kept under lock, and in the large pantry next to the kitchen, where he sat at the head of a big table and monitored the comings and goings through the informal entrance to the house. He installed a 25-cent slot machine in the pantry and played it contentedly for hours while the staff bustled around him. Whenever a visitor or delivery person passed through, he'd call out, "Hey, pal, you got a quarter?" and motion him over to join him. Visitors could put money in, but not take any away. If they hit a jackpot, they had to turn over their winnings to Gussie before they left. Money was at the root of another amusing ritual. Each morning as his valet was getting him dressed, Gussie would ask, "Did you get my money off the dresser?"

"Yes, Mr. Busch," the valet always replied.

"Did you count it?"

"Yes, sir, I did."

"Is it all there?"

"Yes, sir. Fifteen dollars, the same as yesterday."

When he felt up to it, Gussie was taken on carriage rides around the property. Prior to setting out, he would flip a switch in his bedroom that set off a siren mounted on the house outside his bedroom window, announcing to all creatures on the estate that he was about to emerge. He had to be hoisted into the driver's seat, and no longer had the strength to control the team, but he insisted on holding the reins once they got going. As his carriage passed them, workers would stop what they were doing and wave, salute, or bow their heads in tribute. They knew the old man loved the attention.

Gussie's two youngest sons, Billy and Andy, still lived in the big house with him, as did Billy's six-year-old daughter Scarlett. The little girl was at the center of a lurid, highly publicized custody battle between Billy and an ex-girlfriend named Angela Whitson, a troubled young woman with a taste for drugs and a rap sheet that included arrests for lewd and lascivious behavior and endangering the welfare of her seven-year-old son. After Scarlett's birth in 1983, Billy supported Whitson—providing an $80,000 condo, a car, and $3,500 a month—and made his daughter part of the life at Grant's Farm, where she was given her own room, her own horse, and riding lessons beginning at age two. But in September 1987, Whitson, by then a full-blown crystal methamphetamine addict, abruptly moved with her children to southern California, where she lived in five different places, including a motel, over the next eight months, and took up with a reputed drug dealer named Gino.

In July 1988, after receiving a call from Whitson's great-aunt saying the children were being neglected and physically abused, Billy flew to California, scooped them both up, and brought them back to Grant's Farm. A juvenile court awarded him temporary custody, but Whitson challenged the ruling in a case that went to the Missouri Supreme Court and produced some of the most salacious testimony that judicial body had ever heard. Billy's attorneys brought out the fact that Whitson had been "pregnant six times by three men to whom she was not married at the time of conception," including Gino, whose baby she brought to the April 1989 closed-door hearing. Whitson also admitted to once having a sexual affair with an escapee from an Indiana prison.

Whitson's attorney in turn grilled Billy in uncomfortable detail about his numerous sex partners, including a woman named Ginger:

"Do you recall her last name?" he was asked.

"No."

"Was Ginger one time, or more than one time?"

"More than once."

"About how many times?"

"Fifteen."

The court found that Whitson was "absolutely unfit to be the custodian of this child" (the reference was to Scarlett only because, in an odd twist, the county prosecuting attorney had ordered Billy to return Whitson's son to her, and he had complied), but the court's chief justice didn't disguise his distaste for Billy and his lifestyle. "I cannot say very much in Busch's favor," he said in his ruling. "He is the archetypal playboy. . . . He lives and 'works' at

Grant's Farm helping to train elephants and dogs for the public shows and attending crops and gardens. . . . He is the beneficiary of a family trust to which he resorts when he needs money. . . . I doubt that he will allow his daughter to stand in the way of his transient pleasures."

Although Billy would prove him wrong on that last point,* the judge was accurately reflecting the public's perception of Billy at the time, based largely on an incident that occurred in 1981, when he was twenty-two.

Following an arm-wrestling contest in the bar where he later met Angela Whitson, Billy was challenged to a fight by the man he'd bested, and in the course of the subsequent rolling-around-on-the-ground melee—and supposedly at the urging of the chanting crowd—he bit off the top half of his opponent's ear. No charges were filed because Billy had not started the fight, and he paid the man $25,000 for his injury. But news reports of the bloody brawl became so embedded in the public consciousness that even today, after more than two decades as a model citizen and devoted father, Billy still is commonly differentiated from his brothers by the descriptor, "the one who bit off the guy's ear."

Not surprisingly, press coverage of the custody battle played up the sensational revelations and the Busch wealth rather than the story of a young single father trying to protect and provide for an out-of-wedlock child.

It wasn't clear how much Gussie grasped about the latest "scandal" swirling around his family because his health took a turn for the worse around the time of the custody hearing in April 1989, and thereafter he was bedridden most of the time. It's unlikely he would have judged Billy in any case. Of his five sons, Billy was the

---

* Billy raised Scarlett to adulthood along with his six other children from his long-term marriage to his wife Christina.

one who most resembled him physically and behaviorally, down to his love of Grant's Farm and devotion to the animals, particularly the elephants. (Billy would in fact be the last Busch to move from the estate.)

Gussie's relationship with August III warmed as his time grew short. Nothing brightened his mood more than the sound of August's helicopter setting down on the front lawn of the big house. Toward the end, August came at least once a week and sat with Gussie for an hour or so, always taking the time to inspect the antique wood-and-marble "beer box" in the pantry where the house supply of Budweiser was kept. "And if he found a bottle past its freshness date, then you were in trouble," said a former household staff member.

By all accounts, there was now genuine affection between father and son, and no trace of the anger and resentment that had characterized their relationship for more than three decades. On Gussie's part, the rapprochement was due as much to forgetfulness as forgiveness. He just didn't remember the unpleasant details anymore, and instead basked in the glow of August's constant praise: "All of this happened because of you, Dad; none of it would have been possible without you."

August seemed to go out of his way to pay tribute to Gussie at every opportunity. "The person who put us—the recent management team that is here today—in a position to be able to do the things that we've done, is my father," he told a *Post-Dispatch* reporter when a local nonprofit organization named him their "Man of the Year" in 1987. "He is the one who set the base for this corporation and set the standards for this corporation. We simply picked up the fundamentals and stretched them to more distant horizons." He added, "He's the one I try to model myself after."

According to family and friends, August's newfound appreciation for the father who once delighted in undermining and countermanding him sprang in part from guilt. Although time and events had proved him right in deciding to depose his dad, and even his half brothers now agreed he'd had no choice, he continued to feel badly about it. "As hard-nosed as he liked to present himself," said Adolphus IV, "he still had that [guilt] going on inside and it would slip out in comments from time to time."

Of course, August was still the steely-eyed executive who planned and calculated his every move, and some saw self-interest in his public displays of affection for the old man. The *Post-Dispatch* "Man of the Year" article that quoted him praising Gussie, for example, also quoted Gussie as saying of the firstborn son who'd engineered his overthrow, "He's a great kid. But more than that, he is doing a great job of keeping up the tradition of the family and the company. If my grandfather Adolphus were here, he would be proud as hell. I know I am." Anyone familiar with the way the A-B public relations machine worked knew the statement most likely was written and dictated to the reporter by a Fleishman-Hillard rep and approved by August, quite possibly without the old man even knowing about it.

The Busch family began gathering at Grant's Farm during the last week of September 1989. Gussie was suffering from pneumonia and congestive heart failure, confined to bed, and breathing oxygen through a tube in his nose; they knew it wouldn't be long. On September 28, according to Billy, Gussie spoke on the phone to Trudy and asked her to forgive him. The next day, September 29, with nine of his surviving children at his bedside (Adolphus IV was driving back to St. Louis from Houston), he died in the same room where his father had shot himself to death fifty-five years before. According to an account written by a *Post-Dispatch* reporter, moments before Gussie passed away, a bright red cardinal alighted on the bird feeder outside his bedroom window overlooking the deer park.

In its obituary the next morning, the *New York Times* described him definitively as "the master showman and irrepressible salesman who turned a small family operation into the world's largest brewing company." The *Post-Dispatch* dubbed him "Mr. St. Louis."

In addition to his ten children, Gussie was survived by twenty-seven grandchildren and nine great-grandchildren. So the family filled the big house for the private funeral service, which began with a Catholic Mass in the great hall (living room). Afterward, a team of Clydesdales pulling a bright red Budweiser wagon with two drivers and a Dalmatian accompanied the funeral cortege down the long lane from the house to the iron front gates of the estate, and from there a procession of limousines carried the family a mile up the road to Sunset Cemetery, where Gussie's father was buried. As Gussie was lowered into the ground between his daughter Christina and his fourth wife, Margaret, a scarlet-coated groomsman blew Taps on a silver trumpet while one of Gussie's favorite coach-and-pony teams slowly circled the funeral party, and his favorite jumping horse, Stocking Stuffer, stood nearby. His grave was one of eleven that formed a semicircle facing a heavily symbolic artifact his father had acquired from the 1904 St. Louis World's Fair—a statue of a young boy feeding a fawn.

Two days later, the city got its chance to say good-bye at a public memorial in the St. Louis Cathedral on Lindell Boulevard, just a few blocks from where Gussie had delivered his famous address to the nation the night beer went back on sale in April 1933. Among the 1,700 who filled the Basilica for the Catholic High Mass were Missouri governor John Ashcroft, *Tonight Show* sidekick Ed McMahon, New York Yankees legend Joe DiMaggio, five busloads of workers from the brewery (which shut down for the day at 2:00 p.m.), and twenty-four Catholic clerics, including Archbishop John May and Gussie's old friend Father Paul Reinert, the chancellor of St. Louis University. In his homily, Reinert said he'd seen Gussie grow spiritually over the years, from a "self-centered" individual into a socially conscious community leader who "gradually discovered the joy and thrill of giving."

"He had a very beautiful death," Reinert said. "He was resigned and well prepared."

Gussie died a very wealthy man, far richer than his grandfather Adolphus. As the company's largest stockholder, he controlled 35,452,142 shares, or about 12.5 percent of A-B common stock, worth about $1.3 billion. Upon his death, virtually all of it passed to Busch family members and relatives, including Orthweins, von Gontards, Hermanns, Flannigans, and Reisingers.

In accordance with a will Gussie had signed in 1987, each of his ten children—including August III, whom he claimed to have disinherited—received 400,000 shares from a trust that was set up in 1932. With the stock then valued at approximately $37 a share, each child's portion was worth nearly $15 million.

In addition, each of Gussie's six surviving children by Trudy received 337,464 shares from another trust set up in 1936. There were restrictions on the proceeds of the 1936 trust, however. Half of the amount—1,012,392 shares, or 168,723 shares per child—had to be placed in trust for the next generation, though the heirs could continue to draw income from the shares. So the Grant's Farm children each inherited more than $21 million worth of stock, plus an income of more than $100,000 a year, with another $6 million worth of stock held in trust for their children.

Most of Gussie's personal property was divided among the Grant's Farm children as well. Adolphus IV and Billy inherited Belleau Farm, while Peter and Andy were given ownership of 140 acres of land that abutted Grant's Farm. The two girls, Beatrice and Trudy, each got $250,000 in cash. And in his most bedeviling bequest, Gussie left Grant's Farm itself to the six of them jointly, with the restriction that it could not be broken up or sold to anyone outside the immediate family. His expectation was that the four brothers would eventually buy out their sisters and then reach an agreement about ownership among themselves. (It has not worked out that way.)

Gussie's four older children by his first two wives didn't fare nearly as well their younger half siblings. From the large art collection at Grant's Farm, each of the sisters—Lilly, Lotsie, and Elizabeth—received a Western-themed watercolor by St. Louis–born artist Oscar E. Berninghaus. And August III got the golden telegram that brewery employees had presented to his great-grandfather Adolphus for his fiftieth wedding anniversary.

When all was divided, the only real losers were August's children—Susan, Virginia, Steven, and August IV—who received nothing from their grandfather's vast estate. It appeared that Gussie had disinherited them for the sins of their father.

HERE COMES THE SON

In the spring of 1990, Anheuser-Busch simultaneously introduced two new products, each the result of careful planning and promotion.

One was Bud Dry, a brand whose name derived from a brewing process that was all the rage in Japan. "Dry" beer was produced by fermenting the malt, grain, water, and yeast mixture, called wort, longer and more thoroughly, allowing the yeast to consume more of the residual sugar. The result was a light-bodied beer with slightly fewer calories than regular beer, but with higher alcohol content (5 percent), a drier, less malty taste, and little to no aftertaste. As the estimable London beer expert Michael ("the Beer Hunter") Jackson put it, dry beer was "notable for having scarcely any taste, and no finish."

Dry beer itself was nothing new. The process was a modification of one used to make a German lager called Diät Pils, originally brewed specifically with diabetics in mind because of its lower sugar content. Several regional American brewers had produced dry beers over the years, but the style had not caught on with U.S. beer drinkers. In 1987, however, Japan's Asahi Brewery introduced a dry beer in that country, hoping to sell 1 million barrels the first year. Instead, Asahi Dry Draft sold 13.5 million barrels. Asahi's three competitors—Kirin, Suntory, and Sapporo—quickly introduced their own dry beers, and within a year, 39 percent of the beer sold in Japan was dry-brewed, and all four brewers began exporting their new dry brands to the United States.

August III was not about to get caught flat-footed again on a new style of beer, no matter how bland it tasted or oxymoronic it sounded. He put dry beer on the fast track, and Michelob Dry was rushed into five test markets in September 1988. By April 1990, A-B was convinced there was a big enough market for another American-made dry beer, and the company announced the national launch of Bud Dry Draft, backed by a $70 million marketing and advertising budget—the most any brewer had ever spent to promote a new beer, the company said.

The other new product A-B introduced in April 1990 was a revamped version of August IV. Last seen publicly as a defendant on trial for assaulting police officers, the Fourth, now twenty-five, had been made over into the spitting corporate image of his father. From the short, slicked-down hair to the buttoned-down oxford-cloth white dress shirts, the resemblance was almost eerie in the publicity photos Fleishman-Hillard released, announcing that, in his first managerial role with the company, August IV was being put in charge of the Bud Dry rollout and its record budget.

The Fourth was emerging from three years of image rehab, having completed a series of assignments that read like a checklist his father might have given him titled "Things You Need to Do to Redeem Yourself and Follow in My Footsteps." He had graduated from St. Louis University. He'd completed an apprenticeship as a member of Brewers and Maltsters Local Union No. 6, working in the brew house. He'd taken a course of study at Versuchs und Lehranstalt fur Brauerei, a brewing institute in Berlin, where he earned a master brewer certificate. He'd spent a year as assistant to A-B's vice president of brewing, Gerhardt Kraemer, and another year as assistant to marketing vice president Mike Roarty. And he appeared to have settled down in his personal life by becoming engaged to a local model named Judy Buchmiller, as chronicled by *Post-Dispatch* gossip columnist Jerry Berger in his frothy Top of the Town column:

"Bud Dry was on the house at Dominic's on The Hill Saturday night, courtesy of August Busch IV, twogether [*sic*] with his fiancée, who toasted the countdown to their middle-aisling November 17 at Our Lady of Lourdes, followed by a pouring at the St. Louis Country Club."

Two months later, Berger reported that the Fourth and Buchmiller were "off and running to join August III in the Florida Keys to catch *Miss Budweiser* in an offshore race," and he noted offhandedly that their wedding had been postponed. "We're still, hopefully, going to get married," the Fourth said, as if trying to placate his father, who'd been pushing for the marriage. "We're very much in love. I want to marry the girl." But it never happened.

Publicity surrounding the Fourth's reemergence was tightly controlled by Fleishman-Hillard, which doled out access and information to news outlets and reporters that could be counted on not to dredge up his reckless past. For the most part, the media gave him a break and focused on the present. But even Fleishman-Hillard couldn't control all the reporters all the time, and in one of the Fourth's first arranged interviews, he was asked whether the unusually large $70 million Bud Dry budget was the company's way of ensuring success for the boss's son. "No, no, no, no," he responded. "This brand had tremendous success in test markets." Then he all but confirmed that he'd been given special treatment with the promotion, blurting out, "I've only been on the [Bud Dry] team two or three months."

The Fourth initially earned kudos from his coworkers merely for being nicer than his father. "He was very personable," said a former A-B middle manager who first met him during the Bud Dry rollout. "He was walking through the brewery, shaking hands, and asking people questions and actually listening to them. I felt like he was trying to learn, and not from the way his dad did things. He didn't go around looking for old beer. It was more the way Gussie had done it."

There was still that other side to the Fourth, however, the one that came out at night, when he was running with his friends in St. Louis's Central West End or traveling on company business away from the prying eyes of his father and the higher-ups in the home office. This was the side that a group of A-B marketing employees saw during the company's spring break promotion in Palm Springs in 1989.

A team of about ten of them had been in the desert resort town for two weeks, spreading goodwill and free beer among the thousands of "contemporary adults" who were taking a breather from their educational pursuits, when they were told that the heir apparent was flying in to check out the festivities. "He was in training at the time," one member of the team recalled later. "The word was that Three Sticks (August III) was grooming him, and he was on the straight and narrow."

Spring break was serious business because A-B drew 17 percent of its sales from the twenty-one-to-thirty-year-old segment of the population, or the so-called Generation X. Historically, twenty-one-to-thirty-year-olds consumed the most beer, an average of 45 gallons a year per person, compared to 36 gallons for those in the thirty-to-forty age range and 20 gallons in the forty-to-sixty-year-old segment.

Six months worth of planning and preparation had gone into A-B's promotional events in Palm Springs and other college-break hotspots around the country. News that the CEO's son was coming to town for the weekend and wanted to be included in "evening calls" to key accounts only added to the stress on the marketing team and the local distributor, as they now had to prepare for the Fourth's arrival. It fell to the distributor to round up a handful of "models" from Los Angeles—all long-legged and large-breasted but with an array of skin and hair colors—to serve as the Fourth's personal retinue of Bud Girls during his visit. The marketing team got the impression this was a standing order among distributors whenever the Fourth hit town. "Your responsibility was to help him have a good time."

The Fourth checked into the Villas at the Oasis, where the A-B team was staying, but for reasons that soon became clear, his quarters were located apart from the others, on the far side of the property. On Saturday night, the marketing team made a call at Pompeii, the largest-volume club in the area. They worked the crowded room for several hours, buying rounds, handing out promotional items, shaking hands, and making friends. To the inebriated patrons, it was a giant party; to the marketing team, it was a job, more enjoyable than other jobs perhaps, but still grueling in its own way.

Midway through their most important call of the week, however, "all of a sudden we were told that the Fourth wanted us to leave," one team member recounted later. "The distributor came to us and said, 'Gather all your personnel and go. He wants you out of here.' It was all because he was partying and didn't want us to see what he was doing."

The Fourth apparently took the party back to his private villa later that night. The next day, the place was trashed, the Fourth and the models were gone, and the A-B distributor was settling up with Oasis management over the damages.

Bud Dry was a success out of the gate, selling 3.2 million barrels in its first nine months. The company boasted that the new brand accounted for 3.4 percent of sales and had "the best start of any beer since Bud Light in 1982."

Fleishman-Hillard hyped the Fourth's role in the launch, telling the media that he had "helped develop the company's dry brewing method" and heroically promoted the brand by piloting Bud Dry's forty-foot Skater catamaran in six offshore races "at speeds of up to 140 miles an hour" until his father insisted he quit because of the danger. The latter revelation led reporters to describe him as "daring" and "risk-loving." The PR firm also put it out that the Fourth flew planes and helicopters, rose at 5:00 a.m., jogged daily, worked out twice a day, held black belts in aikido, tae kwon do, and hapkido "for security reasons," rode a Harley, owned two manly dogs—a German shepherd and a rottweiler—and wore cowboy boots to work. It was as if they had cast him in his own beer commercial: the most interesting contemporary adult male in the world.

Despite its fast start, Bud Dry sales dropped off in 1991, and the brand, like dry beer in general, ultimately proved a disappointment. But that didn't affect the Fourth's trajectory at the company. In July 1991 he was named brand director for Budweiser, prompting the *Fortune* magazine headline "King of Beer Taps Crown Prince." It was a big promotion that coincided with the first decline in Budweiser sales in fifteen years. The drop was sizable, nearly 6 percent, and the company blamed the doubling of the federal excise tax on beer—to $18 a barrel—that occurred in January 1991, and the economic recession, which caused beer drinkers to switch to cheaper brands. But A-B's research showed it was more than that: the company's flagship brand, which produced nearly 40 percent of its sales and half of its $1.7 billion in operating profits, was falling out of favor with contemporary adult drinkers, the Fourth's peers, who were turning to upstart American microbrew brands such as Samuel Adams and imports like Corona Extra, which had experienced a tenfold increase in sales on the strength of its TV commercials showing sexy young couples relaxing on a tropical beach.

The research threw a scare into A-B's aging management, causing fifty-four-year-old August III to admit, "I've lost the ability to understand the 21- to 30-year-olds the way I used to." Again, the Fourth seemed perfectly cast. "He was young and they thought he could relate to that group," said a former marketing staffer. "He was one of them; they figured he could feel the pulse." Still, inside the company and out, the question hung in the air: was this twenty-six-year-old with less than two years of managerial experience and lingering personal "issues" up to the task? There were some clear signs that he wasn't.

In early media interviews about his promotions, the Fourth came across as defensive and even self-pitying. An article in the *Chicago Tribune* quoted him as saying, "Everybody thinks, 'it must be easy to be you,' but it's probably the hardest thing in the world to be me, and to work under the pressure you have to be under. You have to do three times as good as the next guy to be considered to be doing the same job as he does."

He hit on the hard-to-be-me theme again in an interview with *Fortune* magazine, saying, "You don't know how different it is walking in these shoes, versus what people perceive it to be. People think, 'Here's a guy who's got it all—the Busch name, the best job in the world' [but]; it's a very different reality."

He was alluding to what it was like to work for his father. "There's not a day in the week where he doesn't ask me a question or give me a hard time about something," he told *Business Week* magazine.

The *Business Week* interview was intended to highlight their supposedly close working relationship, but the resultant article failed to conceal the tension between them. "When asked about the [Tucson] accident, the father clenches his fists and lightly pounds a table," the magazine reported, quoting the son as saying, "It was tough for a while . . . that's all I want to say." The Fourth acknowledged that he would like "to step into my father's shoes someday," and his father told the reporter that someday would not be soon. "You're looking at a guy who's 54 years old," he said. "I intend to be around here a long time." He appeared to be quoting Gussie verbatim when he added, "There is no guarantee that August [IV] has a direct line of succession in this corporation."

In the saga of Busch fathers and sons, history was repeating itself, and in remarkable detail. The Fourth's coming of age mirrored that of August III. His parents, too, had split up when he was five, and from then on he lived primarily with his mother and visited his father on weekends, when his father wasn't traveling. His bonding with August III had occurred in duck blinds on the farm and during day trips to the brewery, where "Little August" was allowed to sit in on executive meetings. When the Fourth was a teenager, his father remarried and started a new family, which included another son, Steven, with whom he spent more time and developed a closer relationship, just as Gussie had done with Adolphus IV.

In the Busch family, it seemed as if the firstborn son was offered in sacrifice to the company. The Fourth knew from the age of cognizance that he was expected to become CEO one day. He had no choice in the matter; doing something else with his life was not an option. He also knew he would only become CEO if and when his father judged him worthy. The job was his to lose, every day. The scrutiny was unrelenting, the criticism constant.

At the office, the Fourth's interaction with his father also followed the pattern established by August III and Gussie, with the son struggling to prove himself and the father only grudgingly acknowledging his effort. As a result, the Fourth regarded "the Chief" with an equal measure of hero worship and resentment. He had pictures of the two of them in happy poses all over his office and home, yet he told people, "I never had a father-son relationship, ever; it was purely business," echoing his father's comment about Gussie years before: "I never had a daddy."

The Fourth constantly sought paternal approval but rarely received it to his satisfaction. Even when he emulated his dad by wearing boots at work, he fell short of expectations. He showed up for a meeting with A-B's California wholesalers at the Los Angeles brewery one afternoon sporting a pair of pointy-toed lizard-skin cowboy boots, and his father immediately bawled him out in front of a subordinate. "When the fuck are you going to learn to dress like a business person?" he barked. The Fourth pointed to his father's feet and said, "Well, what do you call those?" August III looked down at his hand-tooled Lucchese dress boots with tastefully rounded toes and said, "*These* are aristocrat boots." Pointing at his son's feet, he declared, "*Those* are shit-kickers."

Such scenes were not uncommon. But even as August III focused his laserlike attention, sharp tongue, and short temper on his son, he continued to reward him with plum promotions that few in the company felt he deserved. In 1993, after less than two years as Budweiser brand director, the Fourth was elevated to senior director of the Budweiser family of brands—Budweiser, Bud Light, Bud Dry, and Bud Ice Draft, a new higher-alcohol brand aimed at the adult contemporary segment. In February 1994 he was named vice president and director of all A-B brands (including Michelob, Busch, and imported brands) and became part of his father's so-called strategy committee, the inner circle of about a dozen top executives.

The promotions weren't tied to any obvious accomplishments on his part, since the company experienced comparatively anemic growth in those years (an increase of only 200,000 barrels in 1993) and Budweiser continued to lose market share (another 0.5 percent in 1993). But the Fourth exhibited a talent for managing up. Having inherited a bright and experienced team of brand managers and sales executives, he used them adroitly, letting them know from the start that a big part of their jobs was to make him look good to his father and the board of directors. If they did that, then he would take care of them, and they all would rise in the company together. "We'll either be famous or fired," he told them. It was a strategy his father would have approved, and it paid off.

In late summer 1994, one of August's team, the new Budweiser brand director Mike Brooks, sent a memo to two top executives at D'Arcy Advertising, Jim Palumbo and Mark Choate, telling them that A-B wanted a new campaign for Bud, one that would "contemporize" the brand and make it more appealing to the twenty-one- to thirty-year-old segment. He asked them to give the assignment out to creative teams in all D'Arcy's offices—New York, Detroit, and Los Angeles, in addition to St. Louis—and present their best work within a month. Thirty days later, Choate, Palumbo, and a handful of D'Arcy creative types presented Brooks with dozens of campaign ideas in a session that lasted several hours. Brooks was struck by one concept in particular from a young creative team in St. Louis, Dave Swaine and Michael Smith. Presented on an "art card," a twelve-by-sixteen-inch piece of white foam board, it was a four-panel drawing of frogs sitting on lily pads with a Budweiser sign in the background. The card was augmented by a thirty-second cassette recording of frogs croaking, "Bud . . . bud . . . weis . . . bud . . . weis . . . bud . . . weis . . . bud . . . weis . . . er."

It was beautifully simple and so totally off-the-wall that Brooks couldn't help laughing at the absurdity. Of all the things he was shown, "Frogs" stood out.

The next day, Brooks, Choate, and Palumbo presented "Frogs"

and two or three other concepts to Brooks's boss, Bob Lachky, the senior director of Budweiser brands, and Lachky's boss, August IV. Both men agreed that "Frogs" was fall-down funny and the best of the lot. They instructed Brooks to take it up the line to Patrick Stokes, the president of the brewing division. One of August III's original stable of MBAs, Stokes had run the Campbell Taggart baking operation before August III put him in Denny Long's old job in 1990. He was seen as a competent, if colorless, placeholder until the Fourth was judged ready to assume the presidency. Inside the company, Stokes was jokingly called "the Tommy Newsom of the beer business," a reference to the buttoned-up, perpetually brown-suited backup bandleader on *The Tonight Show*, who host Johnny Carson delighted in introducing as "the man from bland" and "Mr. Excitement." Brooks was surprised when Stokes, too, laughed at "Frogs" and said he would support the concept as an ad campaign for Budweiser.

That left only August III to convince. The four executives would have been hard pressed at that moment to say exactly why they thought "Frogs" would help sell Budweiser to twenty-five-year-olds. It was certainly a unique concept; they'd never seen anything like it before. It wasn't anyone's father's idea of a Budweiser commercial. There would be no Dalmatians riding on red beer wagons, no Clydesdales galloping slo-mo through the snow, no blue-collar worker tossing back a cold one at the end of a long day, no jiggling Bud Girls on the beach, no beer really, no classic "pour shot" with a punchy voiceover tagline talking about taste or quality or tradition, none of the things that August III liked in a Bud commercial. But they all sensed that if the concept were properly executed, then people would not only remember it, they'd likely never forget it.

It was decided that Brooks should make the pitch to August III at the annual weeklong planning meeting in September, when every brand director presented his advertising and marketing plans for the upcoming year. The meeting was held in the big conference room at the Soccer Park, where more than forty executives, including the entire strategy committee and the creative team from D'Arcy, sat in a U-shaped arrangement of tables, with the presenter in the middle facing August III, who was sitting at the center of the head table.

About halfway through his four-hour presentation, Brooks introduced "Frogs" as "an idea for a thirty-second commercial, for your approval." He held the art card with the drawing of the frogs across his chest and pushed the start button on the cassette player next to him.

When the tape ended, all eyes turned to August III, who did not react. He stared at the art card, and then glanced up at Brooks, then back at the card. He didn't smile. Neither did Stokes or Lachky or the Fourth or any member of the strategy committee. They all just sat there, stone silent.

Finally, August said, "I don't get it, Brooks."

"Sir, I'd like to play the tape again," Brooks replied.

"You do that."

Still holding the art card across his chest, Brooks rewound the tape and pressed the start button again, all the while thinking, "I'm in big trouble here; this was *my* recommendation."

Halfway through the replay, however, a smile flickered across August's face; by the end, he was laughing, and so was everyone else in the room, out of relief if nothing else.

"What's the message of that, Brooks?" August asked.

"Sir, the message is that Budweiser is so attractive that even frogs are drawn to it."

"That's fantastic. What's it gonna cost?"

"Two point three million, sir."

"What?"

"Two point three million," Brooks repeated, launching into

a detailed description of all the animatronics, robotics, and hydraulics that would be required to bring the amphibians to life. August listened intently and jotted notes. Brooks explained that the cost also included $1.2 million for the first airing of the commercial.

"Where's it going to run?" August asked.

"In position 1-A during the Super Bowl," Brooks said. "That's the first thirty-second commercial break after the first possession in the first quarter. It will be the first commercial anyone sees."

"You believe in this?" August asked.

"Yes, sir, I do."

"You willing to stake your job on it?"

"I am."

August III broke into a broad smile and said, "Well, then go get 'em, Brooksie."

As it turned out, D'Arcy didn't get the chance to execute the "Frogs" concept. On November 13, 1994, August III, Pat Stokes, Bob Lachky, and Mike Brooks were visiting the A-B plant in Baldwinsville, New York, when Lachky got a call from D'Arcy's Jim Palumbo, telling him that someone in the agency's New York office had made a deal to buy media (print advertising space and TV commercial time) for Miller Brewing. Palumbo apologized and said he had not been consulted.

On the corporate jet during the flight home to St. Louis, August sat with the others and said calmly, "Gentlemen, I'm going to teach you a business lesson. This corporation has spent millions and millions of dollars with D'Arcy Advertising over a seventy-nine-year period of time. They have done some great things for this company. But after they were bought [by New York-based Benton & Bowles in 1986] we became very unimportant to them. They have now made a business decision to support our biggest competitor, and they did it without even telling us. That is disrespectful.

"So they made their choice, and now we are going to make ours. We will no longer conduct business with that company. When we are on the ground, I want you get hold of the head of PR, and have a statement prepared. And get [D'Arcy managing director] Charlie Claggett out to our hangar at Spirit of St. Louis Airport for a meeting at eight a.m. tomorrow. I will tell him this relationship is over and why. Are there any questions?"

There were plenty, but the three executives were too stunned to ask them. The big question in their minds was what would become of D'Arcy's St. Louis office, which depended on A-B for 80 percent of its business, nearly $150 million a year. Losing that could cost as many as a hundred people their jobs, some of them, like Palumbo and Choate, good friends of theirs. Lives were about to be upended, careers derailed, houses sold, and families relocated. In the St. Louis business community, this was a calamity.

It had been a long time coming. August III had been harboring resentment toward D'Arcy since 1983, when the agency ousted his cousin James Orthwein as chairman, forcing him to retire at age fifty-nine in a manner that August considered disrespectful. Orthwein had gone on to become owner of the New England Patriots and was one of the largest individual owners of A-B stock, with more than a million shares, so he was hardly hurting. But August III had not forgotten how D'Arcy had once treated a member of his family. And now it was payback time.

"Get me Jimmy Orthwein on the phone," he called up to the cockpit. A few minutes later, the pilot said, "We have Mr. Orthwein on the line, sir." August was grinning like a schoolboy as he took the call. "Jimmy, I've got some good news for you. It's retribution day. Can I land my machine [helicopter] in your yard? Great. See you this afternoon."

On January 29, 1995, quarterback Steve Young threw a record six touchdown passes to lead his San Francisco 49ers to a 49–26 victory over the San Diego Chargers in Super Bowl XXIX. But the real winning team that day may have been the Budweiser Frogs, who outscored even the legendary Spuds MacKenzie in *USA Today*'s weekly Ad Track poll, which measured the popularity and effectiveness of ad campaigns. Ad Track rated "Frogs" No. 1 for three months running, with more than 50 percent of poll respondents saying they recalled the commercial and liked it "a lot." *Advertising Age* reported that the frogs had tripled the awareness of Budweiser among the target group of twenty-one- to thirty-year-olds. The advertising industry honored the agency that produced the commercial, DDB Needham of Chicago, with a handful of Clio Awards (the ad industry's version of the Oscars) as well as the Silver Lion award at the Cannes International Festival of Creativity.

The "Frogs" campaign spawned the even more popular "Louie the Lizard" campaign, which began with a thirty-second commercial in which a green-with-envy chameleon complained to his pal Frank:

"I can't believe they went with the frogs. Our audition was flawless. We did the look. We did the tongue thing. It was great."

"Louie," Frank cut in. "Frogs sell beer. That's it, man, the number one rule of marketing."

"The Budweiser Lizards," Louie continued, in his heavy Brooklyn patois. "We coulda been huge . . . those frogs are going to pay."

Subsequent thirty-second spots revealed Louie to be a wiseguy wannabe who hires a ferret hit man to whack the frogs, in the process delivering such memorable lines as "Eventually, every frog has to croak" and "Never hire a ferret to do a weasel's job."

"Louie the Lizard" topped *USA Today*'s Ad Track and won six Clios and another Silver Lion award in Cannes. Together the frogs and lizards pulled Budweiser out of its slump and reinvigorated the brand's image among contemporary adults, who responded to the campaign's ironic humor and the sophisticated extended spoof of show business, the Mafia, and beer advertising itself. Suddenly, Anheuser-Busch wasn't just the world's largest brewer, it was also the hippest. The mood inside the company was euphoric.

"Our ads were on the lips of virtually every adult contemporary consumer," said a former A-B sales executive. "Which made it a lot easier when our sales guys walked into Krogers, or Ralphs or Albertsons. They'd bring a VCR along on the call and pop in a tape and play the commercials, and the retail people thought they were hysterical. The retailers would show the commercials at their senior management meetings. The momentum behind our brands was huge."

It wasn't only Budweiser. In December 1994, Bud Light finally surpassed Miller Lite in sales, giving A-B the No. 1 and No. 2 selling beers in the world.

At the height of the "Louie the Lizard" campaign, August IV received another promotion, to vice president of marketing, a position that had been vacant since Mike Roarty retired in 1990.

The myth-making machinery at Fleischman-Hillard immediately shifted into high gear to assure that he got the credit for the company's recent success. In the press release announcing his promotion, the PR agency wrote, "Throughout his brand management tenure, Busch has been noted for creating innovative advertising and marketing strategies. The most recent successes include the popular 'Frogs.'"

For a full telling of the story, Fleishman-Hillard turned to a trusted reporter, *Fortune* magazine's Patricia Sellers, who had visited Waldmeister and written the long and laudatory profile of August in 1987 following the A-B kickback scandal and Denny Long's resignation.

August III did nothing without a strategy behind it. When he sat down with Sellers for a 7:00 a.m. interview in his aircraft hangar at Spirit of St. Louis Airport, he had several specific messages he wanted to deliver to the financial community. Sellers delivered one of them right at the top of the article, reporting that "the chairman finds this an opportune morning to disclose publicly, for the first time, a big piece of news. 'I'll be retired by 65. At that point, this is a younger person's game.'"

He didn't say the Fourth would succeed him; he got his oldest daughter, Susan, to say it for him. "If my brother continues to perform as he has, it's 100% certain he'll have the job," Sellers quoted her as saying. In a separate interview conducted in his "all-black bachelor pad–style office," the Fourth sent out a cringe-worthy thank-you to his father, revealing to Sellers that he kept five letters in an inside pocket of his briefcase. "Five notes of compliment from the Chief over ten years of full-time employment here," he said. "They're few and far between. But I cherish them. As demanding and challenging as he is, the moments of victory and his acknowledgement of my success mean so much to me." Asked if his father knew of the letters in the briefcase, the Fourth said no. "But he will now." It was almost as if the two men were using the reporter to conduct a conversation they weren't comfortable having face-to-face.

August III couldn't help but be pleased with the *Fortune* article, which described his son as "the hotshot vice president of marketing" who had "toned down his wild ways," and "recharged Anheuser-Busch" by "pumping up beer sales to record levels." Sellers reported that the Fourth's colleagues and clients "praised him as a team player, a consensus builder, and a terrific idea man" (without quoting a single person saying any such thing) and stated (without attribution) that it had been the Fourth's idea "to take Budweiser off its pedestal and move it onto . . . the toadstool."

"The chairman thought his son was nuts two years ago when he saw the monosyllabic frogs who croak 'Bud . . . weis . . . er,'" Sellers wrote. "The Fourth, who can be as unrelenting as his father, insisted the frogs would make Bud hip. He poured on research, and August III gave in."

Seller's account of the campaign's provenance would be repeated as gospel in numerous publications over the next fifteen years, including the 2011 book *Dethroning the King*, which said that the Fourth pitched the concept to his father "behind closed doors," with no one else present, and that the two men had argued about it, but the Fourth prevailed. "That story is an absolute falsehood," Mike Brooks said recently. "August IV was a member of the management team that supported the Frogs campaign. The agency created the work, and we bought it. He did not create the work or present it."

August III likely was relieved that the *Fortune* magazine article touched only lightly on the Fourth's run-ins with the law more than a decade earlier, with Sellers reporting that he was "still haunted by the tragedy" of the Tucson crash, in which "his passenger, a waitress from another bar, flew through the sunroof and died."

"They couldn't prove blame," she quoted the Fourth as saying. "I had a bad head injury. I don't remember that part of my life."

His father hoped everyone else would soon forget it as well, especially the business community, at whom the article was aimed. He was really talking to them when he said to Sellers, with finality, "His past isn't an issue anymore."

He was dead wrong about that.

19

"WAY, WAY, *WAY* BEYOND TIGER WOODS"

After a forty-three-year marriage characterized by exhilarating triumphs, heated disagreements, and bitter disappointments, St. Louis's most beloved couple, the Redbirds and "the Brewery," broke up. In the spring of 1996, Anheuser-Busch sold the Cardinals.

In a way, it wasn't surprising. August III's heart was never really in the relationship, and he'd threatened to walk away a number of times. The issue was always the same—money. Even in the Cardinals' best years, when they won championships and sold more tickets than most other teams, their profits were piddling compared to those of the beer company. The team lost $12 million in 1994, the company claimed, and came in fourth in their division in 1995, with a losing percentage of .434. For August, it just wasn't working. As a spokesman for the company put it, "We have concluded that this is no longer a compatible fit."

Still, August handled the split with grace. He didn't just sell out to the highest bidder; he personally solicited prospective buyers, making sure the team would remain in St. Louis. (He expected that Gussie would roll over in his grave, but he didn't want to risk the old man clawing his way out of the coffin.) He chose a group of local businessmen and set the price for the team and the stadium and parking at $150 million. The sale was *the* topic of public discourse for weeks, but there was no backlash against the company because the citizens were assured that almost everything would remain the same for them—from Busch Stadium with its Clydesdale-drawn beer wagon and giant A & Eagle scoreboard to the brewery's sponsorship of the Cardinals' TV and radio broadcasts to the familiar voices of announcers Jack Buck and former Cardinal right fielder Mike Shannon talking about Bud and Bud Light in between the play-by-play. The fans were told, in effect, that Mom and Dad still loved one another, they just wouldn't be sleeping in the same bed anymore.

Extensive media coverage of the Cardinals sale helped to obscure the news that August simultaneously unloaded two other struggling subsidiaries. After fourteen years of losses, he spun off A-B's Campbell Taggart baking operation into a separate publicly traded company in a stock-swap deal with shareholders. Unable to find a buyer for Eagle Snacks, he shut down the operation and let go all of its 150 employees. (Frito-Lay eventually purchased four of the five Eagle Snacks plants, and Procter & Gamble acquired the trademark and brand name.)

August's grand plan for turning A-B into a fully diversified package-goods company in the style of Procter & Gamble—a strategy inspired by his grandfather's successful diversification of the company during Prohibition—had proved a dismal failure. But he was not one to dwell on failure, especially his own, and he often preached that mistakes were the greatest teacher. He pivoted to a plan that might well have been inspired by the letter his great-grandfather Adolphus wrote to his son (August's grandfather) ninety years before, reminding him that the family's welfare depended "solely on the success of our brewery." August updated the sentiment to a punchier slogan, "Beer is why we are here," and announced to shareholders in the spring of 1996 that his goal was to capture 60 percent of the domestic beer market by the year 2005. He then took to the task with the energy and determination of a man half his age.

He carried a Dictaphone wherever he went, recording an endless stream of questions, critiques, and complaints that his secretaries transcribed and forwarded to the targeted executives in the form of e-mails and interoffice memos marked "from AAB3 executape" and usually accompanied by a demand for an immediate response. He called his executives at all hours, even on Sundays and holidays. "My beeper once went off on Christmas morning when I was opening presents with my kids," sighed a longtime executive. "I knew he'd probably sent out the query to six other people, too, and you didn't want to be the last to respond."

There was no corner of the business that escaped his attention. He traveled to Idaho's remote Teton Valley every summer to personally inspect the hops and barley crops that were destined for his beer, hopping from farm to farm in his helicopter. He conducted similar examinations of his suppliers' rice fields in Arkansas and Mississippi. And when the annual shipments of European hops arrived by train at Pestalozzi Street, he dug right in, rolling the buds in his hands and holding them up to his nose to inhale the bouquet. "He understood the relationship between the ingredients and the processing," said a former employee. "His father didn't even have that sort of technical command of the business."

Mike Brooks recalled accompanying August on an inspection tour of the company's marketing presence at the Indianapolis 500 one year. After checking out the ad signage and meeting the Budweiser racing team owner and driver, August was headed back to his helicopter when he spotted a large trashcan overflowing with empty beer bottles. Brooks watched in astonishment as the boss whipped out his Dictaphone and began fishing out Bud and Bud Light empties, reading the date codes aloud so someone could check to see if the beer being sold at Indy was fresh. "That's how focused he was on quality," Brooks said.

"So there he was, the chairman of the company in his sunglasses, $500 slacks, and $1,000 boots, digging through the trash," said Brooks, still marveling at the image years later, "when this drunk, tattooed biker walks up, stares at him like he's from the moon, and says, 'Hey, buddy, if you need a beer that bad, I'll buy you one.' August almost fell down laughing."

When it came to the company's award-winning ad campaigns, the Fourth may have been claiming the credit, but no commercial went on the air without August III's approval. "He watched everything, and he could be very intimidating, aggressive and uncompromising," said a veteran of many commercial viewing sessions with him. "But he invited opinion. He genuinely wanted to know what *you* thought. I remember one marketing meeting when he said, 'I don't get it, but I'm not a contemporary adult. All the people in here under thirty, stand up and you tell me what you thought about that commercial.' He synthesized opinions; he energized you. He was engaged."

The executive recalled one time when August sought his opinion about a commercial at a particularly inopportune moment. "We had just finished a meeting and I was in the executive washroom, in a stall, when he walked in and said, 'Who's in there? Hey, what did you think? Was that the damnedest thing you ever saw?' He didn't stand on ceremony. His head was working on something, and he didn't care that I was taking a dump," the former executive said, adding with a laugh, "And I was never comfortable using that restroom after that."

August continued to press his personal war on drugs. Few companies had stricter or more comprehensive drug policies than A-B. All union employees were required to undergo a drug test once a year, and nonunion and management employees were subject to random testing without notice. Other companies required employees to provide blood and urine samples for testing, but A-B required them to surrender a hair sample as well, which could be used to detect drug use up to three months prior. The official company policy stated that workers who tested positive for drugs would be given unpaid leave and could be reinstated after completing an employee assistance program and testing clean. In practice, few were reinstated. "The company would pay for rehab, but the minute you completed it, they let you go, so it was really one strike and you're out."

Despite a family history rife with substance abuse (his great-grandfather, uncle, mother, and, arguably, his father), August didn't buy the idea that alcoholism and drug addiction were a disease with a hereditary component. "He believed they were the result of personal weakness, not illness," said a colleague. "I heard him say it many times. He thought it was all a matter of willpower."

In the summer of 1995, August ordered a drug "search and seizure" raid at the Los Angeles brewery, conducted by A-B security and human resources personnel with the help of a private investigation agency, Wells Fargo security guards, and drug-sniffing dogs. The task force swept into the plant during a shift change at 4:30 p.m. and locked down the employee parking lot, preventing anyone from leaving for more than two hours while the dogs went from car to car. If the dogs reacted to a car, indicating that drugs might be present, the owner was located and brought to a room in the administration building, where he was told to sign a consent form authorizing a search of his vehicle or face being fired.

One longtime employee was fired on the spot for refusing to

sign, and another was fired after he consented to a search and security guards found a marijuana roach clip in the glove compartment of his truck. In the parking lot, a handful of workers were ordered to remove their shoes and socks and sit on the ground while their vehicles were being searched.

The operation turned into a debacle as detained employees began calling their spouses to say they would be late for dinner because the company was holding them "hostage." Family members called reporters, and reporters called Fleishman-Hillard for comment. "I think A-B expected to find a shit-load of dope," said a former Fleishman-Hillard executive involved in the damage control. "Instead, they stepped in a load of shit."

A group of more than twenty employees sued the company for false imprisonment, false arrest, assault and battery, invasion of privacy, and defamation, among other things. "The whole operation was reminiscent of some of the horror stories emanating from Germany during World War II," said the workers' attorney, Andrew M. Wyatt, at a press conference announcing the lawsuit, which named August III and A-B security chief Gary Prindiville.

In legal papers, Wyatt cited a sworn statement by the head of the private investigation firm, saying he was told by an A-B executive that "the corporation's legal department had approved [the raid]" and that August III had said "the search better be conducted or (expletive) heads would roll."

But for the embarrassing news stories, August III should have been pleased with the outcome of the raid. No cache of drugs was found, just some traces of marijuana under the seat of one car, which would suggest that there was no significant drug problem at the Los Angeles plant. You could expect to find more than that in any random employee parking lot in America.

Contrary to PR-generated press reports, August IV had not "toned down his wild ways." He had just become more circumspect. As his star rose inside the company, he began gathering his own team of executives. They were a little younger than the team he inherited, by about five years, and he seemed to choose them more for their fealty to him than their knowledge of the business. One of them was Jim Sprick, a former member of the millionaires' boys club. "Sprick was given a VP position and moved up to the ninth floor, and no one could figure out why, other than he was close to the Fourth," said one of the older executives, who was unaware that Sprick's testimony had helped sway the jury in the Fourth's 1986 car chase trial.

Sprick and a handful of the younger executives formed a protective, enabling circle around the Fourth. Whether he was out having dinner, watching football games on TV at home, or traveling on company business, they were ever-present. He called them "my guys." Others in the company called them "the entourage," and several of his friends referred to them as "the jackals." On business trips, they drove the car, carried his money and credit cards, picked up the tabs, and made sure that young women were on the evening's menu. They usually accomplished the latter task by placing an order with the local distributor, telling him what August liked and instructing him to be certain to have several women available. Most of the distributors didn't like it, especially the older married ones. They weren't being asked to provide hookers, just beautiful young women who might want to party with a rich young beer baron, but it felt uncomfortably close to pimping. They felt they couldn't say no to the young man destined to inherit the company in a few years, or complain to his father. If they had been around long enough, they knew that August III and Gussie both had operated in a similar fashion back in the day, though not with the Fourth's singleness of purpose.

In fact, sex seemed to be the one thing that the Fourth and his father bonded over. The two would get into discussions on the subject with such discomfiting specificity that their fellow A-B executives would sometimes excuse themselves from the table, saying they had to go to the restroom, rather than hear more. "It was like listening to Satan talk," said one former colleague. Another remembered having breakfast with them on a business trip in Europe. "August IV had been out to a bar the night before, and he said he'd met a beautiful girl who spoke English beautifully, and he gave her a $100 bill and asked her to go to the room with him, but she tore it in half and gave it back to him. I said, 'Good for her,' and they both looked at me and said, 'What do you mean?'"

The Fourth's relentless womanizing made for great cocktail chatter at company social gatherings, where his colleagues and their wives watched to see what manner of pretty young thing he would bring. They were generally "nice girls" caught up in the thrill of dating the Busch brewery heir and naively hoping there might be a place for them in the kingdom. Most often they were wannabe models, actresses, or beauty queens. "He had a weakness for pageant girls," a friend said. The A-B wives learned not to get attached to them because they tended to disappear without notice. One girl arrived in New Orleans with him, expecting to spend the week as his date at the company's Super Bowl festivities. Instead, she found herself packed up and put on the plane back to St. Louis in less than twenty-four hours. The next night another beautiful young woman was sitting by his side at the dinner table.

The Fourth once picked up a girl in a nightclub in Dallas and flew her back to St. Louis with him on the company jet. After a few days, he sent the jet back to Dallas to fetch the woman's two toy poodles. Just as quickly, the woman and her dogs were headed back to Texas. "August IV fell in love with whomever he was with," said a friend of more than fifteen years.

After breaking up with his fiancée Judy Buchmiller, the Fourth dated an aspiring actress named Sage Linville, who moved from southern California to St. Louis to be with him. "There's a girl I'm very much in love with and she may be the one," he told a reporter, adding playfully. "Sage Busch is an interesting name, isn't it? I'm not making predictions about that." He also dated a stunning blonde named Shandi Finnessy, a Miss Missouri who went on to become Miss USA and a runner-up in Donald Trump's Miss Universe competition.

One relatively long-term relationship ended on an ugly note when the Fourth's rottweiler horribly bit the young woman on the face. The attack occurred late at night in his home on Lindell Boulevard, across from Forest Park. As the Fourth was rushing the woman to the emergency room, he called one of his guys, frantic, and told him to go to the house and "clean up the mess."

"What do you mean?" the other man asked.

"You'll see; just go," the Fourth replied.

The man later told another executive that he found cocaine at the house and evidence of kinky sex, suggesting that the dog might have attacked the girl because he perceived that she was hurting his master. The Fourth told people that she had gotten up in the middle of the night to get a drink of water, and the dog must have mistaken her for an intruder. The girl vanished from his life, supposedly with a hefty financial settlement. The dog stayed.

The media has long characterized August IV's sexual escapades as a "playboy" lifestyle, often employing that old-school adjective as a kind of editorial wink, telegraphing an unmistakable admiration for his accomplishment, as if to say we should all be so lucky. Several of his colleagues even coined a secret nickname for him that was intended as a humorous reference to his seemingly constant priapic state. "How's Woody doing?" they'd say. Or, "Has Woody weighed in on this yet?" But to some who knew him over a number of years, the Fourth's incessant coupling seemed more a sad compulsion born of a deep psychological wound. A female friend suggested that his need to win over beautiful women constantly stemmed from a severe case of acne that had marred his looks and played havoc with his self-confidence when he was a teenager. A male friend opined that it was because "he could never get a hug from his dad."

Whatever the cause, one result was that between the ever-changing women and the ubiquitous entourage, August IV was rarely if ever by himself, almost as if he were terrified of being alone.

Fortunately for him, he could afford not to be. In the late 1990s, he began hosting weekend parties at the company's luxury compound on the Lake of the Ozarks, a 55,000-acre man-made lake in the Ozark Mountains about a forty-five-minute helicopter flight from St. Louis. Started by August III in 1982, the woodsy compound featured four separate residential units, a tennis court, a helicopter landing pad, an elaborate boat dock with a full-service kitchen, and a fleet of half a dozen watercraft, including a large cabin cruiser, a high speed powerboat, and two houseboats. With a staff of twenty-one in the summer months, the complex could accommodate up to a hundred guests.

The lake property was not a place that A-B's rank-and-file workers or middle managers ever visited. August III used it primarily as a conference center for his highest-ranking executives, members of the strategy committee, who would be flown to the lake on corporate aircraft, sometimes with their wives, for several days of meetings and relaxation. He also hosted Busch family gatherings, birthdays, and holiday celebrations at the compound, all sumptuously provisioned but low-key affairs. There were no wild parties when August III was in residence at No. 4, the largest residential unit on the property. Key executives, important distributors, close Busch friends, and even some Cardinals players also were allowed to reserve units for getaways with their families.

The atmosphere at the compound started to change, however, after the Fourth became vice president of marketing and began showing up at the lake with "his guys" nearly every weekend. According to a former supervisor of the household staff, "the work hours got a lot longer because he would stay up late partying, and the staff had to stay on the job until he was done and dismissed them."

Unlike his father, who preferred barbecuing his own steaks to going out to eat, the Fourth hit all the hot spots in the area, from the Blue Heron restaurant, where you could find a $1,200 cabernet on the wine list, to the Horny Toad, a raucous roadhouse hookup joint where cocaine and oxycodone (known as "hillbilly heroin") could be purchased in the crowd almost as easily as a Bud could be bought at the bar. According to local legend, the Fourth once paid a cocktail waitress at the Horny Toad $1,000 to deliver a round of drinks topless.

When the clubs closed, the Fourth and the entourage usually brought some patrons back to the compound, where they liked to fire guns across the water from the boat dock and set off fireworks. "They set the place on fire once," said the former staffer. During the day on weekends, they hopped into one or more of the company boats and headed for "Party Cove," which the *New York Times* called "the oldest established permanent floating bacchanal in the country." The party took place in Anderson Hollow Cove, where more than a thousand boats would be anchored so closely together that you could step from one to another amid much mooning, "titty flashing," and public fornication to the cheers of spectators.

In his posh fifty-foot cruiser or conspicuously branded Budweiser powerboat, the Fourth was always the biggest fish in the cove, and he reveled in his celebrity. The bikinied females who flocked aboard his boat were not the same as the girls he picked up in Central West End bars or brought to company parties. "They were a different class of women altogether," said a friend. "These were more the 'rode hard and put up wet' gals, coarser and more worn. And they reacted to him as if he were a god."

In an interview with a local magazine, the Fourth described a typical lake weekend from an entirely different perspective. "Here we can work in a non-traditional, natural setting," he said. "The great thing about the Lake is that we can walk into any bar or restaurant and just talk to people, engaging consumers while they're enjoying our beverages. It's a tremendous opportunity to get people's honest feedback about a particular product."

The lake became the Fourth's refuge, a place where he was always surrounded by people who catered to him and protected him, including local sheriff's deputies, whom he paid to moonlight as his personal bodyguards and weekend security detail at the compound. "His father had no security," said a former compound employee. "The Fourth was kind of obsessed with it, especially after 9-11." That sort of patronage bought a lot of indulgence from law enforcement in the small rural community of Lake Ozark, Mo. "The Fourth liked the lake because he felt he could control the environment there, and no one in authority was watching or judging him," said a friend.

Over the period of a few years, the Fourth literally took over the lake facility. His father used the compound less frequently, and other A-B executives were uncomfortable with the increasingly rowdy atmosphere. Eventually, management of the property came under the purview of A-B's vice president of hospitality, Jim Sprick. From then on, the Fourth "operated it like a little party palace," said a former company employee.

The Fourth changed the atmosphere at the St. Louis office, too, as he moved to solidify his position in the hierarchy of the company. Buoyed by his accolades for A-B's ad campaigns, he morphed into a "hard-charging, aggressive, assumptive guy, entitled and arrogant," according to one executive who worked with him at the time. "He'd have dinner with his father on Sunday night and then come in on Monday and say, 'My dad and I talked and this is what we are doing.' His father inadvertently empowered him. People knew he was probably going to be chairman one day, so they got out of his way; they deferred to him even though his actual position didn't dictate that deference."

Inevitably, resentments sprang up between the older members of the management team and the younger men the Fourth was bringing in to the mix.

"You had the big brothers and the little brothers," said one observer of the dynamic. The big brothers were, for the most part, loyal to August III, and felt that helping the Fourth succeed was part of their duty to the Chief. The little brothers felt they owed allegiance solely to the Fourth, and they saw his father as a tyrant intent on holding on to power for as long as he could. It was a repeat of the pattern established thirty years earlier, when a young August III and his corporate planners butted heads with Gussie and his buddies up on the third floor of the old administration building.

The big brothers thought the Fourth was too caught up in the glamour aspects of the business—the cool TV commercials, sports sponsorships, and lavish Super Bowl parties—and didn't pay enough attention to the sales functions of the brewery and its distributors, the gritty work that moved the product out of the plants and into the beer coolers of America. They looked askance at the Fourth's growing relationship with Ron Burkle, a onetime California supermarket magnate turned billionaire investor whose reputation for womanizing matched or exceeded his own and whose parties at his Beverly Hills mansion, "Green Acres," featured the sort of guests the Fourth would never have bumped into at the Horny Toad, including former president and Mrs. Clinton and the Reverend Jesse Jackson and his sons Yusef and Jonathan. The

Fourth hosted Burkle on at least one occasion at the lake compound, where the staff had no idea who he was but took to calling him "the rich guy."

The big brothers grumbled that while the Fourth was hobnobbing with Burkle, he avoided mixing with people far more important to the company. "He did not respect our distributors," said one. "He viewed them as hired help rather than the wealthy independent businessmen that they were."

"He had the attention span of a flea," said another. "He could *not* finish a dinner or a round of golf with important clients or wholesalers. He was always saying, 'I gotta go.'"

At a meeting with executives of 7-Eleven at the company's offices in Dallas, for example, the Fourth "got up and walked out when the discussion went longer than he'd planned," said an executive who was present. "Everyone was shocked because they wanted to share their strategy with us. The meeting went on for another hour without him, and when we got back to the airport he was waiting on the plane. We asked, 'How could you walk out on one of our largest customers?' He said, 'I'm sorry, but I just couldn't sit there anymore.'"

(In contrast, August III once waited several hours for the CEO of 7-Eleven, whom he was supposed to meet for dinner at the Ritz-Carlton. But the other man was flying in on his own plane, and there was some delay. "So after about an hour, August asked, 'How much business do we do with 7-Eleven?'" said a former executive who was present. "I told him twenty-four million cases a year, and he said, 'Holy shit! I'll wait all night for someone who buys that much beer from us.'")

Sometimes the Fourth wouldn't show up for meetings at all. When his father and all the other senior executives gathered in Palm Springs for a long-scheduled golf weekend with one of A-B's biggest customers, the vice president of marketing had his assistant phone in his regrets at the last minute. "Where's August?" his father asked a subordinate at the kickoff cocktail party. "He was supposed be here." The Fourth was forty-five minutes away by corporate jet, hanging out with his new best friend Ron Burkle in Los Angeles, where he remained for the entire weekend. To the big brothers, it was another example of his lack of work ethic.

The little brothers had an entirely different view of their boss. They saw him—and by extension themselves—as the hip breath of fresh air the company needed to blow away the smell of the Clydesdale stables that seemed to cling to everything. They pointed to the success of the Bud Light "I Love You, Man" and "Real Men of Genius" campaigns as evidence that the Fourth was himself a marketing genius, capable of leading the company to new heights of success if his father would just support him and not keep undermining him all the time. The Fourth fostered the latter sentiment by posting some personal notes his father had sent him on the wall in his home, where others could see them. "They were painful to read, stern and businesslike," said a frequent visitor to his house.

The most loyal of the little brothers sometimes characterized the Fourth as a "visionary" or even a "great man," but at the same time they ignored or covered up behavior that belied such descriptions. They knew, for example, that his partying was beginning to interfere with his job performance. "Did it ever make sense to you why he would never attend a meeting before noon? It was because he'd gotten wrecked the night before and he couldn't make one before that," one of the little brothers confided to a big brother years later, after the takeover deal went down. "And how many meetings did he cancel out on?"

The older, married executives missed the signs because they didn't stay up with Fourth into the wee hours, when his demeanor changed and he got a little loopy and poignant, and stood with his face a little too close, as if something more than alcohol was at work. The big brothers attributed his unavailability to laziness. The little brothers didn't tell them what was really going on for fear they would tell Dad.

The Fourth's mother, Susie, apparently knew enough to call several of the older executives and ask them to help her arrange an intervention for her son. They thought she was being overly dramatic. Besides, they'd never seen the Fourth any more impaired than a lot of them got on occasion. It sort of went with the territory. They respectfully declined Susie's request, figuring that if they tried to rope the Fourth into an intervention and he didn't go for it, then they'd be looking for another job pretty quickly.

In 2001 the Fourth took half a dozen or so members of his executive team on a working vacation to Key West, Florida, where they found a new safe haven for misbehaving. They rented a secure floor on one wing of the Hilton and, with the 172-foot *Big Eagle* yacht and *Little Eagle* speedboat docked nearby for their use, commenced two weeks of epic partying that seared them into the memories of the locals. They quickly made themselves known at Rick's, the town's largest nightclub complex, which boasted half a dozen separately operated bars, including a topless one called the Red Garter.

"The Budweiser guys," as they became known around town, usually ate dinner in private rooms at the Fourth's two favorite restaurants, Shula's on the Beach and Benihana, running up bills of $5,000 to $6,000 a night. They threw parties on the *Big Eagle* that cost "a couple hundred grand," according to a local business owner who helped provision the boat. "They would send people out to get them cases of Cristal champagne and Opus One wine. Big-ticket items. Sometimes they'd have people drive to Miami and buy it all out, *magnums* of Cristal. There'd be none left anywhere, all the way up the coast to Ft. Lauderdale."

They once sent someone on an emergency helicopter flight to

Joe's Stone Crab Restaurant in Miami after the Fourth complained that the crab claws that were about to be served at a large dinner party were too small. When the bigger ones arrived in time, he instructed that they were to be served "only to my guys," not the other guests. "He took care of his boys; he showed them a good time."

The Fourth's first sojourn to Key West resembled one of his grandfather Gussie's booze-and-broads cruises—on steroids. But when the Budweiser guys came back to town a few months later— and on subsequent biannual trips—the nightly entertainment program would have shocked the old man. The A-B men no longer had to pick up women in the bars because unbeknownst to company higher-ups, women were provided for them through several local escort agencies. According to a Key West business owner who was involved in the supply chain, a midlevel manager in A-B's St. Louis office made the initial contact with the escort agencies and then arranged for a local distributor to write checks to "cash" in the amount of $20,000 upon request. The distributor gave the checks to an intermediary, who cashed them and paid the women directly. The distributor then billed A-B $20,000 for "models."

How much the women were paid depended on whether they were "good girls" or "bad girls." As one participant explained, "Good girls were arm candy, pretty and intelligent." They worked the early shift. They attended dinner parties, mixed with guests and business clients, were generally charming, and then went home with $400 or $500 for their night's work. The "bad girls" worked the late shift. The A-B executives jokingly referred to them as "the finishers." They were expected to provide sexual services, for which they received $1,500 to $2,000 per night. "All the girls were very high class. That's what they liked, even for bad girls." They would request six to eight women a night. "Some nights they'd go through the entire $20,000."

One year, Yusef Jackson, Jesse Jackson's son, joined in the fun.

Having met the Fourth at one of Ron Burkle's Green Acres soirées, Yusef and his brother Jonathan had been allowed to purchase a successful A-B distributorship in the section of Chicago that was home to both the Bulls and the Blackhawks. The 1998 deal raised eyebrows in the city because of the brothers' ages, twenty-eight and thirty-two, respectively, their lack of business experience, beer or otherwise, and the fact that they appeared to have paid far less than market value for the company. Their father, who once threatened a national boycott of Anheuser-Busch over its minority hiring policies, reacted angrily when the media questioned the deal, saying it amounted to "racial profiling" of his sons.

Typically, the Fourth "fell head over heels in love" with one of the escorts in Key West. "She looked like Audrey Hepburn. He wanted her to meet his family. He said, 'Leave your job and come to St. Louis with me.' He seemed to be looking for something he could never find."

According to the intermediary, escorts who worked for different agencies and didn't know one another "all told the same story" about their experience with the Fourth. "He had some deep-seated stuff going on, a sexual dependency that went way, way, *way* beyond Tiger Woods."

For all the money the A-B executives spread around town, they did not make many friends among the serving class in Key West. "They were like cowboys coming off a cattle drive," said one former bar employee. "People were like, 'Oh, great, here come the Budweiser guys again,' and they'd roll their eyes because they were the cheapest sons of bitches. They wouldn't tip. They didn't feel that they had to. No one would want to wait on them.

"The bellhops at the Hilton hated it when they came down. [The Fourth] was never expected to pay for anything. They'd always say, 'I got this. I got this,' and they'd shoo him away. And then we got stiffed.

"We hated the Budweiser people. They thought the whole town should stop because they were there. We were working for a living, and they would treat us like shit."

The former workers drew a sharp distinction between the Fourth and his guys, however. "They were obnoxious pricks who acted like everyone was beneath them. He wasn't that way. He was always smiling, asking people how they were doing. His guys didn't give a shit."

"He was the nice, easygoing, mellow, fun-loving one who never asked for anything. He worked out every day. He'd party until three a.m. and be in the gym at five a.m. I never seen him drunk or high or anything. The other guys were drunk all the time, staggering, trashed."

Amid the bacchanalia, August apparently tried to maintain a level of control. "He made sure no one brought drugs on the [*Big Eagle*]," said one observer. "It was a big thing with him. You were not allowed to be on drugs or possess them." Once, when he learned that one of the escorts had called a cabdriver to bring her some coke, "he had her removed from the boat." The removal was effected by local police officers that worked off-duty security details for the Fourth. One of them was assigned to wrangle the escorts. He "made sure the girls got where they were supposed to be or got rid of a girl if [the A-B executives] decided they didn't like her." He also made sure they didn't carry any recording devices or cameras after one escort obtained pictures of the Fourth "in a compromising situation, and she was made to leave town."

The Fourth's concern about people bringing drugs on board may have sprung from the fact that both boats belonged to Bernie Little, A-B's longtime distributor in north-central Florida, and one of his father's closest friends. And it could have been because he was on thin ice with his father for flunking one of the company's random drug tests. According to the story he told to at least one of his closest associates, he tested positive for cocaine, and the results were relayed up the line from the human resources department to Pat Stokes's office to his father and the board of directors. But he'd managed to avoid the usual consequences—company-ordered counseling and subsequent dismissal—by vehemently denying that he had knowingly taken the drug. "He claimed that somebody spiked his drink; that he was at a party and someone must have given him something without his knowing it. He didn't report it because he didn't know it had happened."

The story was not credible, as anyone familiar with the properties and effects of cocaine would know. But August III and the board apparently bought it. "After some kind of negotiation, an agreement was reached in which the Fourth signed an affidavit swearing that he did not knowingly consume drugs and did not have a drug problem. He said it was an isolated incident and that he would never be involved in anything like it again."

In the 1997 *Fortune* magazine article, August III explained his philosophy on employee discipline. "Make sure your standards are high," he was quoted as saying, "and if someone doesn't meet those standards, take them out. I don't care whether it's family or not."

In 2002, in the wake of the failed drug test, he approved the Fourth's promotion to president of Anheuser-Busch, Inc., the position once held by Denny Long.

20

"A BAD APPLE AT THE TOP"

On June 16, 2002, August III turned sixty-five. He'd promised to be retired by then, telling *Fortune* magazine in 1997, "At that point, this is a younger person's game." Having seen what happened when his father stayed in the job too long, he always said he would never put the company or his successor through something like that again.

When the time came, however, he reneged. Rather than retire, he simply relinquished the title of CEO and stepped away from the day-to-day duties of running the company, while retaining chairmanship of the board. To no one's surprise, Patrick Stokes was named CEO, marking the first time in the company's 126-year history that a non–family member was placed in operational control. August IV was elevated to president of Anheuser-Busch, Inc., the brewing division of the company.

Business Week magazine called it "a succession process as tightly orchestrated as any in the House of Windsor," with the Fourth in effect being given five years—until the sixty-year-old Stokes retired at sixty-five—to get his act together, while his twenty-five-year-old half brother, Steven, worked at their father's side to learn the business in case he didn't.

The Fourth was thirty-eight, the same age his father had been when he ousted Gussie and took over the company. With the possible exception of the Fourth and his team, however, no one thought he was ready to run the company. *Business Week* credited him with "showing an instinctive understanding of the kind of advertisements that stirred young men," but noted that "he hasn't made a name for himself in any other way": "He has never operated the company's network of a dozen breweries, managed its complex relations with independent wholesalers or run its international and theme park units."

August III declined to talk to *Business Week* for the November 2002 article about the management changes, leaving it to the Fourth and Pat Stokes to speak for the company and assure the financial community that all was well within the beer kingdom. The reporter pretty much ignored whatever Stokes had to say and pressed the Fourth about his reputation as a "hard-partying guy," pointing out that it could prove a "hindrance" for a company supposedly trying a promote the responsible use of its products, and asking him to respond to stories about his frequent business trips with "female companions."

It's unlikely the Fourth had ever been confronted so directly by a reporter about his private life, and it apparently caused him to lose his affable cool momentarily. Claiming that he paid for the expenses of any guests who traveled with him and always engaged in "responsible consumption of our products," he snapped, "I didn't get where I am today without performing."

Besides, he argued, his vaunted partying was actually a valuable form of research. "I think I have benefited from my lifestyle [by] being able to be very active in the marketplace," he said. "That has allowed me to understand our customer better and, hopefully, do a better job of creating products and images that are attractive to that customer."

The Fourth always dreaded the inevitable questions from reporters about his Tucson accident and the death of Michele Frederick. "Why do they keep bringing that up?" he often complained to his colleagues. "Why do you keep doing the interviews?" they sometimes replied. This time, he responded to *Business Week* with a spin that could only have been crafted by A-B's public relations department.

"That's a chapter that's never gone, that I will always remember," he said, apparently forgetting that he'd long claimed total amnesia about that night. "But I honestly believe that, as painful as the memory is, that experience will make me a better keeper of responsibility for our products." He seemed to be saying that some good had come from the tragedy after all, that Michele had not died in vain.

Business Week rubbed more salt into the Fourth's wounds by pointing out that his father apparently shared a closer bond with his younger half brother Steven and that his stepmother, Ginny, "has made no secret of her wish to see her son Steven take over the company."

"[Steven] spends a great deal of time with my father," the Fourth acknowledged. "He is a very smart guy and he does a great job for my father. Other than that, I can't really comment." Asked what he thought Steven's next job with the company might be, he replied tersely, "I don't know." Of his own future, he would only say, "I don't take anything for granted in this company. It's not a foregone conclusion that I'll go any farther.

"I love my father," he said. "Take a walk through my house and it looks like a father museum. Every picture on the wall is of my father, or me and my father—to the point where Mom comes over and says, 'where are all my pictures?'" (One Father's Day, he gave his dad a twenty-minute video he'd commissioned, showing moments they'd shared over the years, and he told friends that his father had cried when he viewed it.) "But he's been extremely tough on me," he told *Business Week*. "Maybe you can call it tough love."

Or indulgence. After all, his father had spent millions of dollars and an enormous amount of time and energy shielding him from the consequences of his actions. And now, with three strikes against him—Tucson, the St. Louis police chase, and a flunked drug test—he was getting yet another swing of the bat in a position that paid him nearly $2 million a year (in salary, bonus, and stock), with a ridiculously generous expense account and the use of a helicopter and a private jet. His father had even helped him acquire a new $3 million mansion on ten wooded acres in Huntleigh Village, where his grandfather Gussie and great-grandfather August A. once rode after the foxes in the Bridlespur Hunt.

The Fourth bought the 6,500-square-foot, six-bedroom home from hockey star Brett Hull and turned it into a high-fenced fortress with an elaborate security system that featured surveillance cameras around the house and grounds and ballpark-style banks of outdoor lights that lit up the entire property at night so that no one could approach the house without been seen, recorded, and very likely set upon by his dogs. He created yet another safe haven where he could do what he wanted without fear of interference from any higher authority. All it lacked was a moat.

More than just fodder for the financial media, the relationship between the Fourth and his father was a matter of constant conversation inside the company and the Busch family. Among the latter group, there had long been concern that August III was in denial about the nature and extent of the Fourth's partying. In 1984, Adolphus IV went to August III about rumors of his son's cocaine use. "I need to talk to you because I am hearing that August IV has a serious drug problem," he said. "I don't have any agenda; I'm not thinking you are going to can his ass and ask me to come down there and go to work. But if people are telling me about it, then it has to be all over the whole city." August III confronted the Fourth, who said the rumors were not true.

By 2002 August III should have had, at the very least, a strong suspicion that the Fourth had a predilection for overindulgence. And yet, despite all he knew or suspected, August still put his son in charge of the brewing division, which accounted for 77 percent of the company's $12.9 billion in sales and 94 percent of its net income.

What was he thinking? He was not a reckless man. In business at least, he carefully planned and vetted every move. So why then did he risk handing the Fourth more responsibility, more authority, indeed, more temptation? "That's the biggest contradiction in the man," said Adophus IV. "He held everyone accountable. He held everyone to the line, except when it came to his own son, who would take over the company, even though [August] knew for twenty-seven years the problem his son had."

The most logical, credible explanation was that even after all the heartache and embarrassment the Fourth had caused, and in spite of the disappointment, frustration, and rage that August felt, he still believed in his son. So he doubled down on the bloodline, betting that his firstborn would finally emerge from his wild oats phase, settle down, get married, and run the hell out of the company the way four generations of Busch males had done before him. And he hedged his bet by staying on as chairman longer than he'd planned. The media speculated it was because he couldn't bring himself to relinquish control, and while that may have been true, it was just as likely that he felt he had no choice.

The five years preceding the Fourth's promotion to president had been good ones for the company. While the industry had grown by an anemic 2 percent, A-B's net income had increased by nearly 12 percent. "We were driving the growth in the industry," said one executive. "Without us, the industry would have shown a decline." During a time when the S&P 500 had remained flat, the price of A-B shares had risen 61 percent, and the stock had split two-for-one twice. For the first time, A-B passed the 100 million–barrel mark. Its total of 101.8 million barrels in 2002 bested second-place Miller by more than 63 million barrels and added up to a 49.2 percent share of the U.S. market.

A-B's continued dominance helped move Miller's parent company, Philip Morris, to finally throw in the towel in its thirty-one-year adventure in the beer business. In May, the cigarette maker sold Miller to London-based South African Breweries Ltd in a deal valued at $5.6 billion in stock, cash, and assumed debt. The merged companies would be called SABMiller.

August III no doubt took considerable pride in the fact that A-B had vanquished a competitor as formidable as Philip Morris, and he surely felt a measure of personal satisfaction in *Forbes* magazine ranking him as the best-compensated CEO in the food, drink, and tobacco industry, averaging $13.5 million per year in salary, bonus, and stock benefits. But the creation of SABMiller was a troubling development. It pointed up A-B's main vulnerability.

Prior to the merger, SAB had been the world's fourth-largest brewer, and Miller the sixth. Together they constituted the second-largest brewing operation on the planet, behind Anheuser-Busch. A-B's No.1 ranking was based on the volume of beer it produced, however, not the breadth and scope of its operation, and the company sold 90 percent of its beer inside the United States, making it a powerhouse domestically but a comparative weakling overseas. With U.S. per capita consumption trending downward, brewing industry experts scoffed at August's idea of achieving a 60 percent share of the market, believing that A-B was rapidly approaching saturation level at 50 percent. In order to grow, the company needed to expand in the international marketplace. SABMiller made that more difficult.

August had begun moving cautiously into foreign markets in the late 1980s, usually by entering into equity-based partnerships with leading breweries that gave A-B a controlling interest in a joint venture to brew and distribute Budweiser in their country and a minority stake in the brewery itself. It was a conservative strategy that allowed A-B to control the quality of its product while avoiding the debt that would result from buying the breweries outright. In this way, A-B gained a foothold in the 1990s in three of the world's highest potential markets, acquiring a 10 percent stake in Tsingtao, the largest brewery in China, a 37 percent interest in Grupo Modelo, the largest brewery in Mexico, and a 10 percent interest in Antarctica, the second-largest brewery in Brazil.

At the same time, however, August had passed up a chance to buy South African Breweries before it began gobbling up smaller breweries in Central Europe—including Pilsner Urquell—on its way to becoming a global player capable of mounting a multibillion-dollar purchase of Miller. He could have gone after Guinness before it was acquired by the British food and beverage giant Grad Metropolitan, but he didn't. Nor did he make a play for Canada's No. 1 brewer and A-B's longtime Canadian distribution partner, Labatt, when it became the target of a hostile takeover attempt in 1995 and ultimately agreed to be bought by the Belgian powerhouse Interbrew SA for $2 billion.

August's unwillingness to risk more of A-B's enormous wealth to acquire controlling interests in foreign breweries frustrated and sometimes infuriated some members of his strategy committee who worried that he was being penny wise but pound foolish at a time when the industry was consolidating globally. After buying Labatt, for example, Interbrew scooped up two of England's biggest brewers, Whitbread (for $600 million) and Bass ($3.47 billion), along with Germany's Beck's ($1.58 billion). SABMiller acquired a controlling interest in Italy's Peroni ($256 million) and Holland's Grolsch ($1.2 billion). Closer to home, SAB Miller acquired Grupo Bavaria, Colombia's largest brewery (and the second largest in South America) for $7.8 billion in 2005, the same year that Adolph Coors Co., America's third largest brewer, merged with Canada's largest, Molson, in a stock swap deal worth $6 billion. Prior to the merger, Molson and Coors were controlled by the families that founded them (in 1786 and 1873, respectively).

And yet, amid all the rapid consolidation, August III seemed to be channeling his father toward the end of the old man's reign, trying to avoid spending money by scuttling deals that members of the strategy committee brought to the table.

As one former committee member recalled, "At the last minute, twenty-four hours before the deal was to be signed, he would say, 'We are not going with that price; we are going with this price.' We'd say, 'But then you are going to crater the deal,' and he would say, 'Fine, we will crater the deal, but I am not going to pay that price.'"

Even August's corporate planning mentor and longtime consultant Robert Weinberg agreed that, in hindsight, his foreign expansion strategy was too cautious.

"August is a damned smart man, one of the few people in the business who was significantly smarter than he thought he was," the eighty-four-year-old Weinberg said recently. "And he could move mountains if someone could convince him the mountains could be moved and this is the way to move them. But I don't think he was willing to take big enough chances. When push came to shove, he was too conservative. And when you are too conservative, you are throwing away opportunity."

August's Brazilian adventure in the 1990s is a case in point.

A-B was the first American brewer to invest in Brazil, which was then the world's fastest-growing beer market, increasing at a rate of 15 percent a year. August first attempted to strike a deal with Brazil's biggest brewery, Brahma, which was owned by a trio of investment bankers—Marcel Telles, Carlos Sicupira, and Jorge Lemann. With a combined personal net worth of $10.6 billion, the three men also controlled the retail giant Lojas Americanas, known as "the Wal-Mart of Brazil." August hosted Telles and Lemann at A-B's theme park resort in Williamsburg, Virginia, and gave them a personal tour of the brewery there. In the end, however, he invested $105 million in Antarctica instead because, typically, he thought Brahma's price was too high.

Several years later, Telles, Lemann, and Sicupria approached August with an audacious proposal to merge Anheuser-Busch, Brahma, and Antarctica into a western hemisphere behemoth that they characterized "the Coca-Cola of beer." August said no to the idea, and two years later, in 1999, the brash Brazilians bought Antarctica out from under him and merged it with Brahma to form AmBev, becoming the world's third-largest brewer. August still could have joined the merger because A-B's deal with Antarctica gave it the option to increase its stake to 30 percent and place a representative on the board. Once again, however, August thought the price was too high, and he opted to sell back A-B's minority stake in Antarctica.

"The evaluation he got from his corporate planning analysts and consultants convinced him that if he bought into AmBev, the impact on the stock would be a 10 to 20 percent decline in the short term," a former executive said. "It would have a negative impact on corporate earnings, so stock analysts would hammer them."

Passing up the opportunity to be a partner in AmBev is regarded as one of August III's two great professional mistakes. Five years later, the Brazilians merged AmBev with Belgium-based

InterBrew to form InBev, which knocked A-B out of its long-held spot as the world's largest brewer (by volume)—"The New King of Beers," *Money* magazine proclaimed—and set the table for its eventual takeover. Had August been willing to pay the price in 1999—a mere $210 million—he might have been able to head off the takeover.

His other great mistake, of course, was continuing to promote his son.

When August IV was named president in 2002, the company's fortunes had begun to turn. All the award-winning TV commercials had managed to halt the decline in Budweiser sales, but not increase them. For the first time in nearly fifty years, Gussie's beloved Budweiser had fallen to second place, overtaken by Bud Light, the upstart offspring that no one in the family had wanted in the beginning. A-B could still boast the two top-selling brands, but the switch in places was worrisome because Budweiser, not Bud Light, was the spearhead in the company's foreign expansion plan. As the Fourth said when he was promoted to vice president of marketing, "The question isn't 'Can Budweiser grow again?' We must grow Budweiser again. Budweiser is our ticket to go international. Budweiser is our Coca-Cola."

In the first year of the Fourth's presidency, however, A-B's sales and stock price flattened as Budweiser began to sink again. He responded by pouring money into image marketing, ad campaigns, and new product development. With wine and spirit sales on the rise and cutting into beer sales industry-wide, he approved a $60 million promotional budget for a new product called Bacardi Silver, a clear malt-based, rum-and-citrus-flavored beverage developed in partnership with the world's leading rum distiller. With the Fourth overseeing the rollout, the budget naturally covered the cost of a garishly branded Bacardi Silver high-speed powerboat and racing team.

Beverage industry analysts noted that A-B was a little late to the races with Bacardi Silver; sales of so-called malternative or alcopop beverages—Smirnoff Ice, Captain Morgan Gold, Sauza Diablo, Skyy Blue—peaked just as Bacardi Silver hit the market. The *New York Times* said the new beverage category was "starting to show signs it is a fad rather than a trend."

A-B sales managers grumbled that pushing a product so strongly identified with a distilled spirit seemed counterproductive. Hadn't America's brewers been battling with distillers over the alcohol consumer's buck since back before prohibition? But now they were encouraging people to pick up a bottle that said Bacardi rather than Budweiser or Bud Light? It seemed like bad business.

The Fourth apparently disagreed. In September 2005, A-B established a wholly owned subsidiary specifically tasked with developing and marketing distilled spirits. The subsidiary was called Long Tail Libations, Inc. after the best-selling book *The Long Tail: The New Economics of Culture and Commerce*, which referred to "the long tail of the fast-falling demand curve in economics," and posited the theory that in the new economics of viral marketing and Internet sales, an offering of numerous smaller-selling products could equal or exceed the value of a blockbuster.

"A challenging time calls for looking at things differently," the Fourth told *Fortune* magazine.

Long Tail Libations' first libation, called Jekyll & Hyde, was definitely different. Aimed at twenty-one- to twenty-seven-year-old consumers, it came packaged in two "nesting" bottles—one containing a 60 proof berry-flavored scarlet liquor (Jekyll), and the other a jet-black 80 proof liquor tasting of spices, herbs, and licorice (Hyde). The two liquids were supposed to be combined in a shot glass, where they separated into layers, with Hyde on top. J&H was marketed to bars and nightclubs as a sexy "back bar" display item and sold in retail stores for as much as $24. It was not a drink any self-respecting veteran of the Great Beer War would ever lift to his lips, but it apparently appealed to at least one forty-one-year-old beer company president who'd spent a lot of time "researching" twenty-one- to twenty-seven-year-old women in bars and nightclubs.

At the same time the Fourth was spending millions developing and marketing "innovative" new drinks, he further alienated his veteran sales force by slashing budgets for basic merchandising programs that were the traditional nuts and bolts of selling beer. He ordered a 50 percent cutback in the national account menu program, through which A-B covered the cost of producing menus for national restaurant chains such as T.G.I. Friday's, Bennigan's, and Hooter's in exchange for product visibility in the menus— encouraging patrons to order a cold Bud or Bud Light with their hot wings. The big chains had no trouble finding other beverage companies to pick up their menu tab, and the sale of A-B products went down in their restaurants.

"The Fourth had no appreciation or respect for the fundamentals of sales," said a former sales executive. "If it wasn't glamorous, he wasn't interested. He never missed a chance to fly to the Grammy Awards or the MTV Awards and spend three days in Los Angeles. He loved that juice. But the MTV Awards didn't sell beer for us. The menu program did."

The proof was in the performance. A-B's sales fell by more than 2 million barrels in 2005, causing net income to drop nearly 18 percent, the first significant decline in ten years.

Toward the end of 2005, A-B began test marketing another Long Tail product called Spykes, a caffeine-infused malt beverage containing 12 percent alcohol that was designed to compete with sweet-tasting energy drinks such as Red Bull and Rock Star. A-B promoted it as a dual-purpose drink that could be either used as a mixer or tossed back neat: "It gives kick to your beer, flavor to your drink, and is a perfect shot." The trouble was, Spykes came in mango, melon, peach, raspberry, and hot chocolate flavors and was packaged in candy-colored two-ounce bottles that resembled nothing so much as nail polish and could be secreted in the smallest of purses. At a price of less than $1 per bottle, Spykes was, as one critic noted sarcastically, "The perfect drink for a child."

The initial Spykes rollout was low-key and mostly confined to the Internet through the website spykeme.com. In keeping with the Long Tail theory, A-B executives were hoping the new product would take off virally, which it did, but not in the way they wanted.

"A shameless ploy to market malt liquor to the Lunchables set," said one writer. "A predatory move to attract underage drinking," said Joseph Califano, the secretary of health, education and welfare in the Carter administration and the subsequent founder of the National Center on Addiction and Substance Abuse.

"No thirty- or forty-year-old beer drinker is going to add hot chocolate or some other flavor to make beer more palatable," said Califano, "but kids will, and when they do they will get two drinks in one."

"Anheuser-Busch is practically begging to be investigated, subpoenaed, sued, or hauled before a congressional committee to explain this one," said George Hacker, the director of alcohol policies at the Center for Science in the Public Interest (CSPI).

The Michigan State Police put out a bulletin to its troopers warning that "these new products appear to be marketed for young people and could be easily overlooked by patrol officers, especially in a woman's purse."

The U.S. Alcohol and Tobacco Tax and Trade Bureau wrote to A-B saying the tiny, almost unreadable alcohol warning labeling on Spykes bottles violated federal law.

A group of twenty-nine state attorneys general from around the country sent a letter to August IV saying, "In our view, the labeling for Spykes is inadequate, and the content of its advertising is irresponsible, reflecting a basic disregard for consumer safety and welfare.

"Spykes exhibits all the indicia of a youth-oriented 'starter drink,' while posing the additional risks that arise from combining energy drinks with alcohol," the letter stated. The attorneys general pointed out that A-B was promoting Spykes online with free ring-tone and wallpaper downloads "that primarily appeal to adolescents, on a website with no meaningful barriers to youth access."

In an online article headlined "A Booze Buzz for Teenyboppers," MSNBC.com posted some purported customer comments pulled off the spykeme Web site:

LAURA: This stuff is sweeet! It comes in a tiny little bottle you can take with you . . . so cute!

MURMUR6: I wonder if it still tastes good if you heat it up lol

ELNINA2000: I agree with Laura . . . the bottles are adorable

MYTY: I'm gonna try putting one in the microwave . . . see what happens? lol

STEVIE7: Actually this is my girlfriend's favorite too . . . she takes them in her purse everywhere.

Whether the postings were the cynical compositions of company-paid ad copywriters or the sentiments of real customers, they weren't written in the voice of twenty-one- to twenty-seven-year-old women.

Perhaps the most surprising aspect of the Spykes controversy was the company's tin-eared response. A-B's vice president of communications and consumer affairs, Francine Katz, released a statement calling the critics "perennial fear-mongering, anti-alcohol groups whose members are in the business of spreading misinformation."

Katz was A-B's highest-ranking female executive, the first

woman to serve on the strategy committee, and a member of the Fourth's management team.* As such, she was tasked with delivering the official reply to the attorney general's letter to the boss. The content and tone of her response pointed up that A-B had parted ways with Fleishman-Hillard and was handling its public relations in-house.

Spykes was designed for "contemporary adult consumers" who were "looking for innovative alcohol beverages to match their active lifestyles," the statement said. "Those who criticize Spykes fundamentally misunderstand the behavior of many illegal underage drinkers. They drink for instant impact. The fact that Spykes are sold in 2-ounce bottles and have a total alcohol content equivalent to only one-third of a glass of wine makes it much less likely that illegal underage drinkers will choose Spykes as opposed to similarly colored and similarly flavored products that are 70 to 80 proof hard liquor.

"Those who are concerned about the concealability of small containers should focus on those hard-liquor beverages [such as airline mini-bottles] already on the market that have three to four times greater concentration of alcohol by volume than Spykes," the statement went on. "If the attorneys general believe that 50-ml bottles are a problem because their size makes them easily concealable, this standard should apply not just to malt-based products, but to hard liquor as well.

"One would think that if there were going to be a double standard applied, it would favor the lower alcohol content products, not the type of hard-liquor products made by Beam Global and other hard liquor manufacturers."

---

* Katz would later file a multimillion-dollar gender-discrimination lawsuit against the company, claiming, among other things, that management encouraged and maintained a "locker room" and "frat party" atmosphere. The case is pending as this book goes to press.

One would also think that a 129-year-old alcoholic beverage company could come up with a more mature and measured response to a large group of concerned law enforcement officials, a response that didn't sound so put-upon, and didn't miss the point so completely. Katz's name was on the statement, but the Fourth's fingerprints were all over it. He apparently didn't grasp that the critics weren't so much worried about underage college girls carrying around Spykes in their purses as they were about their twelve- and thirteen-year-old daughters who had nail polish bottles on their makeup tables that looked almost exactly like Spykes. Perhaps if he'd been married with children, he would have understood.

It was not a battle that A-B could win; the optics were just too damning. A week after receiving the attorney general's letter, the company issued a statement saying that August IV had decided to pull Spykes off the market. But it was left to another member of his management team to explain why. "Spykes has not performed up to expectations," said Michael Owens, A-B's vice president of marketing. "Due to its limited volume potential and unfounded criticism, we are ceasing production." He insisted that there was nothing wrong with Spykes or how it was marketed, and repeated that it had been "unduly attacked by perennial anti-alcohol groups."

Critics applauded the move but not the company. "The real question is how this ill-considered product slithered from the drawing board to the assembly line in the first place," said George Hacker of the CSPI. "One also wonders whether the company truly hit bottom with Spykes, or whether it will again stoop to market kid-friendly drinks after the furor subsides."

Indeed, the fact that A-B management remained petulant and unapologetic to the end—and that the Fourth took no responsibility for the decisions that led to the debacle—pointed up just how far the company had drifted from Gussie's belief that serving the public good always served the company best. It appeared that

Anheuser-Busch had lost more than its ranking as the world's largest brewer; it had lost its moral compass as well.

In July 2006, St. Louisans learned that the town's most notorious bachelor, the legendary "playboy" of the Central West End, was once again engaged to be married. Readers of the local newspapers had been able to follow the Fourth's chain of dalliances through the years—from previous fiancée Judy Buchmiller to California girl Sage Linville to local beauty queen Shandi Finnessy ("the pride of Florrisant") to an East St. Louis topless dancer name Karla Stratton. Now the *Post-Dispatch* reported that the next potential Mrs. Busch was twenty-five-year-old Kathryn ("Kate") Thatcher, who held a marketing degree from Boston College and hailed from the tiny town of Fairlee, Vermont (population 967), where her father was a high school athletic director and coach of the boys' basketball team.

Kate appeared tailor-made to please August III. She was tall and blond and radiated the same fresh-faced, All-American good looks as the two women he'd married—the Fourth's mother, Susie, and stepmother, Ginny.

"The Fourth met Kate in the company's VIP suite at a Cardinal-Red Sox game," said one of August's friends. "I think she was Miss Boston or something, a broad with a title. It was when he was on the prowl and needed to find a wife."

The friend confirmed widespread speculation in the company and the media that the Fourth felt pressured to get married because his father had made it a prerequisite for his taking over as chief executive, much as Gussie had done with him.

"The weekend he left for his wedding, he told me, 'I don't want to do this.' He said that his father was making him, that he had to 'fulfill the contract.'"

The wedding was set for August 5, 2006, but prior to the event, the Fourth's seemingly guaranteed ascension to CEO was threatened by a rumor that spread through the executive ranks.

"I heard about him failing two drug tests," said a former executive, "one that he was put on notice for, and a second one that was covered up. The story was known below the strategy committee level, because *I* heard about it, and I wasn't on the committee. It was one of those things where senior executives would close their office door and say, 'I just heard that . . .'"

Part of the rumor was not true. The Fourth had not flunked a second drug test, but only because he had conspired with a handful of his underlings to falsify the test results. "The Fourth's name was pulled again randomly, and he knew that he was going to test positive," said a former executive who learned about the scheme from one of the participants. "The tests were always done at an independent contractor's location, and you had to make an appointment and go there. So they delayed and delayed and kept concocting scheduling conflicts for him, saying he was traveling, until they finally got the drug testing contractor to send someone to the offices of A-B's owned distributor in Boston, where they controlled the situation and were able to switch his test samples with those of a guy who worked there." So the Fourth passed with flying colors, and apparently neither August III nor the board ever learned of the deception.

The wedding of August IV and Kate Thatcher took place in Bradbury, Vermont, followed by an elegant reception in nearby Hanover, the home of Dartmouth College, where the wedding party had taken over the picturesque Hanover Inn for the week. Anheuser-Busch made its presence felt by sending in a hitch of eight Clydesdales and a classic red Budweiser beer wagon with two uniformed drivers and a Dalmatian perched up top, big white satin bows fastened along the sides, and a "Just Married" sign hanging on the back. The Clydesdales were supposed to parade around the Dartmouth Green in the center of town, but instead they remained stationary at the corner of Wentworth Avenue and Main Street, where a large crowd gathered to admire the famous animals. A-B representatives had pressured the proprietors of Molly's Restaurant, the Canoe Club, Murphy's on the Green, and other establishments to feature A-B products more prominently while the wedding party was in town, and most complied, some even replacing more popular local beers to accommodate the request. As he stood with his bride posing for wedding pictures with the beer wagon as a backdrop, the Fourth was careful to have a perfectly poured glass of Budweiser in his hand. The local newspaper put it all into perspective with the headline "Clydesdales Grace Green for Wedding."

Back home in Missouri, the Fourth and his new bride settled into the Huntleigh Village mansion, which he was remodeling to accommodate his growing collections of guns and cars. They spent most warm weekends at the Lake of the Ozarks, where they were celebrated as the Royal Couple, smiling from the cover of a slick new local magazine, *L.O. Profile*. The accompanying article— "Mr. and Mrs. August Busch IV: Newlyweds at Home"—was a fawning promo for Anheuser-Busch, but in what may have been an unintended moment of candor, Kate let slip a sad fact of their life together.

"When August first told me about the Lake, I had visions of long romantic and quiet weekends," she said. "Little did I know that it would be the two of us and several Anheuser-Busch executives." Then, brightening, she added, "After the initial surprise, though, it didn't take long to get used to spending our weekends with everyone. We always have a great group of people with us."

"He really wanted to be true to Kate," said one of the Fourth's male friends. "I think that lasted three months."

By then, of course, he'd been promoted to CEO.

THE LAST WATCH

The long-awaited coronation of August IV as chief executive officer of Anheuser-Busch came on September 29, 2006, beginning with a statement from the board of directors.

"After careful consideration, we selected August Busch IV as the individual most qualified to assume that role. We believe that the company, its employees and its shareholders will be well served by his leadership."

August III, who was resigning from all executive responsibilities at age sixty-eight, said of his son, "August IV has successfully prepared himself by leading the U.S. beer company through a period of great change and challenge. He brings with him the new thinking of his generation yet appreciation for the great traditions and values of the company."

For sheer disingenuousness, the two statements would be hard to top. The board members knew better than anyone that the Fourth's record of leadership was questionable. His five years as president had been marked by flat sales, an underperforming stock, and a series of expensive TV commercials that won rave reviews but relatively few new customers. At least two key longtime sales executives had resigned during his presidency, each stating in their official exit interview—one directly to August III—that they were leaving because they had no faith in the Fourth's ability to lead the brewing division. The board's decision to elect Pat Stokes as chairman of the board and to allow August III to stay on as a member even after he retired was a clear sign that they didn't trust the Fourth's ability or his judgment. To say that he was "the individual most qualified" for the job fell somewhere between dishonest and delusional.

The statements were boilerplate corporate blather, of course, fashioned by public relations consultants intent on assuring the investing world that all things were as they should be. But August III's statement contained a paragraph that no one would have dared to write for him. It stands out as perhaps the most emotional published remark of his forty-five-year career.

"This company is like no other," he said. "For me, this has never been just a job, it has been my passion. I've taken great pleasure in working with people of character, creativity and commitment who have become my second family. Above all, it is the men and women with whom I have worked that I will miss most."

August IV's official statement contained the requisite expressions of gratitude and respect for his predecessors—"I am proud to accept this challenge that carries a great deal of personal meaning for me . . . my father and Pat [Stokes] leave behind a legacy of unparalleled excellence"—but privately he was deeply disappointed at the way things worked out. When he walked into his first board of directors meeting in December, the two men he'd reported to for the past twenty years would be sitting there, still judging his performance. Both had taken big retirement packages—$34.6 million for Stokes and $64 million for August III—but August III was going to serve as a consultant for another six years, during which time the company would continue to cover the cost of his security and travel, including his jet and helicopter, and maintain his executive office at 1 Busch Place. So his father wasn't even leaving the building. Supposedly, August III was going to serve as just another member of the board. The notion was ridiculous. If August III were in the boardroom, by dint of history and force of personality, he would be the man in charge. The nuclear particles would align.

So the promotion to CEO didn't change much for the Fourth, except that, as he ruefully noted to *Forbes* magazine, "I'm the one who is going to be accountable."

He faced some formidable problems. All the major U.S. brewers were losing young consumers to import brands, microbrews, wine, and distilled spirits. Budweiser had lost 16 percent of its market share since 1996. As president, the Fourth's strategy had been to fight the competition by joining them. In addition to Jekyll & Hyde, Spykes, and Bacardi Silver, he added fourteen microbrew-style beers to a product roster that now numbered more than forty brands, including such seemingly whimsical concoctions as Chelada Bud, Michelob Ultra Lime Cactus, and Michelob Ultra Tuscan Orange Grapefruit. It definitely wasn't his grandfather's beer company anymore.

In his first major move as CEO, the Fourth entered into a deal with Belgium-based InBev that made A-B the exclusive U.S. distributor of InBev's best-known European brands—Beck's, Bass Ale, and Stella Artois. His father objected to the idea when it was first proposed in 2006. He'd dealt directly with InBev's key Brazilian backers and didn't trust them. InBev was now A-B's biggest competitor on the world stage and was widely rumored to be eyeing A-B as a possible takeover target. August III thought it was a bad idea to get into a partnership that would give InBev a window onto A-B's operations. But the Fourth kept pushing for it, and in an uncharacteristic display of restraint, his father didn't try to marshal support on the board to block the deal; he let it happen, and InBev moved into a small office just across Pestalozzi Street from the A-B executive offices at 1 Busch Place.

The takeover rumors were well founded. For years, A-B had been protected by its size and stock price: it was simply too big and too expensive to be swallowed by a competitor. But things had changed. A-B wasn't the biggest brewer anymore. Its stock was undervalued. Its record of 150 years in operation wasn't so intimidating in an industry whose world leader had not even existed four years before. InBev was not so much a brewer as it was an investment portfolio of beer brands—more than two hundred of them—that its owners had amassed by gulping down six-hundred-year-old European breweries for breakfast. So as August IV took over the job he had coveted so for long, he was buffeted from all sides by warnings that, sooner or later, InBev would make a move.

Super Bowl XLI offered him some respite from the doom-and-gloom-sayers. As usual, A-B had gone all out, mounting a total of nine commercials for the broadcast. At a rate of $2.6 million per thirty-second spot, that represented an investment of more than $24 million in commercial time alone. Production costs and a week's worth of festivities in Miami leading up to the game probably added at least another few million to the tab. A-B's exclusive deal with the NFL precluded commercials by any other brewer, so the company was easily the dominant advertiser on America's most-watched TV broadcast. By way of comparison, Coca-Cola had four commercials during the game, General Motors had three, and Doritos and Honda each had two.

In the first Super Bowl marred by rain, the Indiana Colts beat the Chicago Bears 29–17, but the score that mattered to A-B came out a few days later when *USA Today* published its weekly Ad Meter chart. Based on the second-by-second reactions of 238 electronically monitored adult volunteers, A-B logged an unprecedented seven of the ten most liked ads aired during the broadcast, including the top two, both for Budweiser. The top-rated spot was the now famous Budweiser "King Crab" commercial, which featured scores of animatronic red crustaceans crawling out of the ocean on a tropical island to worship around a bright red cooler filled with Budweiser.

The Fourth and his management team were ecstatic. Never mind that Ad Meter measured the opinion of only a few hundred people in Houston and McLean, Virginia; the A-B executives knew that online viewing of the Top Ten commercials exploded in the week after the broadcast. The company estimated that its 2006 ads were viewed on YouTube more than 21 million times in the three days following the game. And that audience skewed a lot younger than the TV audience.

A few days after the Super Bowl broadcast, A-B unveiled a new product that had been in development for nearly a year—an online entertainment network called Bud.TV. Aimed at twenty-one- to twenty-seven-year-old consumers who were hard to reach with traditional broadcast television ads, Bud.TV promised a lineup of one- to three-minute programs that featured the kind of hip, mocking humor that A-B commercials had become famous for, ranging from comedy sketches created by writers from *Saturday Night Live* and *The Howard Stern Show* to short films produced by actor Kevin Spacey's company, Trigger Street Films, to a making-of-a-documentary reality series called *Finish My Film*, which was to be produced by Matt Damon and Ben Affleck's production company, LivePlanet. The premise of *Finish My Film* was that LivePlanet would shoot the first and last minutes of a short film and invite viewers to submit proposals for filling in the middle. Whoever came up with the best proposal would be invited to Los Angeles, where they would be filmed making their film.

For a St. Louis–based beer company, Bud.TV was an undertaking of breathtaking ambition, one that bordered on "creative hubris," said the *New York Times*. But it seemed like the kind of new-generation, outside-the-barrel thinking that August III and the board were hoping for when they promoted the Fourth to CEO. A-B launched Bud.TV with a first-year budget of $30 million—a pittance, considering the company's annual marketing budget of more than $1 billion—and high hopes that within a year or two it would grow into a Top 100 Web site with 2 to 3 million unique visitors per month.

It didn't come close. Plagued by a clumsy age verification system that cross-checked would-be visitors' names against a database of state-issued identification and caused even the Fourth to complain that he couldn't get on, Bud.TV drew 253,000 visitors its first month and only 152,000 its second. One episode of a series called "Replaced by a Chimp" drew only 384 views on YouTube. In April 2007, *Advertising Age* reported that Bud.TV ranked as "the 49,303rd busiest site on the Web, just ahead of pornography site www.jstfu.com, and just behind www.rubber-cal.com, which bills itself as a 'comprehensive source for sheet rubber.'"

The following month, it got worse—traffic to the site was so light that the Web measurement service Comscore could not measure it, according to *Ad Age*. When A-B finally pulled the plug on Bud.TV, the vice president of marketing was quoted as saying, belatedly, "If the [TV] networks can't continuously produce that [volume of content], how can a beer company?"

Coming on the heels of the Spykes debacle, the failure of Bud.TV was especially embarrassing. But August IV had more pressing issues to worry about. His father was chairman of the board's executive committee, which gave him oversight of executive hiring. Even though August III didn't come to the office on a daily basis, he was in the Fourth's ear constantly, calling him several times a day. He objected to two key members of the Fourth's management team and ordered him to get rid of them. The Fourth protested and got him to relent on one executive by moving him to a less prominent job. The other man, who was rumored to have played a role in the Fourth's faked drug test, was allowed to resign with a generous separation package.

As recounted in the book *Dethroning the King*, August III was infuriated when he learned that the Fourth had invited a group of Wall Street investment bankers to attend what was supposed to be an internal meeting of A-B executives at the Ritz-Carlton Hotel in Cancun, Mexico, and asked them to present their ideas about how A-B might remain competitive in the new global beer economy. August III thought it was a terrible tactical error.

"All you did by bringing those bankers in there was send a telegraph wire out to InBev that you're ready to be taken over," he supposedly hollered at the Fourth in front of a group of other executives during a weekend quail-hunting trip in Florida. "You're putting up a For Sale sign. You're giving away too much information. All you did was get everyone in the world to sharpen their knives."

Sure enough, within weeks, the financial press and beverage industry trade publications picked up on the Fourth's meeting with the investment bankers and interpreted it as a sign that A-B was actively seeking a merger partner. *Beverage World* reported that "industry analysts are predicting a 70 percent chance" that A-B would merge with InBev. "They have no choice," one analyst was quoted as saying. "They can introduce new products and they have a number of [cost cutting] initiatives, but they still face execution risk and, at the end of the day, it's a global beer industry." A Brazilian business newspaper reported incorrectly that InBev had already had preliminary merger talks with A-B. In nearly all the early speculative reports, A-B was depicted as on the defensive, vulnerable, running out of room to maneuver.

One journalist who met with the Fourth early during his first few months as CEO thought he came off as a smart, amiable middleweight. "He had boyishness about him, not the gravitas of a CEO. He was like someone I might have played ball with in high school and we'd go have a beer together. He seemed younger than his age. He carried himself like a guy who was trapped in his youth.

"He was clearly very bright," the journalist said. "He had a tremendous memory, and could roll off stats about the industry and stories about the challenges his father had faced through the years, but he tended to go off on tangents in his conversation, jumping around like a jackrabbit, veering from one subject to the next. He didn't shy away from talking about the takeover rumors and the realities the company faced, but he sometimes rambled on about inconsequential beer history."

The takeover story died down during the summer of 2007 when nothing happened, but it heated back up again in October when SABMiller and Molson Coors, the No. 2 and No. 3 brewers in the United States, announced they were merging their domestic operations to better compete with A-B. MillerCoors, a merger of two mergers, would control about 30 percent of the U.S. market, significantly reducing A-B's competitive advantage.

Shortly after the MillerCoors announcement, August IV met in New York with Jorge Paulo Lemann, the most influential of the three Brazilian investment bankers behind the creation of InBev. A Harvard graduate who drank only mineral water, the sixty-eight-year-old Lemann was ranked No. 165 on *Forbes* magazine's list of the world's wealthiest people, with a fortune estimated at $4.9 billion. The Fourth believed the meeting was a casual one. When Lemann mentioned the MillerCoors deal and suggested that A-B and InBev consider a merger, the Fourth apparently didn't perceive it as a serious proposal. He brushed the suggestion aside as if it were an off-the-cuff remark, saying he had other plans for reinvigorating his company. But Lemann was dead serious about a merger, and the fact that the Fourth did not pick up on that or report Lemann's comment back to the A-B board in a way that set off alarm bells was an indication of how unprepared he was to play in this ballpark. Having been rebuffed twice on the idea of a friendly merger—by August III in 1997 and now his son—Lemann and his partners commenced plans to acquire A-B by less friendly means.

It appears that the Fourth similarly misjudged the situation with Carlos Brito, the man Lemann put in place as CEO of InBev. The forty-eight-year-old Brazilian, who held a degree in mechanical engineering from the Federal University of Rio de Janeiro and an MBA from Stanford (paid for by Lemann), was in many ways the antithesis of the Fourth. Married with four children, he eschewed the trappings of executive success, avoiding first-class travel and fancy hotels, operating without an assistant, a company car, or even his own desk. "We don't have corporate jets," he pointedly told an auditorium full of Stanford graduate students in February 2008, as InBev was secretly lining up financing to buy A-B. "I don't have an office. I share my table with my vice presidents. I sit with my marketing guy to my left, my sales guy to my right, my finance guy in front of me." Private offices fostered mediocrity, he said. "Mediocre people love to be behind closed doors, playing games and stuff." And there was no free beer at InBev, either. "I don't need the company to buy my beer," he said. "I can afford to buy my own."

During his fifteen years at AmBev, Brito had built a reputation as a ruthless cost cutter and wholehearted proponent of Lemann's "zero-based budgeting" philosophy, which supposedly helped the company achieve an astonishing 50 percent profit margin by requiring every department to justify all costs for each year rather than simply adjusting the baseline spending from the previous year. As he told the grad students at his alma mater, "We say the leaner the business, the more money we will have at the end of the year to share."

And yet the Fourth thought it was a good idea to invite Brito to A-B's annual sales meeting with distributors, the company's most conspicuous display of over-the-top spending.

The merger/takeover rumors reignited in the spring of 2008, fueled by the *Wall Street Journal's* gossipy but usually reliable Heard on the Street column, which reported that A-B and InBev "already have held discussions," according to "people in the industry familiar with both brewers' thinking." Noting that "reports of the talks surfaced as long as a year ago," the column said, "They have become more serious, and a deal is possible this year, people in the industry say."

In truth, the two companies had not had any "talks" other than the brief exchange between August IV and Jorge Lemann in October. In the wake of the item, however, the price of A-B stock briefly jumped 3 percent. The *Journal* kept on the story, reporting on April 11 that during A-B's annual sales meeting with distributors in Chicago a few days earlier, August IV had brought the crowd to its feet by declaring there would be no sale of Anheuser-Busch, "not on my watch."

The *Journal* attributed the story to "sources in the room," but the company refused to confirm or deny the Fourth's statement. "We had a meeting with our wholesalers with the goal of inspiring our sales force," said marketing VP David Peacock, who declined to characterize comments "that were shared in confidence with our distribution system in an effort to keep them focused on performing in support of our business."

The Fourth had blundered again. It was naive of him to think that anything he said to a crowd of five hundred people was confidential, or would stay that way for long. And to publicly reject a buyout offer even before it was made smacked of arrogance or ignorance, or both. No sober, experienced CEO of a publicly traded

Fortune 500 company widely rumored to be the target of a take-over attempt would do such a thing. He didn't have the authority, and it was not in the interest of the stockholders.

Perhaps the pressure was getting to him. The company's domestic market share grew by a paltry one-tenth of a percent in 2007. Sales of Budweiser and Michelob continued to fall. Despite a few brief spikes in response to takeover rumors, the stock remained stuck around $48 a share, the same as it had been for five years—"flatter than two-year-old beer," in the words of one analyst. The company was being investigated and publicly excoriated by eleven state attorneys general, including New York's Andrew Cuomo, for allegedly illegally marketing caffeine-laced alcoholic drinks—Tilt and Bud Extra—to underage consumers.* And A-B department heads were scrambling to find more than $400 million in spending cuts just as the company was preparing to drop a bundle on the rollout of a high-profile new product, Bud Light Lime. Meanwhile, the specter of InBev hovered over everything.

It was not a good time for August IV to pull a disappearing act. But beginning in January 2008, he rarely showed up at the brewery, preferring to work out of the company's suite of offices at the soccer park near the Spirit of St. Louis Airport, which was much closer to his home. A massive construction project on Interstate 64 between West St. Louis County and the city offered a convenient excuse for the change, though several other routes could have provided an easy commute from his house on Lindbergh Boulevard to the plant. His new office offered a fully equipped gym, which he used incessantly as part of a manic physical fitness regimen that included daily sessions with his ever-present Korean bodyguard/martial arts master, Bong Yul Shin, whom the Fourth referred to as "Mr. Shin," as if he were a James Bond character.

---

* The company agreed to pull both products off the market.

Once again, the Fourth had created a safe haven for himself, a secure space where access was restricted to all but a small cadre of devoted and indebted underlings who could be trusted with his secrets. The new office arrangement helped hide from the rest of the company the fact that the chief executive's workday usually didn't begin until the early afternoon and continued into the early morning, the latter hours conducted in bars, restaurants, or, increasingly, his home, where some members of his inner circle gathered nearly every night.

"His guys would come over and they would watch TV; it was work, but they were also like his family," said a confidant who claims he was sometimes there five or six nights a week. "*Scarface* was his favorite movie. They watched it religiously. As the night wore on, he would get more drunk. He drank beer and wine mostly. He usually had a chef there to cook, and a housekeeper, and two A-B security guys."

By then, the Fourth had returned to his playboy ways when he traveled, or when his wife, Kate, was out of town. In the latter case, he made sure the security camera recordings at the house were erased before she returned so she wouldn't find out what went on while she was away. "Kate thought she could change him," said one of August's confidants, "but it was never going to happen."

Given the Fourth's increasingly dissolute behavior, his closest associates were not shocked when he showed up loaded at the National Beer Wholesalers Conference in Washington, D.C. But the five hundred or so A-B distributors who watched as he walked unsteadily into the grand ballroom of the Hyatt on the afternoon of May 13, 2008, were stunned by his condition.

"The wholesalers for all the brands were [at the convention], at least a thousand of them, along with the largest brewers— SABMiller, Molson Coors, InBev," said an A-B distributor who was in the ballroom. "The Fourth was going to be our headliner.

But he didn't get very far. He stumbled over words as if he was reading from a teleprompter in a different language. His speech was slurred, halting, and very deliberate. It was obvious that he could not focus. This was clearly not from overindulging in a 'beverage of moderation.' It wasn't booze; something else was going on. It was painful to see the face of our company in such a state *in public*."

"When it was over, it was all anyone talked about, that evening and for many days afterwards," recalled another distributor who witnessed the meltdown. "I couldn't believe that his people let him get up there like that. Obviously, they were in disarray.

"This was not a home game; we were in the nation's capital," the distributor went on. "There are no secrets in the beer business anyway. No matter what you sell, it's all a big fraternity. So everyone knew about this. I have to believe it factored into what InBev did. They thought, 'If that's the leader, then something is terribly wrong.'"

In all likelihood, Brito and company already knew about the Fourth's weaknesses. They weren't barbarians at the gate, after all; they'd been inside the walls for more than a year. And in any significant corporate acquisition, it is standard practice for the prospective buyer to conduct a due diligence investigation that includes a rigorous vetting of the CEO and his management team to determine whether they should be kept on after the takeover. The investigations usually are conducted either by big law firms or private investigative agencies such as Kroll, which employ former investigative journalists and retired law enforcement officers to gather intelligence. Depending on the size of the company and the risk involved, these due diligence investigations can be exhaustive and expensive, sometimes costing up to half a million dollars or more. And because the investigative report is provided to the client on a confidential basis, its so-called executive summary often contains a good deal of unproven gossip, which can be as significant to a buyer as fact. When it came to gossip, of course, August IV was an open book, with new chapters being written all the time.

On May 22, nine days after the Fourth's disturbing performance in Washington, the InBev board of directors met to discuss the details of their planned merger offer. The following day, the *Financial Times* reported that InBev was readying a cash offer of $65 per share, a total of $46 billion, for all outstanding shares of Anheuser-Busch. InBev expected a "cool reception" from August IV and the A-B board, the *Financial Times* said, and was prepared to follow up with a public appeal directly to A-B shareholders.

The information was attributed to unidentified "sources with a close knowledge" of the deal, but the details were so specific there was little doubt as to the accuracy. The article named the various investment bankers involved in the financing package and said that InBev had approached August IV "informally last October, but [he] insisted he would protect Anheuser's independence and wanted time to show his mettle at a job to which he had only recently been promoted."

The story broke on the Friday morning leading into the Memorial Day weekend. By the time the markets closed, A-B stock had shot up by 8 percent to a record $56.61. A-B management made no official public statement regarding the *Financial Times*' story, but during the day August IV sent a memo to all employees urging them to stay focused on their jobs. "We can't control rumors or speculation," he said. "But we DO control our growth strategies and how we operate our business. It is our job to conduct our business in ways that will keep the company strong, profitable, and growing."

In a defiant flourish that sounded like something his father would say, he added, "Some of our competitors would like nothing better than to see Anheuser-Busch get distracted by rumors over the holiday. They underestimate us."

Out at Belleau Farm in St. Peters, Missouri, the Fourth's uncle, Adolphus Busch IV, read the *Financial Times* story with interest and concern. As the owner of a substantial amount of A-B shares and a financial partner in a large A-B distributorship in Houston, he'd been frustrated for some time with the lackluster performance of the stock. Now, apparently, the A-B board was about to be offered a 34 percent premium on the going price of the shares, and his nephew had already said no. How could he do that?

Adolphus knew A-B had little defense against a serious takeover attempt. The Busch family owned less than 4 percent of the stock, not enough to swing a decision one way or another even in the unlikely event that they all agreed on which way to go. In the past few years, the company had dropped its so-called poison pill provision, which allowed stockholders to buy new stock at a discount in the face of a takeover threat, thereby making an acquisition more expensive for an unwanted suitor. In response to shareholder pressure, the board also had done away with "staggered" elections whereby only a third of its members stood for reelection each year. So now an unfriendly suitor could nominate a new slate of candidates and replace the entire sitting board at a single shareholders' meeting.

Adolphus thought $65 per share was a hell of an offer. He couldn't imagine the current directors turning it down. They'd risk spending the next five years in court defending themselves against shareholder lawsuits. So what was the Fourth doing with that "not on my watch" comment? Over the Memorial Day weekend, he put in several calls to August III and August IV to see what was going on. August III didn't respond, and when the Fourth finally got back to him, his description of the plan for fighting the takeover seemed disconnected from the urgent reality. He said he was confident his management team could build more shareholder value than InBev could offer by improving profitability and stock performance through a cost-cutting program code-named Blue Ocean that would eliminate more than half a billion dollars in spending over the next two years.

"That sounded like bullshit to me," Adolphus said recently, "and it told me that they really didn't have a plan." On Monday, May 26, he contacted David Kesmodel, the *Wall Street Journal* reporter who'd been covering the story, and told him that, contrary to what his nephew had said, some members of the Busch family were open to merger discussions with InBev. "There are members that absolutely want it to stay status quo," he said, "and there are others that say they want to see some kind of chance to enhance shareholder value."

The next morning it became obvious that the Fourth had committed another unforced error. He'd given a phone interview to the *Wall Street Journal* several weeks earlier in which he'd spoken a little too freely. The result was an article in which he seemed to make the InBev story all about him. "Anheuser CEO Fights for His Legacy," the headline read. "As Rival Weighs a Bid, Busch Heir Still Seeks Father's Approval." In what functioned as the company's first public response to the *Financial Times* revelations, the Fourth's every quote dealt with his father and their troubled relationship:

"I never, ever had a father-son relationship," he said. "It's always been purely business."

His transition to CEO had been "a very difficult, fluid situation," he said, because he and his father had clashed over issues ranging from his choices for his executive team—"If I can't have my team then how can you hold me accountable?"—to his scuttled plan to buy the juice beverage manufacturer Hansen Natural Corp. for $7 billion—"He had a big problem with us venturing outside of the beverage beer company."

"He could sell ice cubes to the Eskimos," he said of his father. "He's brilliant and he has so much to offer, [so] long as when he offers it, it comes as advice instead of orders. It's kind of a fine line."

Claiming that August III and Gussie went without speaking to one another for ten years before they finally mended their relationship, he expressed confidence that his father's "love and respect" eventually would come "when I'm ultimately successful." Then he added poignantly, "I honestly do believe if I failed in my professional life, it would be much harder for me to ever gain his respect."

However touching, his comments were not the sort of response the brewing industry, the citizens of St. Louis, or the financial community had expected from the CEO of the $19 billion company. They made him look emotional and weak. His father surely was livid. No one could say whether it was due to this one incident or an accumulation of things, because August III would never say, but relations between the two soon turned so cold they chilled any room they were in together. From then on, the Fourth was on a tight leash.

The board instructed him to send an e-mail to Jorge Lemann seeking clarification about the news reports. Lemann took several days to respond, claiming he had been traveling. They agreed to meet in Tampa on June 2. Some board members worried about sending the Fourth to Florida alone, so several coaching sessions were conducted to make sure he knew what to say and what not to.

The preparation was all for naught, however, as the meeting with Lemann and his longtime investing partner Marcel Telles lasted no more than 10 minutes, during which time the two men politely declined to confirm or deny that InBev was preparing a takeover offer. Back in St. Louis, the board concluded that there was nothing to be done but wait; either a bid would come or it wouldn't.

It came nine days later, on June 11, in the form of a letter from Carlos Brito to August IV, faxed to the Fourth's office at the soccer park and copied to the board.

Dear August,

Over the past several years we have met with you on many occasions to explore ways in which we could deepen the relationship between our two great companies. Jorge Paulo Lemann and Marcel Telles greatly appreciated your taking the time to meet with them on the 2nd of June in Tampa. During the course of that meeting you asked whether we had a formal proposal to make to you and your Board of Directors regarding a potential combination. Although we did not put forward a specific proposal at the time, I am now writing to provide you with proposed terms.

As foretold by the *Financial Times*, InBev's offer was for $65 a share, a total of $46.35 billion in cash. Voicing "the highest respect for Anheuser-Busch, its employees and leadership, as well as the generations of investment that have created the Anheuser-Busch brands, particularly the iconic Budweiser brand," Brito put forward a string of assurances:

We would position Budweiser as our global flagship brand. . . . We would envision making St. Louis the headquarters for the North American region and the global home of the flagship Budweiser brand. . . . We would seek to re-name our combined company to evoke the heritage of your key brands. . . . We will maintain all your existing breweries. . . . We will continue your strong commitment to the communities in which you operate. . . . We would invite a number of your directors to join the board of the new company. . . . We would hope to retain key members of the Anheuser-Busch management team at all levels of seniority.

As one writer put it, Brito "did everything but hand-deliver chocolate and flowers."

It didn't matter. The minute A-B revealed the content of Brito's letter, howls of protest went up from politicians, pundits, and just plain folks. "I am strongly opposed to the sale of Anheuser-Busch, and today's offer to purchase the company is deeply troubling to me," said Missouri governor Matthew Blunt. Vowing she would "do everything in my power" to prevent an InBev takeover, Missouri's Democratic senator Claire McCaskill sent a letter to the A-B board urging members to reject InBev's offer in consideration of "what this great and profitable company represents to St. Louis, the state of Missouri, and the rest of America." Her Republican counterpart, Missouri Senator Christopher "Kit" Bond, couldn't help boasting that he had told Carlos Brito to his face, "This Bud's *not* for you."

Even Democratic presidential candidate—and sometime Bud Light drinker—Barack Obama got pulled into the political posturing when his campaign plane was temporarily grounded at the St. Louis airport due to a mechanical problem. Responding to reporters' questions, the Illinois senator said it would be "a shame" if Anheuser-Busch was sold to a foreign company. "I think we should be able to find an American company that is interested in purchasing Anheuser-Busch, if in fact Anheuser-Busch feels that it is necessary to sell."

"Could anything symbolize America's loss of economic supremacy more clearly than for its favorite beer to fall into foreign hands?" asked the London-based news magazine the *Economist*, adding snarkily, "Hitherto, Budweiser has been at the forefront of the Americanization of the world, often to the dismay of foreign drinkers of traditional beers who regard a Bud as a glass of water wasted."

In the United States, a Web site called Savebudweiser.com

urged Joe and Jane Sixpack to jump onto the jingoistic bandwagon, calling on Bud lovers to "band together as one voice and try to save more than just our beer. We don't want another American icon turned over to a foreign company." Another Web site, SaveAB.com, was launched by Missouri governor Blunt's former chief of staff, Ed Martin, who promised to stage anti-InBev rallies inside Busch Stadium. "Selling out to the Belgians is not worth it," Martin said, "because this is about more than beer: it's about our jobs and our nation."

The strongest reaction to the news of InBev's offer came from the citizens of St. Louis, many of whom were surprised to learn that the Busch family didn't own, or at least control, Anheuser-Busch. The Busches had always acted as if they did. How else could the kid with all the legal problems have ended up in charge?

St. Louisans could be excused for not buying Carlos Brito's assurances that nothing bad would happen as a result of an InBev buyout. They'd heard that kind of talk before, most recently in 2001, when Swiss-based Nestlé acquired St. Louis's Ralston Purina, and in 2005, when Cincinnati-based Federated Department Stores bought the May Company, which operated the city's beloved Famous-Barr department stores. In both cases, the hometown headquarters soon disappeared, along with the jobs they had provided for decades.

"St. Louis has gotten to the point where we have the brewery and the Cardinals—that's it," complained the owner of a restaurant across the street from the brewery. "This is a brewing town, and [A-B] is the last jewel in the crown," said a city worker sitting in a small South Side bar called Crabby's. "If this deal goes through, I won't be buying their beer."

A writer for the *Kansas City Star* succinctly summed up St. Louis's reaction: "It's about hometown pride, purpose, identity—in the face of a soulless global economy."

Back in Adolphus Busch's time, St. Louis had been the fourth-largest city in America, behind New York, Chicago, and Philadelphia. *Time* magazine called it "the midwestern city with an Athenian heart, valuing music and philosophy, nurturing a great university [Washington U], birthing poets [T. S. Eliot, Maya Angelou] and hosting, in one zenith year, both the World's Fair and the Summer Olympics." Unfortunately, as *Time* pointed out, that zenith was in 1904. Subsequently hit hard by Prohibition, the proud "Fourth City" and onetime brewing capital never fully recovered, though the population kept growing until the 1960s, when white flight to the surrounding suburbs began eroding the tax base. From then on, it seemed as if every time St. Louis made the national news, it was in a story about urban decay, inner-city violence, or racial unrest. As *Time* said, "No city in America has slid so far, nor with such dignity."

Through it all, Anheuser-Busch had remained a constant, the city's classiest act, spreading its wealth across the community through charitable donations—a reported $10 million in 2007—and contributions to civic development projects and cultural events. "Anheuser-Busch is so much a part of life at all levels of society that you can hardly walk into a public building without finding 'Anheuser-Busch Hall' or the 'Anheuser-Busch Conference Room,'" said Dan Kopman, the cofounder of Saint Louis Brewery, maker of the locally popular Schlafly brand. Even St. Louisans who preferred Heineken or hated beer felt a flash of pride every time a voiceover at the end of a Bud or Bud Light commercial intoned, "Anheuser-Busch, St. Louis, Missouri."

On June 26, fifteen days after receiving Carlos Brito's letter, the A-B board unanimously rejected InBev's proposal as "financially inadequate and not in the best interest of Anheuser-Busch stockholders."

A-B's written response was friendly, respectful, and firm. "From your standpoint, we see that now could be an opportunistic time for you to make this acquisition, given the weak U.S. dollar and sluggish U.S. stock market," it read. "From the standpoint of the Anheuser-Busch shareholder, however, a transaction with InBev at this time would mean forgoing the greater value obtainable from Anheuser-Busch's strategic growth plan." The letter ended with what appeared to be a personal aside from the Fourth. "As you say yourself, you dream big. We respect your desires to grow your company, but your growth should not come at the expense of our stockholders."

The rejection kicked off an increasingly tense back-and-forth, with both sides invoking the "interest of Anheuser-Busch shareholders" the way U.S. politicians carry on about "the will of the American people." InBev quickly moved to oust the A-B board, putting forward its own slate of candidates, including Adolphus Busch IV, whose statement to the *Wall Street Journal* about being "open to discussions" with InBev was widely interpreted in the media as evidence of a Busch family feud. Adolphus had subsequently come out in favor of InBev's $46 billion offer, saying that Brito's assurances had satisfied his concern about preserving the legacy of the company. "A possible merger is not a family issue," he said. "It is strictly a matter of shareholder value."

His youngest brother Andrew promptly released a statement supporting August III and August IV. "I for one trust the current A-B board to put A-B shareholders first," he said, "and have no reason to think that InBev's proposed board members will have the same devotion to shareholders' interests."

The differences between the two stemmed more from their partnership—along with their brother Billy—in an A-B distributorship in Houston that strained relations among all three of them, but mostly between Adolphus and Andrew, who had rarely spoken in recent years. Other Busch family members were more ambivalent about the potential InBev buyout, and their opinions were evolving rapidly.

"When I first heard there was an offer from Carlos Brito, I was against it," said Billy Busch recently. "The company had meant so much to me and my family, there was so much pride and history involved, that I didn't want to see it go. I thought August IV was just going to have to raise himself up and turn it around somehow. But then I started thinking about it, and as much as I hated to see it go, my business sense told me that maybe this was the time."

It helped that Billy held a large amount of stock, in fact, more than any of his siblings. "I was the only one who never sold any," he admitted. "I guess that's because I remembered that my dad never sold a share in his life." Since each of the Grant's Farm children inherited 400,000 shares that had since split two-for-one twice, Billy now stood to make more than $100 million on a sale to InBev.

It was generally agreed that the A-B board had only one play to make if they wanted avoid the takeover, and that was to acquire the half of Mexico's Grupo Modelo that A-B didn't already own. Such a merger would add anywhere from $10 billion to $15 billion to the value of the company, possibly making it too expensive for InBev to swallow. InBev claimed to have secured $40 billion in financing, mostly from European banks. But the worldwide recession of 2008 was in full swing, and credit was becoming increasingly hard to come by.

The Modelo gambit was a long shot, however. Since 1993, A-B had invested more than $1.6 billion in the brewery, gradually acquiring a 52 percent noncontrolling interest. But the partnership had been an uneasy one, and August III was not exactly beloved by the five Mexican families that controlled their country's largest brewery. Because the Fourth had formed a relationship with Modelo's forty-one-year-old CEO, Carlos Fernandez, he and his strategy committee were assigned the task of trying to negotiate a merger agreement. The Fourth saw it as a last chance to redeem himself, and friends say he got caught up in the idea that he could save Anheuser-Busch for the city, the shareholders, and his family the way his grandfather Gussie had saved the Cardinals. If he pulled it off, he would be the hero of the story, and not held accountable forever for letting the dynasty go down on his watch. He might finally win his father's respect.

Over a period of several weeks, the Fourth and his team hammered out an agreement whereby A-B would pay $15 billion for the remaining 48.5 percent of Modelo and Carlos Fernandez would be named CEO of the merged company, which would be called Anheuser-Busch Modelo. But the A-B board balked at the idea. As much as they believed that Fernandez would be a much better CEO than August IV, they didn't want to pay a premium for Modelo and at the same time appear to turn over control to the Mexicans. They thought that would surely invite shareholder lawsuits. As August III said, "I don't want to spend the rest of my life in depositions."

"I was with the Fourth at his house the night they told him they weren't going to do the Modelo deal and were probably going to sell to InBev," said one of his confidants. "He was devastated."

The InBev deal was sealed when Brito, concerned that A-B might go with Modelo if he didn't sweeten the pot, upped his bid to $70 a share, for a total of $52 billion. That would make it the largest cash transaction in the history of American business. It was an offer too big to turn down.*

On November 8, four days after the election of Barack Obama, Anheuser-Busch shareholders voted to approve InBev's offer and the company surrendered its century and a half of independence, officially becoming Anheuser-Busch InBev, or ABI for short. Two

---

* Five years later, Inbev agreed to pay $20 billion for the remainder of Modelo, or $5 billion more than the deal August IV brought to his father and the A-B board.

days later, ABI announced the layoffs of 1,400 employees, 1,000 of them in St. Louis. Two weeks after that, the company told its suppliers that, in keeping with InBev's traditional practice, they would now have to wait 120 days to be paid, rather than the 30-day basis on which A-B historically had paid.

In the months that followed, ABI divested itself of more than $7 billion in assets, including Busch Entertainment, which operated its theme parks, Busch Gardens and SeaWorld. The division that had sprung from Gussie's passion for colorful, exotic birds was sold for $2.7 billion. The new Brazilian overlords cut back on sports sponsorships, such as the LPGA golf tournament in Williamsburg, Virginia, and reduced charitable contributions in the local community, notably the traditional donation to Gussie Busch's old American Legion post. A company retirees' group that for years had met at the brewery and enjoyed free beer was now asked to pay for both the room and the rounds. Fourteen of the company's top seventeen executives left, most of them as very rich men. The Fourth's payout amounted to more than $100 million, including $120,000 a month in consulting fees and a full-time two-man security detail for three years.

At the same time, the new management announced internally that henceforth salaries would be set at 20 percent below the market rate; that contributions to the pension plan for salaried employees would eventually be frozen; that office trashcans would be emptied only on Mondays, Wednesdays, and Fridays; and that personal plants would not be watered at all. There would be no more first-class travel; BlackBerry cell phone service would be severely curtailed. Management even began posting a sort of shaming list of employees who tipped the most, stayed in the most expensive hotels, or spent the most on cab fare.

The slew of cost-saving directives wreaked havoc on morale among longtime employees who had previously taken pride in working for St. Louis's flagship employer. "Now it's like working for a bunch of accountants, real hard-assed accountants," said one. The biggest blow to employee pride may have come the day the work crews arrived on the ninth floor of the administration building, where the plush decor of the executive offices created a feeling of abundance and prosperity, signaling that all within were a special breed. August had built the building and had it decorated to his taste. Gussie had praised him for it, saying, "It's a fine building, son. You should be proud." But to a cost-obsessed Carlos Brito, the private offices must have seemed anachronistic, extravagant, and dangerously inefficient. His work crews quickly gutted the entire ninth floor, turning it into an austerely functional open-configuration workspace with desks stretching from wall to wall; it looked more like an Internet startup firm working through its first round of venture capital funding than a company with a storied history dating back to the Civil War. If Gussie had lived to see it, he might have dropped dead on the spot. The *St. Louis Post-Dispatch* quoted a twenty-one-year company veteran as saying of the makeover, "The message from InBev is, 'If you don't think we are serious [about cost-cutting], then just look at what we are willing to destroy.'"

There was still one final act of destruction to come, however.

"THEY DIDN'T JUST DROP OUT OF THE SKY"

In November 2009, August IV made his first appearance at the Pestalozzi Street plant in nearly a year. He was supposedly there to attend a board of directors' meeting, but he presented himself to a security guard at a different part of the huge complex and asked to be let into his grandfather Gussie's old office.

It was an odd request, but the guard recognized him and wasn't about to question it. Prior to the InBev takeover, Gussie's office on the third floor of the old executive office building had been preserved just as the old man had left it. The Fourth never had a close relationship with his grandfather, primarily because his father's more than ten-year estrangement from Gussie had limited his exposure to the family patriarch. The Fourth didn't see his grandfather more than a handful of times between 1975 and 1989, when Gussie died, and he didn't visit Grant's Farm once in that time. During his last few years at the company, however, he indicated to family members that he'd always been in awe of the old man, and on a number of occasions he sought and received permission from his uncle, Adolphus IV, the trustee for Grant's Farm, to use the big house to host dinners for A-B executives and distributors. His father had never done that.

When the security guard escorted him to Gussie's office, the Fourth was upset to find it unlocked and empty. The new owners had cleared the space of all Gussie's furnishings and mementos and shipped everything to Grant's Farm, where it now sat in boxes and crates in the ballroom on the third floor of the big house.

The Fourth ordered the guard to leave him there alone. The guard waited outside the door for fifteen minutes, then grew concerned and tried to reenter the office. But the Fourth had propped himself against the door and wouldn't let him in. "Get the hell out of here!" he shouted. "I'm fine; I'm on the phone." When the guard finally gained entrance to the office, he found the former CEO lying on the floor in some sort of emotional state (one of the Fourth's confidants later described it as a "panic attack"). The Fourth pulled himself together and headed off in the direction of the boardroom, hollering over his shoulder to the guard, "You don't have to follow me; I know the way." The guard, an ex-cop, said later that the Fourth appeared gaunt and hollow-eyed. "He looked like a heroin addict."

The Fourth was in a dark place. He was no longer married to Kate. He filed for divorce in November 2008, shortly after A-B shareholders approved the InBev deal, stating in court documents that there was "no reasonable likelihood that the marriage can be preserved and therefore the marriage is irretrievably broken." The court filings revealed that Kate had signed a prenuptial agreement, which had been supplanted by a property settlement. "We were having difficulties in our relationship and then [the takeover] happened and it was just horrible," Kate said later. "He fought the buyout so hard, and he was so upset by it. He felt like he let everybody down."

In addition to retaining his seat on the board of directors, the

Fourth was being paid $120,000 a month in consulting fees supposedly for advising ABI management on new products, marketing programs, beer quality, and the company's relationship with charities. It's not clear if he did any of that, however. He'd only attended the one board meeting. He'd withdrawn from public view and was dividing his time between his Huntleigh mansion and his new $2.8 million waterfront home at the Lake of the Ozarks.

According to friends, he'd fallen into a depression and was being treated by a psychiatrist, who prescribed antidepressant medication. He was also self-medicating with large doses of binge buying. He bought a $1.25 million Bell helicopter and a $2.5 million, fifty-five-foot ocean-worthy cruiser, which he named after his pet mastiff *Waymo* (short for "way more better than you"). He acquired more than twenty high-end automobiles, including several Lamborghinis, Corvettes, Ferraris, and Porsches, a Rolls-Royce, and a $500,000, 600-horsepower Mercedes SLR McLaren with a lightweight carbon fiber body and a top speed of 230 miles per hour. He spent hundreds of thousands of dollars on guns, mostly high-powered, semi-automatic paramilitary weapons, not hunting rifles, including several .50-caliber machine guns with a range of more than a mile. He even built a small house on the Huntleigh property in which to store and display the arsenal. According to longtime *St. Louis Post-Dispatch* gossip columnist Jerry Berger, the gun house featured a full bathroom and a thirty-square-foot safe.

Whether he was at the Huntleigh house or the Lake of the Ozarks, the Fourth presided over constant get-togethers with his "guys," and sometimes their wives and girlfriends. But the revelry and retail therapy apparently did little to fill the hole left by the loss of the company. At some point during the gatherings, the talk inevitably turned to the aborted Modelo deal and how he could have saved the company if only his father hadn't sold them all out for his own personal gain.

Said one regular, sarcastically, "He was feeling sorry for himself, with $100 million in the bank."

When he ventured out in public, he often dressed in pajama bottoms, a T-shirt, dark glasses, a baseball cap, and orange Crocs. "It was sort of his Hugh Hefner outfit," said a friend. "He thought it kept people from recognizing him." He was spotted in the disguise as he shopped for a new Porsche one afternoon and while he was gambling at a West County casino early one morning.

By the fall of 2009, friends and family members were alarmed by his appearance and behavior. "Everyone in the family knew what was going on," said one of the Fourth's friends. "When a member of the family is a disgrace, they want to ignore it, deny it, not talk about it. But Steve Bagwell got them together for an intervention."

Bagwell was A-B's vice president of international marketing and a friend of the Fourth's dating back to their high school days. He was loyal to the boss but not part of the hard-partying "entourage," colleagues say. With Bagwell's help, the Fourth's mother, Susie, and his sister, Susan Busch-Transou, attempted an intervention at the Lake of the Ozarks, enlisting Ron Burkle and another of the Fourth's super-rich friends, Florida-based hotelier Jeffrey Soffer, the boyfriend of Elle MacPherson. Both men flew to Missouri on their private jets to participate in the intervention. When the group confronted the Fourth at his home, he admitted that he'd become dependent on a combination of alcohol, cocaine, oxycodone, and antidepressants. He promised to go into rehab as soon as he returned to St. Louis and got his affairs in order. But he didn't.

By Christmas 2009 the Fourth had taken up with a woman named Adrienne Martin, a twenty-six-year-old divorcee whom he'd met at a notorious downtown dance club called Lure, where she worked as a hostess. An exotic-looking hazel-eyed brunette with a penchant for spandex leggings, Martin maintained an apartment in St. Charles, Missouri, but she lived at the Huntleigh mansion most of the time, along with her eight-year-old son.

According to the Fourth's friends, employees, and regular visitors to the house, Martin soon shared his dependence on drugs, and the couple's behavior began to frighten the household staff. The Fourth's weapons collection seemed to have migrated from the gun house into the main house. "There were guns everywhere, on every table," said one regular visitor to the house. "There were so many guns on one coffee table that you could not see the wood [tabletop]. He had a hundred guns in his bedroom alone."

The arsenal included a Taser gun, which precipitated a trip to the hospital emergency room when Adrienne was shot with a dart that went all the way through her left index finger. The Fourth told friends that she accidentally shot herself, but they weren't sure who really pulled the trigger, since he had discharged weapons in the house multiple times, according to three people who saw the damage and discussed the incidents with him and members of his household staff. "It was at least five times," said one friend. On one occasion he shot up a bookshelf. On another, he fired three or four rounds into his bedroom wall. "He fired a high-powered hunting rifle in the kitchen and it went right through the wall," said a frequent guest at the house. Another time "he emptied an entire gun because he thought something was after him."

There were similar incidents at the lake house, where he installed a dozen "game" cameras in the surrounding woods, like those around the Huntleigh property, so he could see on indoor monitors if anyone approached the house. Friends say he became increasingly paranoid and was beset by what they characterized as wild hallucinations. "He would sit and stare at the security monitors and swear there were people out in the woods watching him," said one. "He said he saw little blue heads floating around in the air," said another. He had a sawed-off shotgun mounted under a countertop in the kitchen where he liked to sit. The gun was aimed at the kitchen door, which was the main delivery entrance to the house.

One day, he supposedly became so enraged by the sound of a leaf blower somewhere in the neighborhood that he donned a bulletproof vest and helmet, strapped on several weapons, and roared off on his motorcycle to find who was responsible. Fortunately, the culprit apparently got away.

Amid all the crazy behavior and guns, it was the regular presence of Martin's young son, Blake, that concerned people the most. "I called A-B security and told them they should do something because there was a little kid walking around with hundreds of loaded guns lying all over the place," said one friend. "They said they were aware of what was going on in general and would look into it."

The Fourth's housekeeper finally took matters into her own hands when she arrived for work one morning in early February 2010 and found the little boy wandering unattended in the midst of all the weaponry while her boss and Adrienne slept in his barricaded bedroom. She called the Fourth's sister, Susan Busch-Transou, in Florida and told her what had been going on in the house. Susan and her mother reacted quickly, contacting the children's division of the Missouri Department of Social Services, which promptly dispatched a social worker to the Huntleigh house, accompanied by a local police officer. But after the social worker interviewed the Fourth and he promised to secure the weapons, the department of social services took no action regarding the child.

Over the next few days, reports from staffers inside the house indicated that the Fourth's paranoia and hallucinations were getting worse, and that he was walking around sweating profusely, with multiple weapons strapped to his body and making threatening comments about finding out who had made the call to social services. His family promptly petitioned the circuit court of St. Louis County to issue an order committing him to involuntary confinement for treatment. Based on written allegations about his "24-hour-a-day" consumption of prescription and illegal drugs, his hallucinations, paranoia, and firing of weapons in the house, the court determined that he presented a likelihood of serious harm to himself or others, and issued a warrant directing the police to take him into custody and transport him to a medical treatment facility for involuntary treatment.

The task of executing the warrant fell to the police department of Frontenac, which provides protection under contract to Huntleigh's 135 homes and 334 well-heeled residents. The officers were told that the Fourth would likely be on drugs, heavily armed, and acutely paranoid, and he would be able to see on his interior monitors whoever buzzed the intercom for admittance through the gates. Somehow they had to gain entrance without alarming him. They were shown the floor plan of the house and warned that if he ran into his heavily fortified bedroom, then they could be in a siege situation.

So they came up with a ruse to fool him into letting them in. They would send the social worker and the police officer who had interviewed him a few days earlier to the front gate on Lindberg Boulevard to say they were just stopping by on a follow-up visit. A contingent of about of about a dozen officers and an emergency medical team would be stationed out of sight. When the Fourth buzzed the social worker and cop through, the others would follow and rush the house to subdue him.

Around noon on Thursday February 11, 2010, a caravan of black SUVs sat idling on Lindbergh Boulevard as the social worker pressed the button on the front gate intercom. A tactical team and a hostage negotiator from the St. Louis County Police Department were standing by a mile up the road at the Frontenac Plaza mall, just in case the commando mission went badly.

The plan worked perfectly. Wearing a bathrobe and armed with five weapons, the Fourth put up no resistance. He was handcuffed and taken to St. John's Hospital, where he was admitted under the name of Sam Stone, the title character of an old John Prine song about a soldier who comes home from Vietnam as an addict and eventually dies of an overdose.

With the Fourth safely locked down in detox, his family moved to clean up the mess he'd left behind. Adrienne Martin was sent packing. "They put her out of the house that day," said one of the Fourth's friends. The family hired a team to go through the house to collect and catalog all the weapons. According to a participant, they found approximately nine hundred weapons and a large cache of ammunition—drawers and buckets full of it. The Fourth had between thirty and forty loaded assault rifles stashed under his bed and a number of semi-automatic pistols fastened by magnets to the headboard. They found a tear gas gun and orange residue indicating that it had been fired inside the house.

After nine days at St. John's Hospital, friends say, the Fourth was flown by private plane to a rehabilitation facility in Phoenix. The only public mention of the entire episode was an item that appeared in Jerry Berger's online gossip column on March 8. Headlined "Busch in Rehab," it reported simply: "August Busch IV is currently in an out-of-state treatment center, confirmed a family source."

Friends say the Fourth made it through twenty-one days in rehab. Then, with his sister and mother in town to visit him, he pronounced himself "cured" and left. Back in St. Louis, he cut off communication with the people who had tried to help him—his mother and sister, Steve Bagwell, Ron Burkle and Jeff Soffer—and picked up his life right where he'd left off. Adrienne Martin and her son moved back into the Huntleigh mansion, and the partying resumed. He even got his guns back because it turned out that they were all legal. It was as if nothing had happened.

Eight months later, on the night of November 18, 2010, the Fourth's longtime friend and A-B underling Jim Sprick got into a domestic dispute with his wife, Michelle, which led to the police being called to their home. While there, the responding officers found a quantity of drugs, including marijuana, methamphetamine, and two large tablets of cocaine molded and professionally packaged to look exactly like Alka-Seltzer, complete with the brand name stamped into it. According to police documents, Michelle admitted that the drugs were hers, and she was taken to the police station, where she said that she and her husband were part of a group of former and current Anheuser-Busch executives and their wives that regularly attended parties at the home of August Busch IV; in fact, they had been at his house that night. Asked where she got the Alka-Seltzer cocaine, she replied that August had given it to her. She said a friend of his, a well-known St. Louis businessman, had it manufactured for his friends so if they got stopped, the police wouldn't know it was drugs. Mrs. Sprick was booked for possession, and the DEA was notified about August's friend with the Alka-Seltzer cocaine.

Thirty days later, at 1:12 p.m. on December 19, a St. Louis County 911 operator took a call from the Huntleigh mansion.

"We need an ambulance to 2832 South Lindbergh," the caller said.

"OK, is that a business or a residence?"

"A residence."

"OK. What's the problem?"

"This girl is not waking up; we can't get her to."

"Is she breathing?"

"Yeah, we don't know. It's dark. I'm going to try and get a light to see."

"OK, all right, I'll get them going right away."

"All right, thanks. Bye."

The caller was Mike Jung, one of the Fourth's household employees. The girl was Adrienne Martin, and she was dead.

An emergency medical team made the official pronouncement fourteen minutes later. They found Adrienne lying on her back fully clothed (including a jacket) on top of the covers on the Fourth's bed. In a short time, five Frontenac police officers and an investigator from the county medical examiner's office were on the scene, bagging evidence, asking questions, and taking notes. Also on hand was one of St. Louis's most prominent criminal attorneys, Arthur Margulis, who was representing the Fourth. Fortunately, Adrienne's son, Blake, was in Springfield, Missouri, visiting relatives.

From the outset, the investigators believed they were looking at a fatal drug overdose. Twenty-seven-year-old women don't often die in their sleep from natural causes. Their suspicion seemed borne out after Adrienne's body was moved to the morgue and the medical investigator found a plastic straw "covered by a white residue" in the right front pocket of her jacket. Police detectives found a similar straw, also encrusted with "a white powdery substance," between the mattress and box springs of the Fourth's bed. They found no cocaine in the room, however, just two empty prescription bottles on a dresser, which were covered inside with a white powder residue.

Detectives saw no signs of trauma on Adrienne's body and no evidence of a struggle, although they noted in their reports that "the entire room appeared to be in disarray. Items were lying throughout the room in no identifiable pattern . . . electronic devices, power cords, television, remote controls, Gatorade bottles, two cups of brown liquid, weapons, ammunition, radios, speakers, shoes, a watch, tools, flashlight batteries." The master bathroom was strewn with similar items, and inside the "toilet room" they found "a loaded shotgun behind the door and a Glock pistol loaded with an extended magazine hanging on a hook next to the toilet paper roll."

Detective James Ford asked to speak to August IV and was told by attorney Margulis that he would allow his client to make a statement and answer limited questions. According to Ford's report, the Fourth offered a brief chronology of the previous eighteen hours: After eating dinner at the house with Adrienne, he went to bed around 6:00 p.m. Saturday, but she did not. He awoke around 2:00 a.m., and she was still awake. He asked her to come to bed and went back to sleep. When he awoke at 12:30 p.m. on Sunday, she was in bed and appeared to be sleeping. He went into the kitchen, made them both a protein shake, and returned to the bedroom around 1:00 p.m. and was unable to wake her. He called Mike Jung into the room, and they both tried to revive her, shaking her, slapping her face. Then they called 911. Detective Ford asked if he knew whether Adrienne abused drugs. He answered no.

Despite all the indications that this was a drug-related death, the Frontenac Police Department did not obtain a warrant to search the rest of the house or obtain blood and urine samples from August IV to see if he had consumed any drugs the night before. Based on the warrant they had executed in February, they had reason to suspect he had.

The next day, December 20, Detective Ford and Detective Matt Brune witnessed the autopsy performed by Dr. Michael Graham, St. Louis County's assistant medical examiner. Graham quickly identified a hole in the septum of Adrienne's nose, which he demonstrated by inserting a surgical tool in one nostril, through the hole in the septum, and out the other nostril. "Snorting a large amount of narcotics over a long period of time" could have caused the condition, he said. It was the only notable finding during the exam, which yielded no apparent cause of death. It would be up to the toxicology reports to tell the tale, and they wouldn't be completed for four to six weeks.

It wasn't until December 23, four days after Martin's death, that the Frontenac Police Department got around to telling the public about it, and even then the disclosure was only in response to a call from a *Post-Dispatch* reporter acting on a tip. Asked why the department had waited so long, Police Chief Tom Becker responded matter-of-factly that the department had released information as soon as it received media inquiries and after approval by the city attorney. The implication was that had it not been for an enterprising reporter, the mysterious death of a young woman in the bed of the town's most notorious "playboy" might have remained a secret indefinitely.

Making matters worse, the department's initial press release stated incorrectly that Martin's body had been discovered on Saturday, making the gap between her death and its disclosure seem even longer. The department quickly corrected the error, but the impression had been created that the authorities were somehow covering for the Busch family. Who else would benefit from keeping the story out of the press? Indeed, the department initially refused to say whether August IV had been in the house when Martin died. On Christmas Eve, the *Post-Dispatch* raised more suspicion when it reported that forty-two minutes had elapsed between the time Adrianne was found unresponsive and paramedics were called. The *Post*'s claim was based on a statement from the medical examiner's office that conflicted with Detective Ford's written report, which put the time at 1:00 p.m. but was not made public.

"I can tell you there is absolutely nothing suspicious about her passing," said the Fourth's attorney, Art Margulis. "It's a tragic and untimely death of a young person. A very kind person, by the way."

Once the news broke, it broke wide. All over the world, wherever Budweiser was sold, so was the story of the handsome, hard-partying brewery scion with a history of having pretty young women die in his company.

Adrienne Martin emerged from all the coverage as a small-town Missouri girl who'd married shortly after graduating from high school and had a baby that same year, a single mom who'd supported herself as a waitress at Hooters, and an undaunted dreamer who entered swimsuit competitions and beauty pageants and who posted glamorous, sexy pictures of herself on a modeling Web site and wrote that she was studying to be an "art therapist" and "hoped to help children."

"I would really like to do beer advertising!" she said. "Since I have only just begun, I can't wait for my exciting times ahead!"

"I never saw Adrienne looking like she did in those pictures," marveled one of the Fourth's friends. "She always looked like a stoned junkie, sitting on the couch, barely able to speak."

In another sad sidebar, Adrienne's death put the name of Michele Frederick back in the media spotlight. Michele's death twenty-seven years before was employed as an ironic device in thousands of news stories, her short life invariably abbreviated to a one-word descriptor, "waitress."

The narrative took an unexpected turn when Adrienne's ex-husband came forward to tell the media and the medical examiner's office that her death might have been caused by a rare heart condition that only he knew about. Kevin Martin, a forty-five-year-old osteopath in Cape Girardeau, Missouri, said that at one point during their marriage, they were in his office after hours and she noticed the EKG machine and asked him to run an EKG on her "to see what it was like." He said the EKG indicated she might have a condition called "long QT syndrome," a congenital disease that affects the heart's electrical rhythm and can result in fainting spells, seizures, or even sudden death. Dr. Martin said he recommended that Adrienne consult a cardiologist, but he didn't think she ever followed up on his advice, nor did he retain a copy of the EKG he ran. He said his ex-wife had been fatigued recently but couldn't sleep. "One of the last things she ever said to me on the phone was, 'I haven't slept in three days now; I am wore [*sic*] OUT!'"

The medical examiner's office dismissed Kevin Martin's long QT theory when he couldn't back it up with any evidence, but the media ran with it, posting headlines such as "Woman Who Died at Busch Home Had Heart Issue." Dr. Martin was downright chatty with reporters, telling them that he and Adrienne "think the world of August. He is a good man." During a recorded interview with detectives Ford and Brune, Dr. Martin stated that he and August IV were "very friendly, almost like brothers." He told them he had taken his son to the Huntleigh mansion the previous evening to visit the Fourth, who seemed depressed and "thinks God is punishing him for what happened to the girl in Arizona."

Dr. Martin also said that August IV had informed him of Adrienne's death shortly after it occurred, calling him on her cell phone. He said his ex-wife had been keeping odd hours and was increasingly difficult to reach in the weeks before her death, but he would be "shocked if it was determined that Adrienne used illegal drugs."

Martin's sudden appearance coincided with a cluster of locally written stories that seemed almost orchestrated to present the Fourth in the best possible light. "August Busch IV Not to Blame for Death, Girlfriend's Mom Says," read the headline of a *Post-Dispatch* article that didn't quote the woman as saying that. The article was followed by an interview that Adrienne's mother, Christine Trampler of Ozark, Missouri, gave to St. Louis TV station KSDK, with the understanding that it would be her "only recorded interview."

Mrs. Trampler volunteered that Adrienne had been taking Trazodone, a prescription drug used mainly to treat depression and anxiety, but sometimes for insomnia and cocaine withdrawal. "She took Trazodone when she couldn't sleep," Mrs. Trampler said. "I didn't find out until after she died that her physician had increased the dosage. That's the only thing I could think of that could have contributed to [her death]." She revealed that on the last day of Adrienne's life, August IV had taken her for her first ride in a helicopter, and Adrienne had sent her pictures of them in the cockpit.

The grieving mother apparently only had good things to say about her late daughter's boyfriend, even though she admitted that she had never met him. "We talk every day on the phone because I feel like he is the only one that semi knows what I'm going through." It seems she gleaned enough from those conversations to say that "August's strengths were Adrienne's weaknesses, and Adrienne's strengths were August's weaknesses. So they balanced each other out perfectly."

A widely published Associated Press article, written by a St. Louis–based correspondent, reported that the Fourth was still held in high regard by the three women you'd least expect it from—his ex-wife, former mother-in-law, and ex-fiancée.

Said the AP: "Those who agreed to talk about [the Fourth] presented a picture of a driven man who seemed thwarted by fate at every turn. The secrecy surrounding him, combined with tales of wild parties, helped perpetuate a misleading portrait of a man who is more diligent, humbler and harder working than most believe, said his former mother-in-law Nancy Thatcher." The article did not actually quote Mrs. Thatcher directly about anything, but it did quote her daughter Kate, the former Mrs. Busch, seeming to defend the Fourth by saying that A-B "was his life. It was everything he knew. . . . I think he's trying to figure out what he wants to do. He just expected that would be his life, and suddenly it wasn't anymore." As a kicker, the article quoted Judy Buchmiller, to whom he was engaged in 1991: "I wouldn't want anything bad to happen to him. He's a good guy. He's really misunderstood."

The capper in the sympathy campaign, however, was a *Post-Dispatch* article based on an interview the Fourth gave to the newspaper's gossip columnist, Deb Peterson. It quoted Busch saying that he "loved this girl with every ounce of my heart. . . . It's the saddest thing I've ever dealt with. . . . I've been through some pretty bad things the past two years, and she was always by my side . . . She was the only girl I've ever been with that I didn't want to have someone on the side. You know, I'm this notorious bachelor who always wanted someone on the side, but I didn't with Adrienne." (The latter comment was so weirdly—and inappropriately— confessional that a local TV station froze it on the screen for a few extra seconds when reporting about the interview.)

Peterson quoted the Fourth as saying he was "falling in love" with Adrienne's son. "I've never spent much time around kids that age before," he said. "They don't care who you are or what you have. They just accept you the way you are."

He said he talked to her mother on the phone every day for few hours. "It's the only thing that makes me feel better." He claimed that he was talking to his father again, too.

" 'I love you,' that's what I told him. 'I love you from the bottom of my heart.' " He said his father responded in kind and advised him to get some grief counseling. "I don't know if individual counseling is the way to go or something else. I've got to figure something out. I can't let this take me down."

The interview apparently was short on hard questioning. If Peterson asked him whether he took drugs with Adrienne, it wasn't indicated. The closest the article came to the topic was the Fourth's admission that he had been in rehab in 2010 for depression and "my other issues," on which "he would not elaborate," Peterson wrote.

In a separate article, the newspaper editorialized on its exclusive, likening the Fourth to "the pitcher yanked from the baseball game too early, just a couple of innings in, left wondering what might have been." The editorial ended by repeating his comment about how kids "just accept you the way you are," then added, "It seems that throughout his life Busch IV has wanted nothing more than this."

The interview turned out to be the Fourth's last words on the subject. A week later, Art Margulis contacted Detective James Ford and informed him that he had advised his client to make no further statements regarding Adrienne's death.

The results of the toxicology reports were finally released on February 9: Adrienne Martin had died from oxycodone intoxication. At a joint press conference the next day, Frontenac police chief Tom Becker and St. Louis County prosecutor Robert McCulloch revealed that her body also contained enough cocaine to kill her. In fact, the tests indicated that she had ingested cocaine within an hour of her death, and oxycodone within six hours. Traces of the drugs were detected in the empty prescription bottles found on the dresser, and cocaine residue was found in the plastic straw discovered under the mattress. Which meant that either Adrienne had snorted the very last line of coke and then lay down on the bed and died, or someone had gotten rid of the rest of it before the paramedics and police arrived.

McCulloch's frustration was palpable when he noted that "neither the oxycodone nor the cocaine were prescribed, and they didn't just drop out of the sky." But because the cause of death was "clearly an accidental overdose" that did not lend itself to a manslaughter prosecution, and because August IV had refused to cooperate, "the investigation as to where the drugs came from is at a dead end," he said. Consequently, no charges would be filed against the Fourth.

The Fourth's attorney, Art Margulis, summed it up smugly for reporters. "If you can reflect back to December, you may recall that we released a statement saying it was an unfortunate tragedy. And it really is," he said. "And we also said in that statement there were no suspicious circumstances. And I think that's now been borne out and it would seem to me that the matter is closed."

In St. Louis and elsewhere, the general reaction to the news was that August IV had gotten away with it yet again; because of his name and his money, he'd avoided the consequences that a less privileged person would have suffered. Among those most upset about the prosecutor's decision to drop the case was George "Larry" Eby of Springfield, Missouri, Adrienne Martin's estranged father, who told the *New York Times* he was "not going to stop" trying to find the answers to why his daughter died. "Mr. Busch doesn't know me, but he will when I'm done."

On March 29, AB InBev made the unsurprising announcement that August IV would not seek reelection to the board of directors in April and was leaving the company "for personal and health reasons."

Two days later, Dr. Kevin Martin filed a wrongful death lawsuit against August IV on behalf of his son, Blake, seeking unspecified damages for "carelessness and neglect." Curiously, the Fourth filed a response almost simultaneously, denying the claims of carelessness and negligence but agreeing to move jurisdiction of the case from St. Louis to Cape Girardeau, where Kevin and Blake Martin lived. Legal experts smelled a deal between the two "almost brothers." Under Missouri law, a family can file only one wrongful death lawsuit. So Kevin Martin's move could be seen as a "rush to the courthouse" to prevent Adrienne's parents, Christine Trampler and Larry Eby, from filing a separate claim. The Fourth quickly offered to pay $1.5 million to settle the suit with no admission of responsibility, and Kevin Martin just as quickly agreed to it. But before a judge approved the settlement, Trampler and Eby filed motions to intervene. Trampler's motion, filed by prominent New York litigator John Q. Kelly, argued that Martin shouldn't be allowed to represent the boy because of his personal relationship with August IV. It also questioned Martin's fitness as a parent and alleged that Busch had provided Adrienne with illegal substances "without her knowledge or consent." That Kelly would take on a client in tiny Ozark, Missouri, reinforced the feeling that, given the Fourth's enormous resources, $1.5 million was a lowball offer for a kid who had lost his mother a few days before Christmas. The court did not approve the proposed settlement agreement, and Adrienne Martin's ex-boyfriend, ex-husband, and divorced parents are still in a legal fight over how much money should be paid to her little boy and who should oversee it.

On a weekday afternoon in the spring of 2012, August IV drew looks from other shoppers as he and a male companion stood in the checkout line at Sam's Club in West St. Louis County. Wearing low-hanging baggy jeans, a white T-shirt, and Crocs, he was just barely recognizable as the formerly trim and handsome head of Anheuser-Busch. He'd gained considerable weight, his hair was clearly dyed, and, an observer said, he gave the distinct impression that he was under the influence of something. When the cashier said to him playfully, "Oh, we've heard of you," he responded, "And I'm sure all of it is bad." He then left his companion to pay for several carts' worth of supplies and walked out of the store. After his companion followed, the cashier said to the next customer in line, "You know who that was, don't you?" Getting an affirmative nod, she said, "He comes in here like that all the time. The world must be just a blur to him."

As described by several people who still see him, the life of August Busch IV these days is not one that many people would choose. Since Adrienne Martin's death, the "guys" don't come to the house anymore. His security detail is gone. All but one or two of his employees have left, either frightened away or fired. Despite what he may tell people, he and his father do not speak. He still talks about August III all the time, however, and lives with the knowledge that he is probably the biggest disappointment of his father's life. As one former A-B executive put it, "All August III ever wanted out of the Fourth was performance, and he never got it."

After the InBev takeover, August III receded from public view for a time, but more recently he's become actively involved in a number of charitable and political endeavors, including the 2012 general election. He's also been robustly involved in building a new $10 million home at Waldmeister Farm. According to family and friends, he maintains a close relationship with his three other children—Susan, Steven, and Ginny—but rarely speaks about August IV. And no one expects that he will ever tell his version of the story.

As for the Fourth, his few remaining friends say that his "issues" are worse than ever before.

"At this point August has no respect for his family or his employees, and he especially doesn't have any respect for himself," said one longtime friend, "I think he will die. He is, in effect, dead already. He doesn't care. He has everything in the world, and he doesn't know it."

Said another long-suffering friend, "I have sat up nights with August so that he wouldn't choke on his own vomit and die. I don't care anymore if he dies. He'd be better off. I just don't want anyone else to die."

AN AMERICAN DREAM

On a hot August day in 1975, Gussie Busch sat in the stone-cool gun room of the big house at Grant's Farm, regaling three *Post-Dispatch* reporters with anecdotes culled from his decades as the patriarch of what *Life* magazine called America's "liveliest, lustiest family dynasty."

The reporters were preparing a lion-in-winter series of articles about the old man's colorful life and times. Al Fleishman was on hand to help Gussie with his memory and his mouth, making sure he didn't slip up and let on about the recent coup d'état engineered by August III. Trudy came and went, checking to see that everyone was comfortable and joining in the conversation when she felt the need.

The room itself was a museum of American history. On display were Tiffany lamps and Remington sculptures; signed photos of Gussie with Presidents Truman, Johnson, and Kennedy; Cardinals' World Series trophies; engraved antique rifles, including a bolt-action Winchester .30-caliber rifle dating back to the days of the buffalo hunts on the Great Plains; and even a beautiful mounted pair of extinct passenger pigeons in a glass case.

Surrounded by all the mementos, Gussie talked about his "granddaddy" Adolphus, who let him smoke and drink whiskey when he was just a boy, and his "good daddy" August A., who had sacrificed his health in steering the company through Prohibition and the Great Depression. He talked about Grant's Farm and Busch Gardens, about the Clydesdales and the Cardinals, about Curt Flood and Steve Carlton, and about the first time he laid eyes on Trudy in her father's restaurant in Switzerland. He couldn't bring himself to talk about Christina, however. He fell silent when the subject of the tragic accident came up, his face tightened with pain as he stared glassy-eyed at a corner of the room. "It was meant to be," Trudy said, putting her hand over his as he struggled to regain his composure. "It [the runaway truck] could have happened a second earlier or later. It was just meant to be. But the experience has made us stronger."

When he recovered, Gussie acknowledged that his net worth was somewhere in the area of $200 million, and he summed up his seventy-six years of living by saying, "Hell, I'd do it all again."

The interview was interrupted when twenty-one-year-old Adolphus IV arrived to serve a round of Budweisers in twelve-ounce bottles. Gussie had several beer-drinking rituals he liked to perform for civilians. One was to demonstrate the proper way to pour a beer—down the center of the glass, not the side—and the other was to give a reverential reading of the company's credo on the Budweiser label: "We know of no other beer produced by any other brewer that costs so much to brew and age. Our exclusive beechwood aging process produces a taste, a smoothness, and a drinkability you will find in no other beers."

This time, however, he dispensed with the usual show. Holding up his half-empty bottle, he kissed it and said, "Gentlemen, *this* is the American dream."

In March 2012, reporters poring over AB InBev's annual 10-K report discovered that CEO Carlos Brito and a group of about forty top executives had qualified for stock option bonuses worth $1.57 billion. Brito's share of the bonus pot—3.2 million shares at $10.52 per share—was worth more than $180 million.

The numbers were stunning. When InBev bought Anheuser-Busch in 2008, a group of seventeen senior A-B executives received more than a billion dollars for their shares. But most of them had amassed the stock over the course of many years with the company, and more than two-thirds of the payout went to three men who'd worked there for decades—August III (forty-eight years, $427.3 million), Patrick Stokes (thirty-nine years, $160.9 million) and August IV (twenty-one years, $91.3 million). Of the new group of stock option recipients, it appeared that only a few had been with A-B prior to the buyout.

Even more stunning, the bonuses were not triggered by increased sales or market share. They were based solely on what the company termed "de-leveraging," or reducing the debt that InBev had incurred in buying Anheuser-Busch in the first place. The company had reduced its total debt by more than $20 billion since 2008—from $56.6 billion to $34.7 billion—by selling off brewing assets in eastern Europe, Korea, and China and non-core businesses such as A-B's theme park division, and by cutting back the St. Louis division's formerly bloated budgets.

In InBev's home base of Belgium, however, rank-and-file workers claimed the company was hitting its budget targets by skimping on repairs and preventive maintenance, and spokesmen expressed outrage at the size of the executive bonuses. "A worker would take

4,500 years to get the bonus of Brito," complained one union official. "No one can be worth that," said a leftist politician, adding, "Companies with the highest bonuses are not necessarily the best run." Oddly, there was no outcry against the bonuses in St. Louis, which had borne the brunt of the company's reduction in its workforce, losing approximately 2,000 jobs.

After nearly four years in charge of the world's largest brewer, Brito and his executive team had shown they were better at buying companies and slashing budgets than selling beer, at least in the United States, where volume fell by more than 3 percent in 2011. For the first time in more than a decade, the company shipped fewer than 100 million barrels domestically, and AB InBev's U.S. market share dropped to 47 percent. Budweiser sales sank another 4.6 per cent, after declining 7 percent in 2010 and 10 percent in 2008.

In July 2012, the company announced that it was buying the remaining 48 percent of Mexico's Modelo brewery for $20.1 billion, or about $5 billion more than the price August IV and his team had negotiated in 2008. The combined companies are expected to yield annual sales of $47 billion, employ 150,000 workers in twenty-four countries, and annually produce as many as 350 million barrels of nearly 300 beers. In an interview about the merger, Carlos Brito referred to the company as a "portfolio of brands."

Also in July 2012, AB InBev revealed that it would be among the first tenants in St. Louis's long-gestating Ballpark Village commercial development adjacent to Busch Stadium. The company has licensed the Budweiser name to a planned industrial-size restaurant featuring "authentic German-inspired cuisine" and a rooftop beer garden with 100 beers on tap. (The dependably irreverent *Riverfront Times* suggested that the company name the restaurant Gussie's instead of Budweiser, and dress the waitresses in skimpy lederhosen outfits).

It is AB Inbev's stated goal to build Budweiser into "the first truly global beer brand," but on Brito's watch, the company's flagship brand has fallen to third place in the United States, surpassed by Coors Light. Bud Light remained the best-selling beer in the United States, and therefore the world, but there are clear signs that the new guys don't have a handle on the American psyche the way previous management had. They spent $30 million on five commercials during the 2012 Super Bowl broadcast, but only one of them—the arguably unclever "Here Weego," which featured a dog of the same name who runs to fetch a Bud Light whenever he's called—made *USA Today*'s Ad Meter Top 10. Two commercials for Bud Light Platinum, the company's new higher-alcohol (6 percent) brand aimed at contemporary adults, ranked in the bottom 10 of the 56 commercials that aired.

In the early days of the takeover, there were rumors that the Brazilian budget cutters were going to do away with the Clydesdales. It seemed only logical, since austerity and carefully bred 2,000-pound show horses don't seem to go together. But the Clydesdales have remained an integral part of the company's promotion effort. There have been changes, however. In 2008, ABI moved the bulk of the 250-head breeding operation out of St. Louis to a farm in Boonville, Missouri, about 140 miles from the circular stable at the brewery, where only a few horses remain on display for the tours. In 2010, the company ended its seventy-six-year practice of providing teams of Clydesdales to public events for free, and began charging $2,000 per day for public appearances. And on New Year's Day 2012, for the first time in fifty-eight years, the Clydesdales were a no-show in the Pasadena Rose Bowl Parade. The company informed parade organizers a month earlier that it preferred to invest "in other types of sponsorships and events that reach a higher concentration of beer drinkers . . . and where [we] can more directly discuss the Budweiser brand."

The Rose Bowl decision did not sit well with the citizens of St. Louis, because it was the city's float that the Clydesdales pulled in the nationally televised parade for all those years. Chalk up another loss, one more blow to civic pride.

The Clydesdales made an appearance during the 2011 World Series, when the Cardinals won their eleventh world championship. At the start of game 2, they clopped along a downtown street and into the newest Busch Stadium (opened in 2006), where they circled the warning track to the cheers of the crowd. But the cheers weren't as loud as they were when Gussie rode shotgun and brought the fans to their feet with his exuberant wave, back when the ball club and the brewery had a personal connection. Some in the 2011 crowd might have recalled the time in the early 1980s when the driver got the team going a little too fast on a turn and the wagon went up on two wheels and nearly toppled the old man off his perch. That was the day, according to company lore, that August III ordered an end to the century-old practice of letting union workers drink free beer on the job, because it turned out that the driver, a Teamster, had downed a few too many Buds before he climbed aboard the red beer wagon.

Colorful stories like that no longer flow from the brewery. A recent *Post-Dispatch* article described a new corporate culture in which "very good financial engineers" emphasize making money as much as they do making beer, and top executives measure the company's performance against such packaged-goods firms as Procter and Gamble and Unilever, "companies that sell soap and toothpaste." The newspaper quoted one former A-B executive as saying the new leadership was "forcing a choice between cutting costs and investing in people and brands."

One 2010 cost cut seems particularly coldhearted in light of the recent "de-leveraging" bonuses: the company reduced by 80 percent its annual donation to a local charity devoted to helping children with mental and physical difficulties, cutting the contribution from $150,000 to $30,000. In defending the action, the company released a statement saying it was part of a new philosophy of "giving larger grants to fewer organizations, which can mean some organizations receive reduced support." The statement went so far as to tout the company's new motto, the one meant to replace the apparently outdated "Making friends is our business."

"This is all part of our dream to be the 'Best Beer Company in a Better World.'"

Whatever the tortured explanation, the move surely didn't make anyone proud to work at the company. And former executives say that is exactly what has been lost in the transition from Anheuser-Busch to AB InBev.

"There was just something about Anheuser-Busch," said eighty-three-year-old Andy Steinhubl, the man who wrote and perfected the recipe for what would become the world's best-selling beer, Bud Light. "It was a feeling that seeped into you when you worked there. I remember when I retired, Jack McDonough, who'd left A-B to run Miller, called and said he wanted me to come work for him, to run the brewing department. But I said no, because it would have made me feel like a traitor."

"There was a magic there that all of us felt, and it's not something you get over," said seventy-five-year-old Denny Long, sitting in his dark wood-paneled office at Sam's Steakhouse, the elegant, old school restaurant he now owns on Gravois Road in South St. Louis. "For years after I left the company, I would be headed out of the house to work and I would say to my wife, 'I'm going to the brewery,' and then catch myself. It's been twenty-five years and I still miss it."

Some of the magic of the Busch beer dynasty can still be seen just across the street from Long's restaurant. On a recent spring afternoon before the opening of the tour season, the sun-dappled 281 acres of Grant's Farm offered a glimpse of what life must have been like during the seventy-plus years that August A. and Gussie were the lords of the manor. Up at the big house, in the second-floor bedroom where both of them died, Adolphus's barber chair still gleamed in the center of the marble bathroom, and Gussie's bright-red Cardinals-Budweiser sport coats hung neatly in the closet, right above his collection of idiosyncratic cowboy boots. A lone visitor's footsteps echoed across the empty courtyard of the Bauernhof, a structure that boggles the modern American mind—a fortress barn with room enough to seat 1,000 dinner guests.

The estate is still owned jointly by the six surviving children who grew up there—Adolphus IV, Beatrice, Peter, Trudy, Billy, and Andrew. Now that the brewery has been sold, it's the one thing that binds them together, however uneasily. The company operates the public portion of the farm under the terms of a lease that doesn't cover the expenses, according to the family, and there is disagreement among the six about what to do when the lease comes up for renewal in 2013. In the meantime, the public tours of the Bauernhof, deer park, and animal compounds go on, while a small staff of longtime Busch family employees maintains the mansion and cottage as if Gussie and Trudy still lived there.

The big house was the scene of a family reunion of sorts in July 2010, when Billy Busch hosted a tasting of the first offerings from the William K. Busch Brewing Company, which he launched with the millions he made when InBev paid him seventy dollars a share for the stock his father left him. His mother, Trudy, was there—her first visit to the house since 1978—along with his oldest brother, Adolphus IV, and members of the von Gontard and Anheuser clans.

St. Louis's newest beer company was officially introduced to the city on the evening of November 6, 2011, during a combined press conference and coming-out party at the World's Fair Pavilion in Forest Park, the site of the city's grandest achievement 107 years before. Dressed in a sport coat and slacks, Billy addressed the public for the first time in his life, telling the crowd of about 500 beer distributors, retailers, local reporters, and civic leaders that, unlike any other American lagers, his two brands, Kräftig (German for "strong") and Kräftig Light, are brewed in adherence to the ancient German Purity Law, or *Reinheitsgebot*. Enacted in Bavaria in 1516, the law decreed that beer be brewed using only four natural ingredients: barley malt, hops, yeast, and water.

Billy also pledged that his company would operate in the civic-minded tradition handed down by his forebears.

"My family was in the beer business for 150 years and was an employer in this city and a supporter of the community for all that time, and now we are not involved, and that didn't seem right," Billy said.

"I am very fortunate to have been the recipient of a lot of wealth because of my family's success in the beer business, and I am willing to put my money at risk to build a company that will create jobs in St. Louis and allow the profits to stay in this city and this country as opposed to a foreign country."

Kräftig and Kräftig Light went on sale in the St. Louis region in October 2011 and quickly captured a measurable share of the market, even managing to gain entry to Busch Stadium, where only a handful of non–AB InBev brands are sold. In July 2012, Adolphus IV bought a 49 percent interest in the Salmon River Brewery, a craft beer maker in Idaho.

On a recent Saturday afternoon, fifty-one-year-old Billy was seen going about the business of making friends during a product tasting at a large, upscale grocery store in West St. Louis County, where he spent an afternoon working the aisles with the energy and enthusiasm reminiscent of his father in his prime. Introducing himself to a woman whose eyes lit up in recognition at the sound of his name, he asked what brand of beer she drank.

"Oh, I really don't drink beer," she replied, apologetically.

"How about your husband? What does he drink?"

Flustered by the unexpected close encounter with a Busch, she couldn't remember her husband's brand. "Why don't we call and ask him?" Billy suggested. And so they did, with Billy doing the talking.

"Hi, this is Billy Busch and I'm here at the grocery store with your wife and she's trying to remember what brand of beer you drink."

"Budweiser Select," the man said. Billy smiled.

A few minutes later, the woman left the store with a good story to tell and a six-pack of a brand-new beer brewed by a member of the Busch family.

Apparently, Gussie's American dream hasn't died.

NOTES

This book is based largely on several hundred hours of interviews with members of the Busch family, their friends and employees, former executives of Anheuser-Busch, brewing industry experts, and former local and federal law enforcement officers. The bulk of the historical background is drawn from the archives of the *St. Louis Post-Dispatch* and the *St. Louis Globe-Democrat*, the longtime newspapers of record regarding Anheuser-Busch and the Busch family, and from the Henry Tobias Brewers and Maltsters Collection, located at the Western Historical Manuscripts Collection at the University of Missouri–St. Louis. The author also relied on court documents, the reporting of the *New York Times*, the *Los Angeles Times*, the *Wall Street Journal*, the *Chicago Tribune*, *Business Week*, *Fortune*, *Forbes*, *Newsweek*, the Associated Press, the *Riverfront Times,* and the books *Making Friends Is Our Business*, by Roland Krebs and Percy J. Orthwein; *Under the Influence*, by former *Post-Dispatch* reporters Peter Hernon and Terry Ganey; *October 1964*, by David Halberstam; and *Dethroning the King*, by former *Financial Times* reporter Julie MacIntosh.

PROLOGUE: "AUGUST IS NOT FEELING WELL"

1–8   Confidential interviews by author.

CHAPTER 1: "BEER IS BACK!"

9   A crowd began gathering: "The Day the Beer Flowed Again," *St. Louis Globe-Democrat*, April 2, 1983.

10   Inside the iron gates: *St. Louis Post-Dispatch Sunday Magazine*, April 3, 1983, 9.

10   On the bottling plant floor: Roland Krebs and Percy J. Orthwein, *Making Friends Is Our Business: 100 Years of Anheuser-Busch* (St. Louis: Anheuser-Busch, 1953).

11   Eager to reestablish: "Reinforcements from Abroad," *St. Louis Post-Dispatch*, December 27, 1969.

12   And now, finally: *St. Louis Post-Dispatch Sunday Magazine*, April 3, 1983.

12   "April seventh is here": Anheuser-Busch archival recording.

13   Back at Kyum Brothers Café: "The Day the Beer Flowed Again," *St. Louis Globe-Democrat*, April 2, 1983

13   At 2:30 a.m: *St. Louis Post-Dispatch Sunday Magazine*, April 3, 1983.

13   By breakfast time: "King of Bottled Beer," *Fortune*, July 1932, 44.

14   "Beer is Back!": Krebs and Orthwein, *Making Friends Is Our Business*, 172–75.

15   "Teutonic tide": "Irish and German Immigration," Independence Hall Association, ushistory.org/us/25f.asp.

15   "A sudden and almost unexpected wave": Mary Jane Quinn, "Local Union #6: Brewing, Malting and General Labor Department," master's thesis, University of Missouri, 1947.

15   St. Louis even had: Ibid.

16   Adolphus worked for two years: "King of Bottled Beer," 48.

16   On March 7, 1861: Peter Hernon and Terry Ganey, *Under the Influence: The Unauthorized Story of the Anheuser-Busch Dynasty* (New York: Simon & Schuster, 1991), 26.

16   It's unlikely that: Gerald Holland, "The King of Beer," *American Mercury*, October 1929, 171.

16   Eberhard rewarded Adolphus: Hernon and Ganey, *Under the Influence*, 33, 34.

17   Of course, Adolphus got an assist: "Irish and German Immigration."

18   Sure enough: Martin H. Stack, "A Concise History of America's Brewing Industry," eh.net/encyclopedia/article/stack.brewing.history.us.

18   the Pasadena estate: Ibid., 46

18   Everything he did: Hernon and Ganey, *Under the Influence*, 120.

19   When he and Lilly celebrated: Ibid., 78

19   *Custer's Last Fight*: Death Notices, *Indianapolis Star*, May 9, 1921.

21   "promoter of villainous dives": Hernon and Ganey, *Under the Influence*, 69.

21   "Mr. President, the demand I speak of": Richard Bartholdt, *From Steerage to Congress: Reminiscences and Reflections* (Philadelphia: Dorrance, 1930): 206–7.

22   On June 10, 1910: "75 Years Ago," *St. Louis Globe-Democrat*, June 10, 1985.

22   Adolphus did not live to see: Hernon and Ganey, *Under the Influence*, 84–87.

23   With an original par value: "King of Bottled Beer," 48.

24   The Busch family's ties: Ibid.

24   Despite these efforts: Ibid., 98.

24   Upon her arrival in Key West: Hernon and Ganey, *Under the Influence*, 100.

25   "an attempt to substitute": Krebs and Orthwein, *Making Friends Is Our Business*, 160.

26   "The temperate use": *The Anheuser-Busch Brewery*, brochure, Henry Tobias Brewers and Maltsters Collection, Western Historical Manuscripts Collection, University of Missouri–St. Louis.

26   "generally innocent": Department of Information, brochure, U.S. Brewers Foundation, Tobias Collection.

26   "You can afford to ride this out": "Gussie Busch: Beer Dynasty Dynamo," *St. Louis Post-Dispatch*, April 19, 1970.

27   "Our whole welfare and happiness": Hernon and Ganey, *Under the Influence*, 64.

27   The estate featured a $250,000: *Grant's Farm: Preliminary Boundary Adjustment Evaluation, Reconnaissance Study*, National Parks Service, U.S Department of the Interior.

27   steeped in American history: Ibid., 6–8.

29   "We ended up as the biggest": Hernon and Ganey, *Under the Influence*, 132.

29   Anheuser-Busch lost: "King of Bottled Beer," 102.

29   He saw Tessie one last time: Hernon and Ganey, *Under the Influence*,158.

30   In June 1922: Krebs and Orthwein, *Making Friends Is Our Business*, 131–34.

30   To President Coolidge: Ibid., 135.

31   His most effective broadside: Hernon and Ganey, *Under the Influence*, 149.

31   In one way: Ibid., 163.

32   At age sixty-eight: Ibid., 161.

33   "with the utmost simplicity": Ibid., 165.

33   August A.'s estate: Ibid., 166.

CHAPTER 2: THE ALPHA BUSCH

35   Marie was twenty-two: "300 Guests See Miss Church and A.A. Busch Jr. Wed," *St. Louis Globe-Democrat*, April 28, 1918.

35   Beautiful, refined, and polished: Hernon and Ganey, *Under the Influence*, 126.

36   One of his cousins: Hernon and Ganey, *Under the Influence*, 171.

37   "recently divorced": "August A. Busch Jr. Weds Mrs. E. O. Dozier, Recently Divorced," Associated Press, September 23, 1933.

37   The second marriage didn't yield: Lotsie Busch Webster, interview by author, 2011.

40   Viewed from an era: Krebs and Orthwein, *Making Friends Is Our Business*, 218–19.

41   "*very* good business": "Busches: 'Too Flamboyant for St. Louis High Society.'" *St. Louis Post-Dispatch*, August 26, 1975.

42   "Grandaddy would take us hunting: " *St. Louis Post-Dispatch*, August 25, 1973.

CHAPTER 3: "BEING SECOND ISN'T WORTH SHIT"

46   hundreds of thousands of olive-drab cans: Krebs and Orthwein, *Making Friends Is Our Business*, 225–26.

47   Per capita consumption: Stack, "Concise History."

47   But all was not well: Webster, interview.

48   Gussie's homecoming: "Col. Busch Won't Run for Mayor," *St. Louis Globe-Democrat*, February 9, 1945.

49   The problem: Hernon and Ganey, *Under the Influence*, 51.

50   Gussie bounded onto the Anheuser-Busch throne: *St. Louis Post-Dispatch*, August 27, 1975.

50   "a Wagnerian air to the whole enterprise": "The Very Last of the Marvelous Beer Barons," *St. Louisan* magazine, January 1976, 40–47.

51   "That's my daughter": Trudy Busch, interview by author, 2011.

53   Gussie and the president: Webster, interview.

53   At Grant's Farm: "Busch Party Receiving Line Ruled Out to Humor Truman." *St. Louis Globe-Democrat*, June 8, 1950.

54   All the while: *St. Louis Globe-Democrat*, December 7, 1948.

54   He finally filed: *St. Louis Globe-Democrat*, August 8, 1951.

54   "how much she paid the yard man": *St. Louis Globe-Democrat*, December 8, 1951.

54   "immaterial": *St. Louis Globe-Democrat*, January 15, 1952.

54   A few weeks later: "Mrs. August A. Busch Jr. Gets Divorce and a Million," *St. Louis Globe-Democrat*, February 21, 1942.

55   One particular antisocial episode: "August A. Busch III Questioned by police in Halloween Fracas," *St. Louis Globe-Democrat*, November 1, 1949.

56   Years later: Confidential interview by author.

CHAPTER 4: "THE MAN WHO SAVED THE CARDINALS"

57   a two-week Florida vacation: "Busch and His Swiss Bride to Honeymoon in Florida." *St. Louis Globe-Democrat*, March 23, 1952.

58   "August A. Busch Jr. Will Marry Swiss Girl Today": *St. Louis Globe-Democrat*, March 22, 1952.

59   Those rights were then held: *St. Louis Globe-Democrat*, April 11, 1953.

60   Done deal: "Busch Sweeps In, Sets Up Regime," *St. Louis Globe-Democrat*, March 11, 1953.

60   On March 10, 1953: Ibid.

61   "recruited from a P. G. Wodehouse March on the Rhine": "Gussie's Move to Save the Cardinals for St. Louis," *St. Louis Post-Dispatch*, April 20, 1970.

61   He donned a Cardinals cap: Ibid.

61   Meeting the players: David Halberstam, *October 1964* (New York: Ballantine, 1995), 57.

62   find some black players, fast: Halberstam, *October 1964*, 57.

62   "Gussie likes me": *St. Louis Post-Dispatch*, April 20, 1970.

62   If the Cardinals thought: *St. Louis Globe-Democrat*, February 23, 1954.

62   "a cold-blooded, beer-peddling business": "Hearing Today on Anti-Busch Bill," *St. Louis Globe-Democrat*, March 18, 1954.

63   "an outstanding leader in St. Louis affairs": "Civic Leaders Protest Charges against Busch," *St. Louis Globe-Democrat*, February 25, 1954.

63   "a lavish and vulgar display": "Move Started to Scrap Baseball-Business Ties," Associated Press, March 19, 1954.

63   "stabilized the national league": "Busch Tells Senator Terms on Which He'd Sell Cardinals," Associated Press, May 26, 1954.

63   Johnson's motives: *St. Louis Globe-Democrat*, February 25, 1954.

64   "I'm through": "Senator Gives Up Fight to Bar Brewery from Owning Team," *St. Louis Post-Dispatch*, May 26, 1954.

65   "August Busch and his beer company": "Beer Won't Sell If Cards Lose, Wrigley Advises," Associated Press, March 9, 1954.

65   "Not many people wrote to me": Al Fleishman, "Conversations with Gussie," *St. Louis Business Journal*, September 27–October 3, 1982.

66   Sportswriters flocked: *St. Louis Post-Dispatch*, April 19, 1970.

66   "the biggest bitch that ever happened": Hernon and Ganey, *Under the Influence*, 169.

CHAPTER 5: THE MAGICAL BEER KINGDOM

67   American millionaire's farmstead: *Grant's Farm*.

68   As luck would have it: Webster, interview.

68   The big house had gone to seed: Trudy Busch, interview.

69   Gussie was not a religious man: Ibid.

70   "magical": Ibid.

71   "My happiness is my business": "Gussie Busch."

72   He was proud of himself, too: Webster, interview.

72   For the first time in his life: Trudy Busch and Adolphus Busch IV, interview by author.

73   Gussie didn't involve: Adolphus Busch IV, interview by author, 2011.

75   "I take sole responsibility": *St. Louis Post-Dispatch*, August 27, 1975.

77   Without seeking the approval: Ibid.

78   In her will: Adolphus Busch IV, interview.

79   "All you had to do": Thomas F. Eagleton, "Recollections of Gussie Busch," *St. Louis Post-Dispatch*, October 3, 1989.

79   "You're supposed to have a lot of pull": *St. Louisan*, January 1976.

CHAPTER 6: THE PRUSSIAN LIEUTENANT

86   "Anybody can ride a horse": Webster, interview.

87   On November 21, 1954: "August A. Busch III Hits Telephone Pole, Two Hurt," *St. Louis Globe-Democrat*, November 22, 1954.

89   "never had a daddy": Confidential interview by author.

89   In truth, he completed: Confidential interview by author.

90   "He didn't trust anyone": Denny Long, interview by author, 2011.

92   Gussie picked up the tab: Webster, interview.

CHAPTER 7: THE OLD MAN AND THE KID

96   Gussie and Trudy: Webster, interview.

96   Back at the hotel: Ibid.

97   "Throw the fucking ball back": "Bob Gibson in The Year of the Pitcher: The Cardinals Right-Hander Dominated 1968," Suite101.com.

98   "You look at this here": *St. Louis Post-Dispatch*, April 19, 1970.

99   "I've never once seen him": Confidential interview by author.

101   "He came to visit me": Robert S. Weinberg, interview by author, 2011.

102   "Traditionally, getting smart": R. S. Weinberg and Associates, "Quantitative Methods for Developing Corporate Strategy."

103   Two weeks later: "All Anheuser-Busch Plants Idled in Strike," *St. Louis Globe-Democrat* May 28, 1969.

105   "I'll give you another chance": Hernon and Ganey, *Under the Influence*, 23.

106   "it just didn't get any better": "Near Beer," *St. Louis Post-Dispatch*, June 13, 1995.

106   "She was the All-American girl": Confidential interview by author.

106   The first public sign of trouble: "Mrs. Busch Injured in Crash," *St. Louis Globe-Democrat*, May 10, 1968.

107   The pair could not have been: Firsthand account by author.

107   "We were a friendship item": *St. Louis Post-Dispatch*, June 13, 1995.

107   When the divorce came: "Mrs. Susan Busch Granted a Divorce": *St. Louis Globe-Democrat*, November 15, 1969.

109   "I don't mean to give you a lecture": Halberstam, *October 1964*, 361–62.

110   "the first class way this club operates": "Birds' Players Get the Message, Applaud Busch," *St. Louis Globe-Democrat*, March 24, 1969.

111   "fresh nigger": Personal correspondence files of Gussie Busch, viewed by author.

111   But the reporters present: Halberstam, *October 1964*, 361–62.

113   There is no record: Adolphus Busch IV, interview.

CHAPTER 8: GUSSIE'S LAST STAND

115   The beer business as a whole: Stack, "Concise History."

116   A-B continued to widen: "Who Rules the Foam?" *Forbes*, December 15, 1972, 39.

116   The man driving the changes: Ibid., 40.

117   Robert Uihlein, August's grandson: Adolphus Busch IV, interview.

118   "get rid of that whole damn department": Long, interview.

119   "When you try to run a company": "A Pregnant Elephant," *Forbes*, May 15, 1971.

119   The announcement was nothing less than: "A Struggle to Stay First in Brewing," *Business Week*, March 24, 1973, 43.

119   Gussie soon was caught up in: "Busch Gardens, Houston Open for Business," *Budcaster*, 1971.

121   "that arrogant little prick": Adolphus Busch IV, interview.

123   "seemed chiefly intent on revenge": "Gussie vs. the Cards," *Newsweek*, June 19, 1972, 61.

124   It got worse: *Business Week*, March 24, 1973, 43.

126   It was a bad start: Ibid.

127   The economic crisis: "Gussie Busch's Bitter Brew," *Forbes*, June 1, 1974.

127   Schlitz quickly became: *Business Week*, March 24, 1973.

128   Of course, Gussie's refusal: Confidential interview by author.

128   The car privileges continued: Ibid.

130   At 4:00 p.m. that afternoon: "Man Is Killed, Busch Daughter Critically Injured in Crash," *St. Louis Globe-Democrat*, December 7, 1974.

CHAPTER 9: CHOOSING SIDES

140   "After more than 50 years": "Grand Old Man of Brewing Steps Aside as Chief Executive," *St. Louis Globe-Democrat*, May 9, 1975.

141   "we might be able to get back": Adolphus Busch IV, interview.

143   The saddest chapter: "Schlitz Recalls Beer Said to 'Taste Funny,'" *St. Louis Post-Dispatch*, September 7, 1975.

144   In the normal brewing process: "What Went Wrong," *Advertising Age*, April 13, 1981, 61–64.

CHAPTER 10: CAMELOT'S END

147   At 1:00 a.m.: Hernon and Ganey, *Under the Influence*, 395.

150   "has cooperated with us fully": "Killing at Busch Estate Is Found an Accident," *St. Louis Post-Dispatch*, June 9, 1976.

151   The grieving Leeker family: Hernon and Ganey, *Under the Influence*, 306.

152   While Peter's case was moving: "Crazy To do Anything Like This, Busch Says of Clydesdale Shooting." *St. Louis Post-Dispatch*, October 10, 1976.

154   "irretrievably broken": "Mrs. Busch Requests an Open Hearing," *St. Louis Post-Dispatch*, January 12, 1978.

154   Trudy obtained an injunction: "Grant's Farm Bars Brother of Mrs. Busch," *St. Louis Globe-Democrat*, February 9, 1976.

155   A divorce was granted: "Busch, Wife Granted Divorce after 25 Years," *St. Louis Globe-Democrat*, February 28, 1978.

CHAPTER 11: "WE ARE AT WAR"

158   Local 6 members had recently ratified: "Beer Strike May Have Broad Labor Impact," *St. Louis Post-Dispatch*, May 18, 1976.

158   "My people are bitter": "Dissident Teamster Leader Hopping Mad at Busch Strike," *St. Louis Post-Dispatch*, March 28, 1976.

159   In June 1881: "100 Years Ago," *St. Louis Globe-Democrat*, June 2, 1981.

159   The Teamsters International in Chicago: "Busch Resuming Beer Production," *St. Louis Post-Dispatch*, March 23, 1976.

159   "This is nothing but scab beer": "Pickets Plan to Block Movement of Busch Beer," *St. Louis Post-Dispatch*, March 24, 1976.

160   Violence flared: "19 Busch Pickets Seized in Blocking of Yeast Trucks," *St. Louis Post-Dispatch*, April 28, 1976.

160   Art Barhorst defended: "Busch Says He'll Fire Lawbreakers," *St. Louis Globe-Democrat*, April 29, 1976.

161   And so it had: "Busch Workers Back after 95-Day Strike," *St. Louis Post-Dispatch*, June 4, 1976.

161   He showed his gratitude: "Busch Firm Forms Political Arm," *St. Louis Post-Dispatch*, July 27, 1976.

164   While Anheuser-Busch management was distracted: "We Missed the Boat: We Were Unsmarted," *Forbes*, August 7, 1978.

166   The marketing guys sheepishly explained: Confidential interview by author.

168   Miller said as much: "Facts of Light Shed on Miller-Busch Feud," *St. Louis Post-Dispatch*, March 23, 1979.

169   Sensing a delicious opportunity: Confidential interviews by author.

170   The two beer companies: *St. Louis Post-Dispatch*, March 23, 1979.

170   Miller finally went with a nuclear option: "Whap! Bam! Zap! The Battle of the Beers Goes On," *St. Louis Globe-Democrat*, February 2, 1979.

171   "a publicity ploy": "Busch Foaming over Latest Miller Attack," *St. Louis Post-Dispatch*, August 15, 1970.

171   "For six years now": *Forbes*, August 7, 1988.

172   "You are not to have anything to do": Confidential interview by author.

172   "Miller is aggressive": "The Battle of the Beers," *Newsweek*, September 4, 1978.

CHAPTER 12: REBIRTHING BUD

173   Their relationship was outwardly polite: Confidential interview by author.

174   Once again, Gussie blew his stack: "Busch's Statement," *St. Louis Globe-Democrat*, June 24, 1978.

175   "cheap shot": "Cheap Shot by Big Eagle," *St. Louis Globe-Democrat*, June 27, 1978.

CHAPTER 13: "TELL ME I'M A HORSE'S ASS"

183   "I want you to make me": Andy Steinhubl, interview by author, 2011.

192   "The clear establishment": "The King of Beers Still Rules," *Business Week*, July 12, 1982, 50.

CHAPTER 14: WARNING SIGN

195   She was a townie: Confidential interview by author.

197   Around 8:30 that Sunday: Ron Benson, interview by author, 2011.

198   August IV told them: "Busch Heir May Be Charged in Fatal Car Crash," *St. Louis Globe-Democrat*, November 15, 1983.

199   After conferring with Benson: Benson, interview.

202   "stonewalling": "Busch Evidence Sought in Crash," *St. Louis Globe-Democrat*, March 7, 1984.

206   "I was devastated": "Near Beer," *St. Louis Post-Dispatch*, June 13, 1995.

249   a bright red cardinal: Hernon and Ganey, *Under the Influence*, 402.

250   In addition to his ten children: "Gussie Busch Buried in Private Service," *St. Louis Post-Dispatch*, October 2, 1989.

250   Two days later: "Busch: Brewer Eulogized as Benevolent Leader," *St. Louis Post-Dispatch*, October 4, 1989.

251   Most of Gussie's personal property: "Final Wish: Busch Urges Heirs to Use Grant's Farm," *St. Louis Post-Dispatch*, October 6, 1989.

CHAPTER 18: HERE COMES THE SON

254   The other new product: "Busch Son Leading Bud Dry Rollout," *St. Louis Post-Dispatch*, February 5, 1990.

255   But even Fleishman-Hillard: "Bud Blooms: New Beer Gets $70 Million Launch," *St. Louis Post-Dispatch*, March 15, 1990.

256   "He was very personable": Confidential interview by author.

256   "He was in training at the time": Confidential interview by author.

259   "Everybody thinks, 'It must be easy'": "Bud Man. Prince of Deer August Busch IV Pours a Little Dash in the Family Business," *Chicago Tribune*, June 14, 1991.

259   "You don't know how different": "Bud-Weis-Heir August Busch IV Is Rebellious, Risk-Taking—and (Nearly) Ready to Rule the World's Largest Brewery," *Fortune*, January 13, 1997.

259   "There's not a day in the week": "A Tall Order for the Prince of Beer," *Business Week*, March 23, 1992.

261   The Fourth constantly sought: Confidential interview by author.

262   "We'll either be famous or fired": Confidential interview by author.

265   "Gentlemen, I'm going to teach you": Confidential interview by author.

268   August III did nothing without a strategy: *Fortune*, January 13, 1997.

CHAPTER 19: WAY, WAY, *WAY* BEYOND TIGER WOODS

Confidential interviews by author.

CHAPTER 20: "A BAD APPLE AT THE TOP"

291   "a succession process as tightly orchestrated": "Is This Bud for You, August IV?" *Business Week*, November 11, 2002.

294   The Fourth bought the 6,500-square-foot: Confidential interview by author.

294   More than just fodder: Adolphus Busch IV, interview.

299   "the Coca-Cola of beer": Julie Macintosh, *Dethroning the King: The Hos-*

tile Takeover of Anheuser-Busch, an American Icon (Hoboken, NJ: John Wylie and Sons, 2010), 119.

301 "A challenging time": "The Son Finally Rises," *Forbes*, March 12, 2007.

302 "The Fourth had no appreciation": Confidential interview by author.

303 as one critic noted: "A Booze Buzz for Teenyboppers? Anheuser-Busch Product So Adorable It Draws Fire from Alcohol Abuse Camp," MSNBC .com, April 3, 2007.

303 "No thirty- or forty-year-old beer drinker": Statement by Joseph A. Califano, Jr., CASA Chairman and President, on Anheuser-Busch's "Spykes," The National Center on Addiction and Substance Abuse, April 4, 2007.

303 "In our view, the labeling": "Anheuser Criticized for Alcohol-Caffeine Drinks," *Bloomberg News*, May 11, 2007.

308 "I heard about him failing two drug tests": Confidential interview by author.

308 Part of the rumor was not true: Ibid.

CHAPTER 21: THE LAST WATCH

313 "I'm the one": *Forbes*, March 12, 2007.

315 A few days after the Super Bowl: "Brew Tube," *New York Times Magazine*, February 4, 2007.

316 It didn't come close: "Anheuser-Busch Pulls Plug on Bud TV," *Ad Age*, February 18, 2009.

317 He objected to two key members: Confidential interview by author.

317 As recounted: Macintosh, *Dethroning the King*, 3.

318 "He had boyishness": Confidential interview by author.

318 Shortly after the MillerCoors announcement: Macintosh, *Dethroning the King*, 140.

320 And yet the Fourth thought: Ibid., 166.

321 The company was being investigated: "Anheuser-Busch to Drop Stimulants from Tilt, Bud Extra to Settle Probe," *Tribune News Service*, June 27, 2008.

322 "His guys would come over": Confidential interview by author.

322 "The wholesalers for all the brands": Confidential interview by author.

325 Out at Belleau Farm: Adolphus Busch IV, interview.

326 The result was an article: "Anheuser CEO Fights for His Legacy," *Wall Street Journal*, May 27, 2008.

327 The board instructed him: Macintosh, *Dethroning the King*, 157.

330 "St. Louis has gotten to the point": "Trouble Is Brewing in St. Louis," *Chicago Tribune*, June 27, 2008.

333 "When I first heard": Billy Busch, interview by author.

337   In November 2009: Confidential interview by author.

338   "We were having difficulties": "Busch Heir's Once-Charmed Life Takes a Tragic Turn," Associated Press, January 8, 2011.

339   According to friends: Confidential interviews by author.

345   Thirty days later: Transcript of 911 call, December 19, 2010.

346   From the outset: City of Frontenac Police Department reports, released February 2011.

348   It wasn't until December 23: "Woman Found Dead in Home of August Busch IV," *St. Louis Post-Dispatch*, December 23, 2010.

348   The *Post*'s claim: Ibid.

349   Adrienne Martin emerged: "Death at Busch Home Investigated," *St. Louis Post-Dispatch*, December 24, 2010.

349   The narrative took an unexpected turn: St. Louis County medical examiner's report, December 24, 2010.

350   Martin's sudden appearance: "Mother of Adrienne Martin Speaks Out About Death in Busch home," radio interview, KSDK, St. Louis, January 5, 1011.

351   A widely published: Associated Press, January 8, 2011.

352   "loved this girl": "Busch IV Talks about Death of Girlfriend, Depression," *St. Louis Post-Dispatch*, January 4, 2011.

353   "the pitcher yanked": "In Busch IV's Words, Confirmation of the Lonely Life of a Former Beer Baron," *St. Louis Post-Dispatch*, January 4, 2011.

INDEX

Buck, Jack, 272
Bud Dry, 253–54, 255–56, 258
Bud Dry Draft, 254
Bud Extra, 321
Bud Ice Draft, 261
Bud Light
  ads for, 190–92
  development of, 187–90, 363
  idea of, 183–84
  promotion of, 168
  rollout of, 190–92
  sales of, 225, 227, 258, 268, 300, 361
  tasting of, 184–86
Bud Light Lime, 321
Bud Light Platinum, 361
Bud.TV, 315–16
Budweiser beer
  ads for (see advertising campaigns)
  brewing process for, 116, 125,
    127–28, 144, 358
  and competition, 49, 75–76, 136,
    165, 268, 300, 313, 361
  customer loyalty to, 20
  distribution of, 17
  and InBev takeover, 328, 329
  label of, 24
  licensing agreement, 360
  as national brand, 17
  as number-one-selling beer, 3, 11, 39,
    225, 268
  nonalcoholic form of, 29
  purity/quality of, 26, 39, 116, 124,
    126, 127, 144, 145, 165, 185, 297
  recipe for, 16–17, 32
  sales of, 3, 11, 24, 32, 51, 59, 70, 95,
    175–76, 258, 262, 321, 360
  tradition of, 189
  in wartime, 46
Budweiser Select, 366
Buford, Tony, 51, 79
Buholzer, Willy, 51–52
Buoniconti, Nick, 179

Burkle, Ron, 283–84, 285, 340, 344
Burnes, Bob, 111
Busch, Adolphus, 173, 358
  A-B founded by, 2, 231
  and ads, 19–20
  arrival in U.S., 15, 35, 331
  brewery business of, 16–22, 38
  and Clydesdales, 11
  and competition, 49, 51
  death of, 22, 28
  estate of, 22–23, 33
  influence of, 42–43, 45, 50, 99,
    272–73
  inspections by, 11
  marriage to Lilly, 16
  and Prohibition, 20–22
  public image of, 19, 41
  standards of, 27, 32, 75
  wealth of, 18, 22–23, 33, 251
Busch, Adolphus III, 2, 10
  as A-B president, 34
  death of, 49
  and Prohibition, 26, 29, 38
  and stock shares, 33
  and tainted beer, 47–48, 50
Busch, Adolphus IV
  and August IV, 294–95, 338
  and Billy's brewery, 364
  birth of, 68, 72
  childhood of, 73
  and Christina's death, 131, 134
  and Gussie, 137, 138–41, 153–54,
    249, 251, 260
  and InBev takeover, 325–26, 332
  and Leeker shooting, 147–49, 151
Busch, Alice (Gussie's sister), 78
Busch, Alice Ziesman (Gussie's
    mother), 48, 68, 77–78
Busch, Andrew (Gussie's son)
  and A-B sale, 332
  birth of, 72
  and car accident, 130

and Gussie, 139, 156, 245, 251
and property, 251, 364
Busch, August Anheuser Sr. "August
A.," 27–34, 173, 231
death of, 32–33, 48, 249
estate of, 33–34, 67, 364
and Great Depression, 358
influence of, 42, 99
and inspections, 11
and Prohibition, 10, 25, 26, 30–31,
180, 358
and social clubs, 36–37
standards of, 32
and stock shares, 22
and World War I, 24
Busch, August Anheuser Jr. "Gussie,"
35–43, 231, 357–59
A-B positions of, 34, 38–39, 49–56,
71
aging of, 95, 99, 100, 117, 129, 134,
136, 138, 153–54, 180, 193,
243–45, 247–49
and Cardinals, 59–65, 71, 80–81,
95–99, 108–13, 122–24, 137,
142–43, 174–75, 192–93,
243–44, 334, 358
charitable works of, 98, 99
and Christina's death, 131, 133–34,
358
and Clydesdales, 11, 71, 152, 244,
250, 358, 362
and competition, 49, 51, 75, 78, 106,
117, 124–25, 127
and cost-cutting measures, 128–29
death of, 249–51
and divorce, 54–55, 57, 68, 78, 121,
153–56
early years of, 35–36
empire of, 78–79
and end of Prohibition, 10, 12–14
estate of, 138, 251–52, 364
and expansion, 102–3, 222, 272

and family, 42–43, 71, 72–75, 78,
261
forced out, 135–43, 154, 177, 239,
249, 292
and hunting, 37, 38, 117, 294
and labor unions, 105, 108–9,
122–23
and Leeker shooting, 148–49, 152,
153
marriage to Elizabeth, 37
marriage to Marie, 35, 36, 37
marriage to Trudy, 57–58
and media, 118–19, 122–23, 127–28,
140–41, 175, 249, 357–58
and modernization, 118–19
office of, 173, 336, 337–38
and politics, 78–79, 130–31
and Prohibition, 26, 29, 38
and the public good, 41, 64, 77, 98,
306
reputation of, 5, 41–42, 50, 65–66,
71, 82–83, 97
standards of, 75, 124–25, 127–28,
129, 145, 358
and stock shares, 33, 68
and succession, 119, 129, 134
and tainted beer, 47–48
and theme parks, 76–77, 119–20,
124, 335
and Uihlein family, 117, 145
in wartime, 47, 51
wealth of, 66, 68, 358
as womanizer, 37, 38, 54, 79–80
Busch, August Anheuser III, 3, 85–94
A-B positions of, 85, 88, 89–90,
91–94, 99–108, 124, 129, 221,
239, 273–74, 284, 291, 296,
312–13, 316–18
and ad campaigns, 177–78, 263–66,
274
aging of, 291
auto accident of, 87

Busch, August Anheuser III *(cont.)*